Bleak Liberalism

Bleak Liberalism

AMANDA ANDERSON

The University of Chicago Press

CHICAGO AND LONDON

The University of Chicago Press, Chicago 60637
The University of Chicago Press, Ltd., London
© 2016 by The University of Chicago
All rights reserved. Published 2016.

Printed and bound by CPI Group (UK) Ltd, Croydon,
CR0 4YY

25 24 23 22 21 20 19 18 17 16   1 2 3 4 5

ISBN-13: 978-0-226-92351-2 (cloth)
ISBN-13: 978-0-226-92352-9 (paper)
ISBN-13: 978-0-226-92353-6 (e-book)
DOI: 10.7208/chicago/9780226923536.001.0001

Library of Congress Cataloging-in-Publication Data

Names: Anderson, Amanda, 1960– author.
Title: Bleak liberalism / Amanda Anderson.
Description: Chicago; London: The University of Chicago Press,
2016. | Includes bibliographical references.
Identifiers: LCCN 2016032592 | ISBN 9780226923512 (cloth: alk. paper) | ISBN
9780226923529 (pbk.: alk. paper) |ISBN 9780226923536 (e-book)
Subjects: LCSH: Liberalism in literature. | American literature—20th century—
History and criticism. | English literature—19th century—History and criticism. |
Realism in literature. | Modernism (Literature) | Politics and literature. |
Literature—Philosophy. | Liberalism.
Classification: LCC PS374.L42 A53 2016 | DDC 810.9/3581—dc23
LC record available at https://lccn.loc.gov/2016032592

♾ This paper meets the requirements of ANSI/NISO Z39.48–1992
(Permanence of Paper).

For Helen

Contents

Acknowledgments

This book has been long in the writing, and many friends and colleagues have been key in helping me think through its central questions. I thank Isobel Armstrong, Jane Bennett, Michael Bérubé, Timothy Bewes, Sharon Cameron, Robert Caserio, Bill Connolly, Simon During, Rita Felski, Frances Ferguson, Regenia Gagnier, Catherine Gallagher, Leela Gandhi, Phil Gould, Richard Halpern, Bonnie Honig, Jacques Khalip, Janet Lyon, Kevin McLaughlin, Ourida Moustefai, Deak Nabers, Jeff Nunokawa, Adela Pinch, Bruce Robbins, and David Thomas. I also thank graduate students in two seminars on liberalism and aesthetics, one at Johns Hopkins University and one at Brown University, who helped me think through the topic at different stages of its development.

During most of the time I was working on this book, I had the great good fortune to serve as director of the School of Criticism and Theory, hosted by Cornell University. The audiences who listened to portions of this project there were enormously helpful, as were the many SCT colleagues who talked with me about my work. I thank Lauren Berlant, John Brenkman, Tim Brennan, Jonathan Culler, Geoff Eley, Jason Frank, Victorian Kahn, Webb Keane, Dominick LaCapra, Saba Mahmood, Tim Murray, Steve Nichols, Robert Pippin, Suzanne Stewart-Steinberg, Kathryn Bond Stockton, Amy Villarejo, Hent de Vries, Michael Warner, and David Wellbery.

I also benefited from the opportunity to present portions of this project on many occasions. I delivered an early version of the arguments as the Ward Phillips Lectures at the University of Notre Dame, and I also gave lectures and colloquiums at Stanford University, Yale University, the School of Criticism and Theory, the National Humanities Center, University of Alberta, University of Cambridge, King's College London, University of California, Davis, University of Chicago, University of Wisconsin–Madison, Brown University, University of Tennessee, Dartmouth College, Concordia University, Southern Methodist University, Ohio State University, Leuven University, American University, University of Utah, University of Connecticut, University of Maryland, University of Virginia, Pennsylvania State University, Columbia University, SUNY, University at Buffalo, and University of California, Berkeley. I thank the organizers and audiences at all these events.

The writing and research for this book were supported by a fellowship from the John Simon Guggenheim Foundation during 2009–10, as well as a sabbatical from Brown University during 2012–13. I also thank Alan Thomas, my editor at the University of Chicago Press, for his early interest in the project and his ongoing engagement with it.

My family was absolutely crucial in helping me finish this book, especially during the extraordinary challenges of the past few years. I especially thank my mother, Sara Anderson, who has influenced my work and my values more than she perhaps knows. Her company remains one of the great gifts of my life. My wonderful father, Philip Anderson, did not live to see this book completed, but we held many conversations about it over several years. The example of his kindness, his intellectual curiosity, and his extraordinary humor guides me every day.

My children, Jackson and Emily, never cease to amaze me and enrich my life with their love and companionship. I am deeply grateful to them both and proud of their insight, creativity, and ongoing achievements.

This book is dedicated to my sister Helen, who has always been there.

Parts of the introduction previously appeared as "The Liberal Aesthetic," in *Theory after "Theory,"* ed. Jane Elliott and Derek Attridge (New York: Routledge, 2011), 249–61. A shorter version of chapter 1 appeared as "Character and Ideology: The Case of Cold War Liberalism," *New Literary History: A Journal of Theory and Interpretation* 42, no. 2 (2011): 209–29. An earlier version of chapter 2's section on Trollope's *The Way We Live Now* appeared as "Trollope's Modernity," *ELH* 74 (2007): 509–34, © 2007 English Literary History, Johns Hopkins University. Some paragraphs of chapter 3 appeared in "Dickens, the Brontës, Gaskell: Politics and Its Limits," in *The Cambridge History of the English Novel,* ed. Robert Caserio and Clement Hawes (Cambridge: Cambridge University Press, 2012). And an earlier version of chapter 4 appeared as "Cold War Aesthetics: The Case of Adorno and Trilling," *Critical Inquiry* 40, no. 4 (2014): 418–38, © 2014 by The University of Chicago.

INTRODUCTION

In this book I advance a specific argument about the character of liberal thought, with the aim of providing a fuller understanding of the way liberal concepts, principles, and aspirations have informed novelistic art of the nineteenth and twentieth centuries. I begin with the premise that liberalism is best understood as a philosophical and political project conceived in an acute awareness of the challenges and often bleak prospects confronting it. Commonly associated with ideas of human perfectibility and assured progressivism, philosophical liberalism is often contrasted not only with radical philosophies that call for wholesale transformation, but also with a conservative tradition that claims a monopoly on tragic, pessimistic, and "realistic" conceptions of humanity. From this perspective, liberalism is seen as naively optimistic, failing to attend to structural inequities or economic, psychological, and political actualities. Moreover, as a theory characterized as "thin" or abstract, liberalism has been seen as unable to register the existential density, and the affiliation-prompting intensity, that other belief systems—especially systems more at home with religious and nationalist rhetoric—have been able to offer. This concern has been central to the influential communitarian critique of liberalism. Some commentators see the problem as endemic to liberalism since its inception; others see a falling away from earlier and more robust forms of civic, welfare, or social democracy.[1]

These critical frameworks typically fail to credit liberalism for the genuineness of its predicaments and the seriousness and complexity of its engagement with them. It must be acknowledged, of course, that very real ideological differences and political commitments undergird the division between the radical Left and the liberal Left and between conservatism and liberalism, both within and outside the academy. But liberalism has a more complex and "thick" array of attitudinal stances, affective dispositions, and political objectives than the conventional contrasts admit. Throughout its history, liberalism has engaged sober and even stark views of historical development, political dynamics, and human and social psychology. This is strikingly evident in American liberalism of the 1930s and 1940s, when liberalism was articulated as a refusal of communism, on the one hand (whose utopianism was seen as entailing grave dangers), and fascism, on the other. More recent theoretical discussions of liberalism, especially those in literary and cultural studies, have tended to misrepresent liberalism's considered engagements with negative social and historical forces.

The complexity of liberal thinking is evident across a spectrum of writers as diverse as Alexis de Tocqueville, John Stuart Mill, Isaiah Berlin, Hannah Arendt, Richard Hofstadter, Reinhold Niebuhr, Lionel Trilling, Judith N. Shklar, and Jürgen Habermas. The work of these writers brings into view a number of undercurrents or persistent perceptions within liberal aspiration: the intractability of liberal vices, the limits of rational argument, the exacting demands of freedom amid value pluralism, the tragedy of history, and the corruptibility of procedure.[2] There has been a tendency at times to read the darker phases or turns within liberal thought simply as moments where writers or texts cease to be liberal. This is, I think, a misguided move. The pessimistic component of Mill's thinking is not a simple anomaly to be cataloged and dismissed along with similar fatalistic turns or odd obsessions in other liberal writers such as Trilling or Berlin. One might object that the major systematic liberals of recent times manifest different attitudes, serenity in the case of John Rawls and stringent rationalism in the case of Habermas. The point is not to disregard important differences among liberal thinkers but rather to press toward an account of the deeper discontents and aspirations that lie behind a pattern of attitudinal forms discernible across the tradition. Fundamentally, I will argue, liberalism is prompted by enduring challenges, often born of crisis, that exert their pressure on the internal dynamics of liberal thought. Properly assessed, liberalism can be seen to encompass, and not simply occasionally to disclose, the psychological, social, and economic barriers to its moral and political ideals. Once we admit this fuller understanding of political and philosophical liberalism, moreover, we can begin to see the formal and conceptual complexity involved in literary engagements with liberal thinking. As I will elaborate, these formal and conceptual features will move us well beyond familiar notions of the liberal temperament, individual fulfillment, or harmonious diversity.

To isolate one central example from nineteenth-century liberalism, John Stuart Mill's thinking importantly combined a faith in the ideal of self-development, on the one hand, and, on the other, a sociological assessment of the dangers associated with mass opinion.[3] This type of split within liberal thinking—its inclusion of both a moral and a sociological perspective—can be attributed in part to its having emerged concomitant with the evolutionary or historical view of social development characteristic of much nineteenth-century European thought. Importantly, the double view promotes a variety of attitudinal stances, not only forms of progressive confidence but also irony and pessimism. Historian John Burrow dates the double vision structure back to the eighteenth century and preeminently to Adam Smith, though of course Mill's version is a kind of reverse Smithism.[4] In place of the gap between the invisible hand and the self-interested individual, that is, we find a gap between the moral agent and darker sociological tendencies: the malevolent hand. Burrow memorably describes the double vision at one point as a persistent disjunction, at the intellectual level, between "what we morally admire and what we sociologically discern" (51). Liberals do not have a monopoly on this split view, but it tends to cause them more angst, especially given their investment in the ideal of progressive enlightenment, an investment which sits uneasily next to the frustrated acknowledgment of persistent sociological and psychological barriers to the projects of individual actualization and collective betterment.

Moreover, liberalism's commitment to the ideal of reflective enlightenment often presents itself not as a mere investment in neutrality, principle, or critical distance, but precisely as a kind of existential challenge. This broad condition is often where we see the affective dimensions of liberal aspiration given heightened expression. In general, the liberal tradition values the examined life in its many dimensions, including the rigorous scrutiny of principles, assumptions, and belief systems; the questioning of authority and tradition; the dedication to argument, debate, and deliberative processes of legitimation and justification; and the commitment to openness and transparency. Turning these principles and practices into a way of life, or infusing them into political institutions, has typically been seen as a challenge for liberalism. Acknowledging the philosophical complexities and existential predicaments attending liberal thought allows us to begin to conceptualize, and to disclose, a richer tradition of liberal aesthetics, especially given the complex ways literary works both register the dual vision and give resonant expression to the lived experience of political aspirations.

*   *   *

It is one of the ironies of contemporary culture in the United States that "liberal" is used as a negative term not only by the Republican Right but also by the academic Left. In the language of the Right, the word is typically used either as a noun designating individual politicians or as an adjective modifying the social and economic policies they support. In the language of the academic Left, by contrast, it is used almost exclusively as an adjective meant to characterize broad ideological and political formations: liberal humanism, the liberal state, the liberal imperial project. In this usage the term is understood not only to denote the core elements of liberal philosophy (free-market principles and a conception of the subject as free-standing and autonomous) but also to signal a view of the world that systematically disavows the structural inequities of the capitalist system, the conditions of power animating the social field, and the ways individuals are always embedded in myriad social relationships and interdependencies.

The academic use of "liberal" has enjoyed considerable staying power and portability throughout the rise and transformations of the interdisciplinary field known as theory. In both their theoretical premises and their political commitments, the dominant forms of literary scholarship in recent decades have not only kept their distance from liberalism, but also constituted liberalism as an assumed stable target of critique. The situation has been further intensified by a tendency to identify neoliberalism as the dominant contemporary regime, a tendency that implicitly identifies liberalism as the fundamental ideological form underwriting the neoliberal order. I will discuss this contributing factor in the following chapter, since the current discussions of neoliberalism are various and important. But there is of course an older and established critique of liberalism, one that predates the assumptions built into the critique of neoliberalism. Anti-humanist critiques of modernity—including structuralist, poststructuralist, and ideological criticism—have sought to dismantle the primacy of the liberal humanist subject and to identify liberalism as a function of capitalist ideology or, in the case of Michel Foucault, modern disciplinary power. Collateral critiques have been waged from the vantage point of communitarianism, feminism (with its critique of rationality and neutrality), and queer theory (with its focus on normativity as normalization). There are, of course, significant earlier critiques of liberal thought, including the tradition of organicist cultural criticism extending from Coleridge, Carlyle, and Arnold up through F. R. Leavis in Britain and the Southern Agrarians in the United States (in a sense the communitarian critique reprises this tradition). And a philosophical prelude to contemporary anti-liberal thought may be found in the work of the Frankfurt school in the postwar years (as I will discuss in chapter 4).

More recently, the critique of liberal modernity has come to focus on proceduralism and state politics, partly in response to the aftermath of 9/11 (specifically the abrogation of civil liberties in the "war on terror" and the expansion of executive power). While, on the one hand, the current geopolitical situation has promoted a closer consideration of proceduralism, on the other hand, the negative judgment of liberalism has essentially not changed. Indeed, the reconsideration of proceduralism has been framed by theories of the state of exception, which read violations of the rule of law and democratic procedure as an unavoidable condition of modern constitutionalism rather than a departure from a progressive democratic norm that merits strong constitutional and philosophical defense.

Giorgio Agamben's work, which draws on the theories of Carl Schmitt as well as on Michel Foucault's concept of biopower, has been central to this renewed critique of liberalism. Agamben insists on the enduring importance of sovereignty (as opposed to disciplinary power), and he argues that the state of exception and the politicization of what he calls bare life are at the heart of the horror of modernity and led inexorably to the Nazi death camps as the paradigmatic political topos in a world where the state of exception has become the norm. Crucially, Agamben sees the politicization of life as encompassing both the rise of liberal democracy and the emergence of totalitarianism. Like Foucault in his late-middle period, Agamben has a negative view of liberalism and the freedoms it pretends to promote, seeing those rights and freedoms as indissolubly linked to the production of more subtle and pervasive forms of power:

> It is almost as if, starting from a certain point, every decisive political event were double-sided: the spaces, the liberties, and the rights won by individuals in their conflicts with central powers always simultaneously prepared a tacit but increasing inscription of individuals' lives within the state order, thus offering a new and more dreadful foundation for the very sovereign power from which they wanted to liberate themselves.[5]

By abandoning the resources of the liberal democratic tradition and assimilating it to a modernity in which a Holocaust hue covers all of political life, Agamben's theory reinscribes the long-standing anti-liberal and anti-proceduralist commitments of much of contemporary literary theory.

Agamben's position has not stood uncontested, and there have also been some important broader critiques of the academic Left's failure to adequately address, and think through, democratic institutions and state politics. These critiques, it should be noted, tend to include at least two lines of argument, often in combination. One line is theoretical and political, stressing that the forms of negative critique dominating the field result in anti-normative, anti-procedural, and consequently anti-statist positions and stances. The most sustained and compelling versions of this argument may be found in Timothy Brennan's *Wars of Position* and John Brenkman's *The Cultural Contradictions of Democracy*.[6] The second criticism responds to what it sees as a romantic temperament driving the theoretical visions under discussion, identifiable in aesthetic concepts or values that fundamentally displace the political. Dominick LaCapra, for example, identifies modes of sublime excess and utopian displacement in Agamben.[7] Brennan faults literary and cultural theorists for aesthetic, poetic, and sublime modes of thinking. And Sean McCann and Michael Szalay emphasize the symbolic, magical, and aesthetic solutions that mark what they also tellingly call "literary thinking" after the New Left.[8]

It is here that we can begin to disclose some of the barriers to understanding the aesthetic forms and energies that characterize literary engagement with liberal thought. An argument structure that faults aesthetic thinking and asserts liberal principles reflects a tacit alliance between aesthetics and radical politics, one that liberalism is poised to diagnose and demystify. But it is worth probing a bit deeper into why theoretical work that valorizes aesthetic concepts and modes gains ascendancy in the literary field, which is a separate issue from the questionable displacement of normative questions by aestheticizing moves. Indeed, there is a genuine and deep problem here, one having to do with the literary Left's core vocational orientation toward the values of the aesthetic. Apart from any question of ideological or philosophical tendencies in the field, that is, we should not be surprised that aesthetic values figure prominently within its analytical frameworks. It is worth considering, moreover, how this particular field condition has played out in broader intellectual historical terms. One way to put this is to ask whether and to what extent the aesthetic investments of the field practitioners have influenced the field's own favored critical and theoretical frameworks. This will allow us to begin to analyze why, within the literary field, there is such difficulty in apprehending or thinking in distinctly aesthetic terms about some of the core concepts and normative values of political liberalism.

To identify what one means by aesthetic values or investments is of course a difficult task, given the long and varied history of thinking on aesthetics. Given the coincidence of the development of the field of literary studies with the modern period, I will emphasize a range of values and concepts that derive from that period and that are recognizably post-Kantian in their self-understandings and internal differentiations. Let us stipulate, then, that the aesthetic, as a governing orientation of the field, involves a broad spectrum of values associated with complexity, difficulty, variousness, ambiguity, undecidability, hermeneutic open-endedness, and threshold experiences — experiences that prompt or tease one into an apprehension of the new, the unrealized, or the buried. While particular readings may assert what seems to be a finalizing authority or narrow certainty, in general we consider aesthetic objects, and especially the complex conceptual forms of literary art, to yield an ongoing richness of interpretive possibilities. And we associate what we call the experience of the aesthetic with the values of incompleteness, complexity, difficulty, excess, aporia. These values shift in emphasis, and they can be mapped in relation to familiar oppositions: beautiful/sublime, liberal/radical, human/inhuman. What is salient for the purposes of this book, however, is that even in their tamer liberal humanist non-sublime forms, these aesthetic values clash with the investments of normative liberal philosophy, democratic proceduralism, and the mundane aspects of participatory and state politics. Within literary and cultural studies, across the liberal and radical camps, there is a kind of temperamental aversion to certain key values of normative philosophy and procedural theory — most especially normative explicitness, reason-giving argument, and transparency. Against these, the aesthetic temperament values the implicit, the tacit, paradox, and a rich opacity.

Thus, apart from the real ideological commitments driving the critique of liberalism, commitments whose relevance I in no way intend to dismiss or demote, there is also at play a temperamental factor, conditioned by field propensities, that favors the forms of critique that target liberalism. Theories and modes of analysis that manage to play out an aesthetic resistance to the values of liberalism and proceduralism are thus often given pride of place. For an example of this broader tendency, one need only look to the influential theoretical readings of Franz Kafka's fable "Before the Law." Kafka's short text, written independently but later situated within *The Trial*, dramatizes a relation between the individual and the law in a way that invites universalization. Viewed in the context of the novel, however, and especially given its precise location there, a more humanizing or existential understanding of the fable becomes possible. I will return to this point a bit later. The fable itself describes an encounter between a man from the country and a doorkeeper who stands "before the law," barring entry yet also speaking as though entry is simply being deferred: not yet may the man enter. The man goes on waiting, his entreaties to pass through endlessly put off by the doorkeeper, until his death. Just as death approaches he asks the doorkeeper why no one else has tried to enter, and the doorkeeper responds: "No one else could gain admittance here, because this entrance was meant solely for you. I'm going to go shut it now."[9]

In his reading of the fable, Jacques Derrida emphasizes the incessant deferral of the decision on whether the man can pass through the door: the law is "a nothing that incessantly defers access to itself," and the subject is always standing before the law, before an incessantly deferred judgment.[10] Additionally, in Derrida's analysis the law is fundamentally subordinated to the more primary conditions of language and literature. For Derrida, while the law is always trying to project an authority that lies beyond or outside narrative or history, it inevitably partakes of the same condition of possibility of literature, the fundamental linguistic conditions of *différance* and undecidability. It is crucial, therefore, that in Kafka's text the law projects its authoritative power and originary status within a fable. In a later and equally influential text, "Force of Law: The 'Mystical Foundation of Authority,'" Derrida juxtaposes law's calculability to the incalculability of justice, arguing for the necessity of acts of decision within a kind of impossible aporia.[11] The law in its calculability is a degraded and limited form, associated with a fundamental violence; by contrast, justice as a kind of ideal stands above and beyond it to show the law's limits and conditioned aspect. It is not possible, given these terms, to talk in any way about a viable procedural politics, since such a politics would, on the one hand, fall beneath the level of the romanticized decision and would, on the other hand, be squarely within the realm of the calculability of the law.

In *Homo Sacer*, Agamben differentiates his reading of Kafka's fable from Derrida's, as part of a broader and longer critique of deconstruction's tendency to rest in aporias. For Agamben, the parable is not an account of an event that never happens, or happens in not happening, but rather a description of "how something has really happened in seeming not to happen": the virtual state of exception becomes real in the eventual closing of the door.[12] The indeterminacy of contemporary politics, evident in the many "zones of indistinction" he identifies, is not an absolute condition of political existence but precisely what needs to be diagnosed and overcome. Whether this methodological distinction ultimately amounts to a difference that makes a difference is of course open to debate. We see a similar theoretical sidestep in Agamben's approach to proceduralism more generally, where its value appears limited to negative diagnosis:

> The correct question to pose concerning the horrors committed in the camps is, therefore, not the hypocritical one of how crimes of such atrocity could be committed against human beings. It would be more honest and, above all, more useful to investigate carefully the juridical procedures and deployments of power by which human beings could be so completely deprived of their rights and prerogatives that no act committed against them could appear any longer as a crime. (171)

By this account, proceduralism operates as a power-laden and dehumanizing instrument for evacuating moral categories. Crucially for our purposes, Agamben's negative critique of liberal modernity is combined with a call to move entirely beyond the logic of modernity: what is required is thinking the relation between potentiality and actuality differently or, as he puts it cryptically, "thinking ontology and politics beyond every figure of relation" (47). Liberal and procedural modernity are themselves beyond redemption.

The approach Derrida and Agamben take to the analysis of law in modernity certainly seems to warrant the claims of those who criticize the displacement of state and institutional politics by romantic, aesthetic, and mystical values. However, if one wishes to reconstruct a literary history of liberalism or imagine possibilities for a distinctly liberal aesthetic, it is unproductive simply to identify and reject a pattern of "aestheticizing" within contemporary theoretical practices. One can certainly fault as obscure and messianic a theory that combines a diagnostic-critical analysis of the state of exception with a call to think beyond any relation. But we need a better understanding of the influence of this work as a function of specific conditions within the literary field. If one wishes to propose an alternative understanding of liberal concepts and forms that will be effective and influential within literary studies, one needs to remain responsive to the field's values and methods, which are, in a word, inescapably oriented toward the aesthetic. And it must be stressed that this is not merely a practical consideration: the history of liberalism, as both a philosophy and a literary topos, is richer, and more amenable to interpretive challenges and complexity, than many of the current critiques allow.

These complexities make themselves felt in the formal dynamics of literary texts as well as through their representation of the lived relation to political commitment or political conditions. It is here that we might return to "Before the Law." While I in no way claim to recruit Kafka to the camp of liberalism, it is arguable that the theoretical readings of "Before the Law" fail to capture what is of most interest in the interplay between the fable and both the immediate scene and the larger narrative surrounding its appearance in *The Trial*. The parable is conveyed by a priest K speaks with, one who ultimately reveals himself to be the "prison chaplain" and therefore belonging to the court that is trying K. In telling the parable, the priest is trying to disabuse K of his misplaced belief that any individual could help him in relation to the law and, correlatively, that trust and openness have any relevance when one is before the law. Afterward K and the priest have a long discussion about the fable, with K falling back into a natural attitude about the two characters' understanding and sincerity, wondering whether they are deceived or simply unknowing. Ultimately the priest insists on the irrelevance of K's characterological and ethical interest in the story, stating that the doorkeeper represents the Law and its necessity, just as he, as prison chaplain, necessarily represents the court as well. Derrida reads this conversation as a repetition of the recursive structure of the fable itself and therefore as simply reinforcing its effects. But K resists the depersonalizing invocation of the Law throughout, just as he has been impelled toward the priest as one who might provide human aid of some sort. K is trying to hold on to an existentialist spar here, one that would make individual choice and character matter and that would make human relations matter. He is fatigued and disoriented by the priest's tendency to invoke the pointlessness of hermeneutic discussion while still engaging in it.

Regardless of the force of the fable, or the force of the Law it represents, the surrounding narrative insists on the significance of living a relation to these difficult conditions, and this is the feature of the text that goes unacknowledged in the theoretical readings.[13] One could say that these readings refuse or ignore the humanist elements at play in Kafka's emphasis on alienation and demoralization, but I would underscore, rather, the significance of the novel's representation of the lived relation to harsh conditions, its emphasis on the effort to hold on to the significance of various principles (in this case of truth, truthfulness, and justice). It is the spirit of this type of narrative project, however pessimistic or bleakly aspirational, that it is of interest to me here, not the precise ideological position of the novel or, to the extent that it is discernible, the author. We will see many versions of this commitment amid bleak conditions throughout the chapters that follow.

*   *   *

It must be conceded that thinkers within the liberal tradition have contributed to the situation in which liberalism is seen to have a deficient if not antagonistic relation to aesthetic values and modes. Indeed, to the extent that self-identified liberal thinkers have implicitly or explicitly taken up the question of liberalism's relation to the aesthetic, there has been a tendency to refuse or at least evade the development of a liberal aesthetics that encompasses the forms and practices of political liberalism itself. In the work of thinkers and critics such as Lionel Trilling, Richard Rorty, and Stefan Collini, for example, a certain humanist emphasis on creative richness ("variousness," to use Trilling's term) and aesthetic temperament has set the terms for what many anti-liberal thinkers view as an easily discernible and tame liberal aesthetic.[14] Trilling and Rorty, moreover, help to entrench a certain gulf between political liberalism and liberal aesthetics. In his influential essay "Private Irony and Liberal Hope," Rorty argues that we should accept and even cultivate a productive division between private and public life, one that precisely turns on the modes, temperaments, and values suitable to each.[15] In opposition to the notion, put forward by Habermas, that postmodernism has been destructive of social hope, Rorty claims that one can be an ironist in private, endlessly re-elaborating one's self-descriptions and one's frameworks of understanding, without jeopardizing the role one needs to adopt in public in order to honor the procedural public sphere or liberal democracy. Here a generative self-fashioning and playful aesthetic mode are given full force in the private realm, then curtailed or muted in public. It is true that Rorty's position acknowledges the ways private irony might generate better forms of understanding and practice in the public sphere, where one constantly needs to negotiate different standpoints and different sets of interests. And his position shifts over time toward a discussion of the ways various aesthetics might animate public discourse.[16] But "Private Irony and Liberal Hope" insists on a division not only between the private and public spheres but also, it is clear, between aesthetics and politics. And even though Rorty stresses irony as opposed to, say, tolerance and appreciation of diversity, his emphasis on individual self-fashioning falls within the broader rubric of the creative liberal individualism that stretches back to John Stuart Mill's emphasis on "experiments of living."[17]

Rorty's position is anticipated by Lionel Trilling, a thinker deeply interested in the relation between liberalism and literature. In *The Liberal Imagination*, Trilling observes that readers in a liberal democratic culture like his own most value works by writers who are actually antagonistic to the culture's social and political ideals (he invokes, as valued writers, Yeats, Eliot, Proust, Joyce, Lawrence, and Gide). He also observes that to the extent that contemporary American literature is politically liberal in orientation, it is not of lasting interest. Trilling's larger point here is that there is a serious aesthetic deficiency in the ideas of political liberalism. There is no insistence that this need be so for all time, but there is a sense that liberalism cannot generate a profound literature, one we would return to or would live with, as Trilling puts it, "in an active reciprocal relation."[18] "It is by no means true," Trilling writes, "that the inadequacy of the literature that connects itself with a body of ideas is the sign of the inadequacy of those ideas, although it is no doubt true that some ideas have less affinity with literature than others" (302).

In the preface to *The Liberal Imagination*, Trilling expresses his project as an internal critique of liberalism that would "recall liberalism to its first essential imagination of variousness and possibility" (xxi). Trilling's conception of political liberalism is broad, including both what we think of as democratic liberalism in the United States and other forms of progressive politics from social democracy to communism.[19] The danger of political liberalism in all its forms, according to Trilling, is its tendency to "organize the elements of life in a rational way":

> When we approach liberalism in a critical spirit we shall fail in critical completeness if we do not take into account the value and necessity of its organizational impulse. But at the same time we must understand that organization means delegation, and agencies, and bureaus, and technicians, and that the ideas that can survive delegation, that can be passed on to agencies and bureaus and technicians, incline to be ideas of a certain kind and of certain simplicity: they give up something of their largeness and modulation and complexity in order to survive. The lively sense of contingency and possibility, and of those exceptions to the rule which may be the beginning of the end of the rule—this sense does not suit well with the impulse to organization.[20]

Trilling's argument resonates with certain claims of literature's superiority to philosophy when it comes to capturing living ideas, but he offers a more specific claim about the poverty of political liberalism as an existential and aesthetic mode of thought.[21] Also evident is the distinction between liberalism as a temperament and liberalism as a body of ideas or a practical orientation toward institutions and the larger political system. The former is enabling for literature and, through literature, enabling for politics: it is the true promise of liberalism. The latter, by contrast, is a problem for vital literary art.

The examples of Rorty and Trilling reveal what is actually a broader and quite consequential phenomenon—an odd gap, often actively elaborated and reflectively endorsed, between political liberalism and liberal aesthetics. This phenomenon has been reinforced by certain systematic liberal philosophers, such as Rawls and Habermas, who have tended not to pay sustained attention to matters aesthetic. Moreover, certain approaches that may appear to overcome or refuse the split in liberalism between the political and the aesthetic registers (the "creative democracy" of John Dewey, for example) tend to support a liberal humanism oriented to the aesthetic register of the beautiful and to ethico-political virtues associated with harmonious diversity.[22] Missing from such visions are the intractable energies of those moods of doubt, despair, and difficulty that frequently accompany the commitment to liberal democratic principles. From this perspective, the motivating skepticism of Trilling and Rorty can be seen both as an important acknowledgment of the specificity of institutional and procedural politics (their distance from common conceptions of the liberal imagination) and as a symptom of an established way of thinking about liberal aesthetics. In this book I will promote an angle of sight capable of discerning the productive difficulty and excess that attend rich literary engagements with liberal politics and the broader values of philosophical modernity that subtend them. The liberal tradition is not as prosaic, rule-governed, and simply hopeful as its critics seem to suppose; certain aspirations and threshold experiences, certain energies at once negative and utopian, are as vital within the liberal aesthetic tradition as they are in the Marxist aesthetics of someone like Theodor Adorno. To put it another way, liberalism manifests its own version of the Gramscian motto, "Pessimism of the intellect, optimism of the will."

This book aims to contribute to reconsiderations of liberalism, both by drawing on existing scholarship and by identifying specific formal and theoretical features of liberalism that have remained unacknowledged or under-examined. I will be particularly interested in attending to concepts and principles associated with political and philosophical liberalism, such as enfranchisement, injustice and harm, critique, argument, and deliberative debate. Some key scholarship in the literary field has identified an underappreciated liberal tradition, most notably in relation to the theory of the public sphere and the practices associated with it.[23] Additionally, some work on nineteenth- and twentieth-century American and British literature has turned its lens on the importance of the state and its institutions (this work could be seen as an accompaniment to the more polemical interventions of critics such as Brennan and McCann and Szalay). Moving away from the Foucauldian model of disciplinarity and surveillance, which productively engaged earlier critics of power such as D. A. Miller and Nancy Armstrong, these studies have insisted on a more differentiated understanding of state power, and some have taken a less suspicious look at forms of social democracy and the welfare state.[24] All these critics explore modes of experience that issue from specific engagements with the institution of the state. My aim, however, is to expand the field of inquiry to include explorations of when, where, and how specific literary forms engage some of the shaping principles of liberal political thought as well as the enduring challenges of liberal political life. As will become apparent, my analyses are more oriented both toward concepts in political philosophy and toward existential questions than the work I mention above.

Other notable reconsiderations of liberalism and literature have focused not on the state and its institutions but on elements we associate with the liberal temperament and its ethico-political features: open-mindedness, tolerance, sympathy, responsiveness, and a set of aesthetic features associated with these postures — perspectivalism, particularity, complexity, density of representation. This approach is represented in David Wayne Thomas's work on "many-sidedness" in Victorian liberal aesthetics, in Stefan Collini's intellectual history of the concept of character in Victorian political thought, and in the ethically oriented literary criticism of Martha Nussbaum and Richard Rorty.[25] Such work certainly contributes to a fuller understanding of the liberal ethos or, better, to an understanding of how central ethos and character are to the liberal tradition. But it tends to have an individualist bias — in this sense reinscribing one of the features of liberalism itself. As a consequence, lost to view are both the systems perspectives associated with liberalism — its larger sociological and political analyses of inequality, injustice, and thwarted actualization — and the struggles or difficulties associated with living an avowed commitment to liberal principles. While a dominantly character-based interpretive approach to literary texts may capture some of the features of lived commitment that interest me here, it will miss some of the more complex formal dynamics at play in literary engagements with liberal thought, such as the interplay between third- and first-person perspectives or the complex use of narratorial and character-character argument.

From a somewhat different perspective but pursuing the same notion of subjective enactment we see in the work on the liberal temperament, Elaine Hadley has analyzed liberal individualism in Victorian culture, showing how forms of cognition and abstract citizenship were imagined and practiced.[26] In addition, Hadley discloses aesthetic manifestations of liberal thinking and liberal selfhood, expanding the field of liberal aesthetics in welcome ways. There are thus affinities between her project and mine. But there is also a key difference in emphasis: Hadley's analyses settle most strenuously on challenges internal to the subjective ideals of liberalism, many of them presented as afflicting individuals with forms of ambivalence or unease, while I am aiming to reconstruct how writers sought to give theoretical and literary form to what they actively and reflectively embraced as constitutive challenges.

The literature that provides the occasion for my analyses will include canonical works of high realism, a representative constellation of political novels from England and the United States, and two works of modernism that themselves dramatize the ideological conflicts of the twentieth century in striking ways. Indeed, a central role in this book is played by the liberalism of the war and cold war era, in that its features shed light on some of the abiding orientations of liberal thinking. In the following chapter I will elaborate the significance of the liberalism of this era, within a broader discussion of the concept and history of bleak liberalism. This opening chapter will aim to provide a context for the literary chapters that follow, exploring not only the complexities of liberalism's engagement with those forces and conditions that most challenge its aspirations, but also the distinctive ethos of liberal thought, its character as a lived commitment. What is especially instructive about the liberalism of the twentieth century is its active engagement with debates over politics and art, not only in discussions about realism and modernism, but also in response to concerns about the role of art in the face of challenging experiences of political disenchantment and renewed aspirations. The hybrid nature of this discursive formation, its fluid movement across the literary, philosophical, and journalistic domains, makes it an especially vibrant enactment of the liberalism this book aims to capture. In this chapter I will also assess the role that the concept of neoliberalism has played in recent cultural analysis of the ideological and political field, showing where critical accounts of neoliberalism stand in relation to the broader phenomenon of bleak liberalism.

In chapter 2 I turn to the place of liberalism in the realist tradition. Coming at the same historical juncture as the rise of liberalism, the nineteenth-century novel takes up some of the same issues that exercise liberalism itself: imagining the critique of custom and convention as a way of life and grappling with its consequences on conceptions of virtue and character; mediating between the moral life of individuals and a long sociological or historical view of communities and societies; finding a way to acknowledge violence and suffering, both natural and social; and engaging the relation between existence and doctrine or between life and theory. In this chapter I consider three major realist texts of the nineteenth century—*Bleak House*, *The Way We Live Now*, and *Middlemarch*—demonstrating the distinctive ways they reflect liberal commitments and dilemmas, paying particular attention to the tension between moral aspiration and systemic critique (Dickens), critique and custom (Trollope), and the gap between ethics and politics (Eliot). One persistent claim of my analyses in this chapter is that liberal principles disallow any easy turn to moral character as the sole site of value or effective action. Strikingly, these writers simultaneously present exemplary individuals and register the limits of a character-based understanding of political practice and political life. As we will see, transpersonal or impersonal forms and practices make their force felt alongside the individual self-actualization so familiar from those strands of liberalism that have heretofore influenced literary studies.

The third chapter reconsiders the role of argument as a distinctive formal feature within the genre of the political or "social problem" novel. Noticeable most within interludes of ideological debate among characters, dialogical argument characterizes the social problem novel from its inception and is sometimes supplemented by forms of narratorial commentary or position taking. As a precursor to the novel of ideas, this subgenre of the novel helps us identify and characterize what often functions as a distinctly liberal formal component—deliberative debate or ideological self-positioning—within the broader constellation of formal features in the novel more generally. As I will argue, it is important to identify the narratological specificity of such forms of argument, which cannot simply be classed as conventional dialogue. Additionally, in its focus on the lived relation to political commitment, the political novel vividly dramatizes the challenges associated with emergent forms of ideological self-consciousness or reflective awareness. Readings of Dickens's *Hard Times*, Elizabeth Gaskell's *North and South*, and E. M. Forster's *Howards End* provide the basis for a set of claims about the aesthetic force and contours of argument within specific novelistic projects. I pay special attention not only to the significance of argument, but also to its perceived limits and to the limits of politics as such, a haunting concern of liberalism that distinguishes it from conservatism.

The final two chapters of the book turn to the twentieth-century context so central to my conceptualization of bleak liberalism. Chapter 4 explores the relation between politics and aesthetics in the war and postwar era through a comparison of liberal and radical responses to the catastrophes of the twentieth century. To illuminate the role played by aesthetics, I compare the Frankfurt school and the bleak liberals, Adorno and Trilling in particular. The aim of this chapter is to expose the striking similarities in attitude and intellectual orientation that characterize these two schools of thought, while at the same time identifying the instructive divergences in their aesthetic and political valuations. This comparison ultimately allows for a fuller understanding of the liberalism of this era and discloses the importance of existential realism to the bleak liberal tradition—its strong interest in capturing through literary art the lived commitment to ideas. As a case study, I turn to Trilling's novel *The Middle of the Journey*, which represents a continuation of the tradition of the political novel analyzed in chapter 3 but also constitutes a new subgenre, the ideological novel of manners, a literary form that aims to capture the sociological and psychological dimensions of ideological commitment in the context of twentieth-century political life.

The final chapter addresses two important political novels of the mid-twentieth century, Ralph Ellison's *Invisible Man* and Doris Lessing's *The Golden Notebook*, showing how the bleak liberal tradition continues its experiments with form in modernist literary art. Literary circles in the postwar period often engaged in vigorous debates about the relative merits of realism and modernism, and both Ellison and Lessing are known for their innovative use of form as well as their strong respect for the moral and intellectual achievements of the realist tradition. These two texts in particular are eloquent in their treatment of continued aspiration in the wake of political disenchantment. In this chapter I aim to show the striking formal and conceptual elements that make up these novels' engagement with political ideals (democratic in the case of Ellison, socialist and liberal-progressive in the case of Lessing). This concluding chapter is meant to open out the discussion of the liberal aesthetic to a potentially limitless field of formal experiments.

CHAPTER ONE

Bleak Liberalism

One of the more basic judgments typically made about authors and texts concerns ideological stance. In both casual intellectual conversation and formal scholarship, the designation of ideological position often plays a significant orienting role, as premise, flanking assertion, or conclusion. The primary characterizations, of course, are conservative, liberal, and radical, but there are an infinite number of shadings and qualifiers, to which the art of analysis is irresistibly drawn: liberal communitarian, Left conservative, Tory radical. If we relax the parameters a bit further, we can include such designations as angry communitarian, charismatic proceduralist, or anti-anticommunist. Indeed, in humanistic analysis, ideological designation tends to take on a descriptive density that allows for the finer discriminations we associate with interpretive insight and individual variation, however fundamentally we may regard the divide between Left and Right. Which is to say ideological designations often take on the quality of more nuanced understandings of embedded character, in that they refer to style and disposition as much as to position or platform.

One doesn't need adjectival flags or descriptive refinements to recognize that the appeal to the character of political ideologies has a long and significant history. In fact, underlying the impulse to finer differentiations are basic assumptions that are themselves characterological. In much intellectual and political discourse, as I discussed in the introduction, liberalism is assumed to project a fundamentally optimistic attitude while conservatism is seen as either realistic or stoical and radicalism as utopian and dogmatic. My claim here is not simply that humanistic analysis tends to accord psychological and ethical nuance to existing political stances, but rather that political orientations and commitments can never be understood or grasped — or even made manifest in the first place — except through forms of human expression that also reflect, and are routinely taken to reflect, attitudes, dispositions, and characterological elements.

Ideology critique, a key practice in the Left academy with a strong influence on trends in the humanities, axiomatically privileges interests over character and aims to remind us that it is necessary to understand the complexities of human response in relation to socioeconomic position. An attention to individual variation typically appears as a feature of any extended ideological analysis of specific thinkers or texts, but imagining that variation is itself a value would be seen as something of a misstep, one associated with the particular ideological blindness of liberalism. I mention this because it is important to recognize at the outset that attention to finely differentiated character is itself associated with the political ideology of liberalism, especially in its aesthetic dimensions. But of course there is also a field propensity in humanistic studies, and probably preeminently in literary studies, to produce variation in scholarship precisely through descriptions that presuppose a near-infinite multiplicity of individual cases of ideological form and expression.

I am not particularly interested in dwelling on this dizzying irony, but I am interested in what it says about the peculiar position of liberalism in much current humanities scholarship. It is well known that liberalism serves negatively to define many theoretical positions in the humanities, not only because it is associated with two faulty ideals, the autonomous individual and the free market, but also because it is seen as a particularly pernicious and efficacious ideology, one that disavows its own interests and violence and perpetuates forms of subjectivity and thought that entrench established interests and mask operations of power. In this sense liberalism is not *an* ideology; it simply *is* ideology and therefore supersedes individuals completely. To the extent that it is lived, it is a structuring illusion. That is, while liberalism historically has accorded value to individual experience and variation, the critique of liberalism has tended to stress its distance from anything we would recognize as authentic experience. To this extent, liberalism is often perceived by the radical Left as worse than conservatism, in that it is seen to legitimate rather than lament capitalist modernity and as failing to capture fundamental human and social needs.

To focus on individual character as an ideological element of a benighted liberalism is to fail to acknowledge the informing textures of liberalism's own characterology or its status as an affirmed stance with its own forms of lived complexity. This chapter will seek to recapture and reframe liberalism as a body of thought and as a lived political commitment, and in doing so it will argue for a more differentiated understanding of both the history of liberalism and its ethos, or character. The chapter will focus especially on liberalism's sense of the challenges it faces and on the cautions it sounds in light of those conditions and forces that threaten its aspirations. I will pay special attention to persistent efforts to expand liberalism beyond the boundaries of what we think of as classical economic liberalism, to acknowledge the limits of reason, and to explore artistic and literary means for expressing political experience. The chapter will explore twentieth-century liberal formations in some depth, largely because liberalism of the interwar, war, and cold war era manifests with striking intensity the features I wish to underscore throughout the book. As I will argue, the liberalism of this era—bleak, chastened, and invested in complex aesthetic expression of its aims and experiential depth—is best viewed not as an anomaly within the history of liberal thought but rather as a heightened example of persistent features of liberal thinking and art. Since this book will culminate in two chapters on the literature and aesthetic theories of this era, this opening chapter importantly sets the stage for both the book as a whole and the final chapters. My hermeneutic wager is that the profound disenchantment of twentieth-century political thought helps light up a persistent feature of liberal aspiration, and this chapter therefore returns to nineteenth-century thinkers only after a discussion of the mid-twentieth century. At the conclusion of this chapter, I will address the relation of neoliberalism to the broad formation of bleak liberalism I am aiming to reconstruct. The final section has two aims: to directly confront the challenge that neoliberalism poses to the project of traditional political liberalism, and to characterize the informing aims and principles of the critics of neoliberalism, who, I will argue, share important features of the bleak liberal tradition and thus could be considered to extend it, if ambivalently.

Before I continue, however, let me provide a brief note on my use of "ethos" and "character." I use these terms throughout the book both to emphasize their close interrelation and to suggest that it is not coherent to treat "ethos" as a valorized term, as much anti-humanistic discourse does, while banning "character."[1] "Ethos" is doubtless privileged by some because it seems to denote habits and practices—or ways of being—without invoking the unified self many associate with "character." And in its meaning as "culture," it also crucially allows for characterizations that extend beyond the individual to the collective or community at large. I will employ both terms because I believe that using "character" along with "ethos" helps us think through the ethical and existential dimensions of intellectual and political positions, precisely because terms we associate with character (particularly adjectival and adverbial ascriptions) often signal moments where the lived aspects of theory are making their force felt. My aim in using both terms is thus to illuminate the way various forms of thought imagine how ideas and commitments might be enacted and lived. In this sense, the characterological dimensions of thought infuse it with experiential vividness, but they are not equivalent to the characterological attributes of a person. My focus here is on the character of forms of thinking as they express what might be called their existential dimensions.

Liberalism's own character can be discerned, I will suggest, only if one sees liberalism not just as a philosophy aiming to set out first principles but also, and almost from the start, as a situated response to historical challenges. Ironically, the recent academic framings of liberalism effect a denial of liberalism's own internal history, even as those who dismiss it call for a careful attention to the situated nature of all thought. From its inception, liberal thinkers were aware of the tension between the abstract value of liberty and the problem of social and economic equality, and that awareness prompted significant systematic shifts in liberal thought beginning in the later nineteenth century. The New Liberalism in Britain associated with T. H. Green, L. T. Hobhouse, and J. A. Hobson involved an attempt to articulate the principles of socioeconomic justice, and the scope of government action, that would allow for any meaningful achievement of liberty within the conditions of the modern economic state. And on the political front, the development of the welfare state in Europe and the New Deal in the United States constituted a major redirection of the liberal project toward social democratic policy. These changes in philosophical outlook and political program also led to replacing the emphasis on the isolated individual with an emphasis on individuals as socially embedded and interdependent. From the organicism of the New Liberals to the pragmatic holism of John Dewey and the communicative ethics of Jürgen Habermas, a major strand of liberal thought foregrounds the embedded nature of social life and the impossibility of imagining an individual agent who can be cleanly separated from the rest of the polity. Moreover, the processual nature of political liberalism, whether viewed as a neutral proceduralism or as a commitment to a positive conception of liberty founded on discussion in the service of assumed values (characterological, intellectual, or political), is fundamentally open-ended and reflective, displacing the passive conceptions of market liberalism and rational self-interest as the guarantors of systemic progress.

Liberalism's self-correcting movements do not merely reflect a progressivist confidence, though they have often been seen that way. On the contrary, the self-critical and transformative nature of liberalism throughout its history, its responsiveness to ethical, philosophical, and historical challenges, brings to the fore an entirely different facet of the liberal character that has been present since the beginning—a pessimism or bleakness of attitude that derives from awareness of all those forces and conditions that threaten the realization of liberal ambitions. This is not to dismiss the exclusions that have attended liberalism throughout its long history, exclusions based on many forms of ascribed and chosen identities. To reconstruct the ways liberalism has engaged recalcitrant social and psychological problems is not to aim to dissolve the differences between consciously avowed problems and those that are ignored or disavowed or even actively created. Figures discussed in this chapter, including preeminently Mill and Trilling, displayed forms of bias and exclusion especially when it came to race. And of course liberalism's advances don't always come from internal questioning but also arise from external pressure. Many accounts of liberalism to date have given great emphasis to these shortcomings, and some have seen such exclusions as constitutive of liberalism.[2] I do not adhere to that view, seeking rather to reconstruct liberalism's doubts about its own project and its understanding of the ways it remains an unfinished project. Elements of internal blindness and identity-based exclusions require acknowledgment, however, and they will come up in several of the writers included here. The discussion of Ralph Ellison and Doris Lessing in chapter 5 will return us centrally to the unaddressed problem of race in many of the liberals of the postwar era.

As I discussed in the introduction, to duly acknowledge liberalism's own internal struggles, its historically situated forms of self-criticism and self-transformation, is to disclose a philosophical and political orientation that has more existential density than it is often presumed to possess. This fact also has significant implications, I will show, for the range of aesthetic forms and effects we associate with liberalism. The complex range of stances and affects manifest throughout liberalism's history is attributable not merely to a governing flexibility of mind that might be classified under the rubric of the liberal temperament, but also to interacting forms of analysis and human response that typically express a dialectic of skepticism and hope. On the one hand, one encounters bleak sociologies, sober psychologies, historical pessimism; on the other, commitments to freedom and equality, to individual and collective self-actualization, to democratic process and the rule of law. To begin to recognize these shaping tensions of liberalism therefore can prompt new ways of thinking about both the liberal ethos and the liberal aesthetic. In this sense, a renewed understanding of liberalism promises to move beyond a restrictive association with a narrow, and ideologically blinkered, valorization of temperament and character. It does so not by dismissing the importance of character in relation to ideology, but by trying to give a fuller understanding of the specific character of liberalism's ongoing relation to its own project.

As I have suggested, this constellation of concerns is perhaps nowhere more evident than in the liberalisms of the twentieth century, particularly in what often goes under the name cold war liberalism. Cold war liberalism is often assumed to simply confirm the bid for power, and the exercise of force, that is perceived to underlie liberalism's disavowal of the fact that power structures all relations and institutions. But a closer look at this passage in the history of liberalism, including the debates that arose in the thirties and forties (in advance of the cold war proper), reveals a complex and considered response to a set of factors: the rise of fascism, the entry into World War II, and the profound disappointment of the Soviet experiment. Many of those who entered the debate, it is striking to note, were as interested in aesthetics, particularly literature, as they were in politics.

The debates that developed in the pages of *Partisan Review* and elsewhere among the group known as the New York intellectuals are generally underrepresented in histories of twentieth-century criticism, and certainly in theory anthologies, which tend to elevate the New Critics as the key precursors to the rise of theory in the sixties, while the frameworks for discussion of aesthetics and politics are drawn from the Frankfurt school, the New Left, and British cultural studies. Tellingly, the *Norton Anthology of Theory and Criticism* includes entries by only three figures from this intellectual context, none of whom were cold war liberals: Leon Trotsky (an important figure in this cultural milieu, and one whose works appeared in its journals), Irving Howe, and Edmund Wilson.[3]

Two forces have contributed to this occlusion: the bitter relationship between the cold war liberals and the New Left, and the rise of theory itself, which incorporated a structuring critique of humanism and liberalism. That many of the cold war liberals had earlier subscribed to more radical positions, either as self-identifying communists or as fellow travelers, has reinforced a common sense on the left that liberalism is itself fundamentally conservative. To adapt the title of a book on Trilling and Whittaker Chambers, everyone seemed to have made a "conservative turn."[4] One cannot emphasize this too sharply: the axiomatic view on the left is that liberals are conservative. And the New York intellectuals as a socio-intellectual and cultural-political phenomenon seem to underscore this point in such a way that the actual content of their debates ends up getting nullified. The move from radical to conservative (or neoconservative) is seen as at once a personal autobiographical tendency and a historical trend, both of which reinforce each other and in turn justify a larger tendency to collapse liberalism and neoconservatism. Thus Alan Wald, in his history of the New York intellectuals, asserts that Irving Kristol "personally embodied neoconservatism's continuity with Cold War liberalism."[5]

The turn from radicalism to conservatism among a number of high-profile New York intellectuals, most prominently Irving Kristol and Norman Podhoretz, is well documented, as is the later tendency for many of these intellectuals to adopt an antagonistic attitude toward the New Left and toward identity politics and multiculturalism.[6] It is also the case that the uncompromising anticommunism of many of these figures was seen to collapse anti-Stalinism and anticommunism in a way that impoverished thought on the liberal Left. By reducing this vital cultural debate to a trend line, however, one loses sight of one of the most significant phases of liberal thought—a notably bleak liberalism, with suggestive aesthetic elements that can be understood only if the broader context of the liberal response is elucidated. As I have stated, liberalism typically manifests an interplay between hope and skepticism, often marked by a tension between moral aspiration and sober apprehension of those historical, sociological, or psychological tendencies that threaten its ambitions. In the case of the New York intellectuals in the thirties and forties, this particular dynamic expresses a deeply felt sense of lived crisis, and it in fact sounds odd to anyone steeped in that period of history to assert that liberalism is bleak—odd because it is so obviously true. From Arthur Schlesinger's *The Vital Center*, which calls for "moderate pessimism," to the darker visions of those such as Reinhold Niebuhr and Lionel Trilling, there was a strong insistence on the negative: as Daniel Bell puts it, "ours, a 'twice-born' generation, finds its wisdom in pessimism, evil, tragedy, and despair."[7] It is precisely the belated and disenchanted quality of this liberalism that requires exegesis so we can better understand it as a response to a historical situation, one that dwells as much in the existential register of crisis and repair as in the normative regions of principle and procedure.

The rise of theory, and in particular the critique of Enlightenment from both the poststructuralist and the Marxist perspectives, also contributed to the conditions under which twentieth-century liberalism was typically either disavowed or simply ignored. Indeed, within theory, the critiques of economic liberalism, instrumental reason, and the liberal subject made it impossible to appraise actually existing liberalisms with any degree of impartiality or openness of mind, while the rejection of existentialist frameworks in the rise of structuralism and poststructuralism made the qualities of this era's felt response to its own history seem particularly foreign and irrelevant. There are some newer elements within the theoretical field that may open the door to a fuller comprehension of this particular phase of liberal thought. First, the recent turn to ethos (as evinced in the later work of Foucault and in ethos-laden concepts such as cosmopolitanism) emphasizes in particular the virtue of restraint (in view of power's force) and the danger of certain ideals, which themselves can lead to violence and unintended results.[8] Second, as I discussed in the introduction, there have been some important critiques of the absolute rejection of liberal principle, especially as it has been represented in Agamben's anti-procedural political theory.[9] Agamben extends and revises the critique of liberal modernity advanced by Foucault, in part by reactivating the significance of sovereignty. He insists on a basic continuity between liberalism and totalitarianism, both of which are involved in the "politicization of life." What such an approach disallows is any meaningful appeal to the rule of law, and in the post-9/11 era this deficiency has made itself sharply felt, especially with respect to the ongoing threat to civil liberties and to the difficulties in conceiving of effective international adjudication of crises. Interestingly, these two elements, the attention to "ethos" and the commitment to basic liberal principles, coincide in a general (but certainly not specific) way with the dynamic blend of ethical and political commitment in the cold war liberals—the emphasis on bleak prospects and reduced expectations, on the one hand, and the absolute necessity of defending basic liberal principles, programs, and institutions, on the other. As I will show in the final section of this chapter, the critics of neoliberalism manifest another version of this dual stance.

Revisiting the debates of the twentieth century reveals that the liberals of this era self-consciously reject what they identify as a steady line of misguided progressivism that leads from the Enlightenment through Victorian liberalism up to early twentieth-century radical utopianism, or communism. Liberalism in this twentieth-century form is thus precisely a rejection of the progressive optimism that was seen to mark nineteenth-century liberalism and its heir, twentieth-century radicalism. In this sense, a certain noncommunist liberalism aims to preserve the democratic project against considerable danger on both the right and the left. A succinct version of this argument appears in Schlesinger's *The Vital Center*:

> The degeneration of the Soviet Union taught us a useful lesson. . . . It broke the bubble of the false optimism of the nineteenth century. Official liberalism had long been almost inextricably identified with a picture of man as perfectible, as endowed with sufficient wisdom and selflessness to endure power and to use it infallibly for the general good. The Soviet experience, on top of the rise of fascism, reminded my generation rather forcibly that man was, indeed, imperfect, and that the corruptions of power could unleash great evil in the world. We discovered a new dimension of experience—the dimension of anxiety, guilt, and corruption.[10]

An assumption that cold war liberals such as Schlesinger are defined by anticommunism, as a structuring negation, makes it difficult to recognize not only the more complex textures of their thought, but also the fact that their experience is fundamentally one of historical crisis, one that forces a rethinking of liberalism's field of action, its broader human and social vision, and its concrete aims. We should note as well that the shift to a grave recognition of the moral and practical difficulties attending all political aspiration was in no way a simple or straightforward matter, with temperamental tensions often coming to the fore. In a special 1947 section in *Partisan Review* titled "The Future of Socialism," for example, Granville Hicks addressed a broad spectrum of attitudes on what he designated the "unaffiliated Left," in recognition of the crisis and disenchantment produced by Stalinism. "Many Leftists are so afraid of being called pessimists that they fail to reckon with the difficulties of their tasks and thus doom themselves to defeat. The kind of optimism that is worked up in Communist and neoliberal circles makes straight thinking impossible. That is why the writings of certain religious thinkers—Toynbee, Niebuhr, Eliot—are so often more impressive than the writings of radicals and liberals."[11] A similar version of this attitude appears in Trilling, whose own form of liberalism was a forceful rejection of progressivism, and who typically worked through stronger, tragic, religious visions without endorsing them directly.[12] I will reserve a fuller discussion of Trilling until later, since his own approach to liberalism was intimately linked to an aesthetic vision and kept its distance from the concrete political projects to which figures like Schlesinger and Hicks are here speaking. But the tenor of Trilling's claims—the insistence that optimism must be seriously checked—was similar to what we see among the political thinkers.

This particular intellectual attitude toward the dangers of optimism and rationalism was not confined to the United States. To glance briefly at France, whose internal debates at this time are highly relevant to the present discussion, the liberal Raymond Aron's *The Opium of the Intellectuals* begins with a critique of radical optimism:

> Both American liberals and the Left in France and Britain share the same illusion: the illusion of the orientation in history in a constant direction, of evolution toward a state of affairs in harmony with an ideal. Marxism is only one version, a simultaneously cataclysmic and determinist version, of an optimism to which rationalists are professionally inclined; it is favoured by the contrast between the promises of industrial civilization and the catastrophes of our time.[13]

In Britain, the key figure within this general discursive formation is Isaiah Berlin, whose influential essay "Two Concepts of Liberty" is crucially inflected by the catastrophes of the twentieth century, of which he had direct personal experience. As is well known, Berlin elaborates a primary distinction between negative and positive liberty. Negative liberty follows the classic liberal conception of freedom understood as freedom from interference by others, or the liberty to do as one pleases beyond the recognized minimal constraints required to prevent harm to others or to the social order more generally. Positive liberty, by contrast, is associated with the individual's desire for self-realization or self-actualization, and it necessarily introduces substantive conceptions of the good. What is striking about Berlin's discussion of positive liberty is the turn from more familiar notions of individual self-actualization (such as we find in Kant and Mill) toward a Platonic focus on the notion of self-mastery or rational imposition. Berlin is especially alert to the risks involved in assuming what is best for individuals or groups, and he links positive liberty in general with a dangerous form of rational control. The totalitarian horrors of the twentieth century thus derive from the general psychological precondition of a will to mastery, the corruption unleashed when one moves from the individual to the collective forms of positive liberty: "The rationalist argument, with its assumption of the single true solution, has led by steps which, if not logically valid, are historically and psychologically intelligible from an ethical doctrine of individual responsibility and individual self-perfection to an authoritarian State obedient to the directives of an élite of Platonic guardians."[14]

The bleak liberals of the cold war era, then, strongly emphasized the need for a historically responsive sense of restraint. And in general, beyond the critique of progressive, rationalist optimism and the dangers it entails, there were two formative elements to the general framework of interwar, war, and early cold war liberalism: a distinct emphasis on tragic limitation and negative forces, on the one hand, and an endorsement of democratic process, piecemeal reform, and limited or ad hoc political measures, on the other. The markedly pragmatic approach to political aims, however, did not necessarily translate into modesty of vision: the liberals under discussion argued for ambitious social programs associated with the welfare state and the New Deal, support of civil liberties and the rule of law, and endorsement of the balance of powers. There were of course differences of emphasis among the thinkers I have mentioned, and some thinkers' views changed significantly over time. As I have stressed, the turn rightward and the inflexible anticommunism among many figures often obscures the more vital dynamic at play in this discursive formation, especially during the thirties and forties. What seems most significant in this early period is the interplay between a tragic ethos and a pragmatic politics, whereby the political commitment is somehow deepened by the subtending existential stance. In the last chapter of *A Vital Center*, Schlesinger worries that democracy can't really become a fighting faith, given its bloodless virtues of rationalism, tolerance, persuasion, and skepticism.[15] But what the bleak liberals in general tend to emphasize is the historical and existential context from which such seemingly thin commitments emerge and necessarily take on importance. Unlike Richard Rorty's advocacy of prosaic proceduralism in the public sphere and ironic self-fashioning in the private, this particular way of thinking justifies its practical politics by appeal to the tragic fact of human limitation and destructiveness, as both a historical and a general condition.[16] The political stance is thus reparative or therapeutic; the force of its commitment is strengthened by the perceived fragility of the project as well as by its necessity in light of historical context. This was one of the key notes in Niebuhr, who gradually moved from socialist sympathies to a strong call for the need to back Great Britain against Hitler and eventually argued for the virtues of a kind of democratic realism: "Democracy is a method of finding proximate solutions for insoluble problems."[17]

There were, it must be noted, more strictly pragmatic positions that refused the bleak mode. In this sense the bleak version of liberalism was under debate even as it was being formulated, as is evident in Sidney Hook's widely cited pair of articles, "The New Failure of Nerve" and "The Failure of the Left," published in *Partisan Review* in 1943.[18] Hook advances a strong critique of the antiscientific thinking and the mysticism, romanticism, and utopianism of many on the left. He in fact groups together the bleak liberals and the more radical Left, inasmuch as he sees the emphasis on antirationalism, especially when linked to an emphasis on evil or sin, as producing a "failure of nerve." For Hook, who was a student of Dewey's, part of what seemed so dangerous about the bleak liberal attack on rationalism was its failure to acknowledge and support the productive power of science and reason.[19] In political terms, Hook emphasizes the need for strategic practical politics: those sympathetic to labor and socialist policies should secure a place at the table rather than refusing engagement with the established government simply out of a misplaced purism (in this he is targeting the more radical Left). The main context for his argument has to do with his disdain for those who fail to see the importance of defeating fascism, or who seek to subordinate that task to the struggle for socialism. Whether to abandon the socialist struggle and make common cause against fascism or to hold out against joining an inter-imperialist war and continue to fight for international socialism was the subject of a heated dispute within the Left at the time. Hook's response was unequivocal: *"Whoever has given up the struggle for democracy here and now against Fascism has already given up the struggle for socialism"* (emphasis in the original).[20]

Aesthetics and literature, and in particular modernism, held a central place for the bleak liberals, in part because literature and art were seen as better poised to register, and give voice to, the existential challenges of political life. Among the writers or critics this view seems natural, and other parties to the debate were broadly influenced by a cultural atmosphere in which literature and aesthetics formed part of the general discussion. For example, directly after the passage in which he states that totalitarianism liquidated man's tragic insights, Schlesinger goes on to cite Ignazio Silone, Arthur Koestler, and André Malraux. Interestingly, the terms that were advanced to deepen the political debate on the left—pessimism, tragedy, irony, paradox, ambiguity, and complexity—were also the aesthetic terms valorized by those on the literary Left, and they coincide in general with the aesthetic values of modernism. In part this feature of bleak liberalism had to do with the rejection of party line aesthetics, in particular Soviet realism. From the perspective of literary and cultural theory of the past several decades, however, the valorization of modernism stands out because modernism and its successors have generally been associated with radical rather than liberal politics. As a result of the general privileging of Adorno over Lukács and the

dominance of literary Foucauldian accounts of modern disciplinary power
and the realist novel, liberalism is almost axiomatically seen as allied with
realism rather than modernism—and moreover this alliance is seen as a
form of ideological enforcement.

As I have indicated, for many who were interested in the place of aesthetics, literature was in some ways aligned with, or especially capable of
expressing, the forms of bleak apprehension that were lost to view in rationalist political theory. This was certainly the case for Trilling, who believed
that art could challenge and disrupt the optimism of the progressivist political mind. For Trilling, art brings into play those features of life that the
political liberal mind fails to value: variousness, possibility, contingency,
complexity. In criticizing the way forms of political thinking had affected
literary art, Trilling singled out the sociological reductionism that treated
individuals as group members in need of special treatment (rather than,
as in the novel of manners, complex and individualized representatives of
social class). Trilling advances a critique of identity politics *avant la lettre*
(focusing on groups such as blacks and Jews, but also "the poor"), and he
sees this as something that has vitiated the power of the novel, particularly
the American novel, leading to a situation where moral and social judgment
becomes distorted or weak for fear of enacting some sort of exclusion. In his
essay on *The Princess Cassamassima,* he praises James for avoiding precisely
this tendency:

> Few of our novelists are able to write about the poor so as to make them some-
> thing more than the pitied objects of our facile sociological minds. The litera-
> ture of our liberal democracy pets and dandles its underprivileged characters,
> and, quite as if it had the right to do so, forgives them what faults they may
> have. But James is sure that in such people, who are numerous, there are the
> usual human gradations of understanding, interest, and goodness.[21]

In his essay on the Kinsey report, Trilling links this habit of mind to
broader intellectual trends obtaining in universities and the foundation
world, isolating the "nearly conscious aversion from making intellectual
distinctions, almost as if out of the belief that an intellectual distinction
must inevitably lead to a social discrimination or exclusion" (241–42).

Trilling ultimately advocates not a rejection of the possibilities of rationalism as an approach to human social life, but a careful consideration of
those ideas that convey the tragic conditions under which we aspire and
the dangers of supposing we can fully will and control a transformation
of political forms. Like John Stuart Mill's insistence on the importance of

considering the ideas of Coleridge and Bentham together, Trilling argues that there are certain ideas, such as T. S. Eliot's conception of the religious life, that we need to consider without granting them our allegiance. A resolutely secular thinker, Trilling believes it is necessary to take into account the whole of human experience, including features that cannot easily be grasped. As he writes in the 1940 essay "Elements That Are Wanted," in the context of a discussion of Wordsworth's artistic vision in the wake of his disenchantment with revolution:

> What is meant negatively is that man cannot be comprehended in a formula; what is meant positively is the sense of complication and possibility, of surprise, intensification, variety, unfoldment, worth. These are things whose more or less abstract impressions we recognize in the arts; in our inability to admit them in social matters lies a great significance. . . . It is a tragic irony that this diminution of the moral possibility, with all that the moral possibility implies of free will and individual value, should spring, as it does, from the notion of the perfectibility of man. The *ultimate man* has become the end for which all temporal men are the means. Such a notion is part of the notion of progress in general, a belief shared by the bourgeois and the Marxist, that the direction of the world is that of a never-ceasing improvement. (emphasis in the original)[22]

Trilling goes on to fault Wordsworth for going too far and making morality absolute, just as he rejects the religious doctrine behind Eliot's views. It is possible, of course, to see Trilling as ultimately in thrall to a vision, and more specifically an art, that would simply register the complexities, but his point is that the complexities of powerful artistic visions should ideally be brought to bear on the political formation of liberalism. Such a demand, moreover, is of a piece with the insistence on differentiated moral judgment in novelistic representations—there is a difference between mere complexity and the complex demands of moral judgment. Trilling may remain somewhat stalled on the threshold of a project of reinvigorated politics, held by a strong anti-ideological and even anti-practical counterforce, but he nonetheless urges an open dialectical dynamic between art and liberal politics. In this he shares the divided impulses of his first scholarly interest, Matthew Arnold, though his own thinking is informed by modern psychology and the response to the unfolding history of the twentieth century. He is especially responsive to art's ability to register the negative, to give expression to the existential density of all human aspiration, and most especially to register the limits of a progressive politics unable to comprehend certain forces at play in human experience—especially forms of experience aligned with psychologically extreme or destructive occurrences such as illness, loss, and aggression. At its most suggestive, Trilling's vision intimates the possibility of a new form of the novel of ideas, something like an ideological novel of manners, where individuals are differentiated according to their concrete individuality, their relation to ideas, and their placement in the social order. I will return in chapter 4 to a fuller consideration of Trilling's aesthetics and to a reading of his own ideological novel of manners, *The Middle of the Journey*. More generally, the expansive aesthetics of the bleak liberals allow us to reconstruct a diverse tradition of writing that spans the realist and modernist eras and engages the demands of liberal experience and liberal commitment.

Interesting to consider next to Trilling is Albert Camus, whose book *The Rebel* (*L'homme révolté*) was published in 1951, almost exactly contemporaneous with Trilling's *The Liberal Imagination*. Camus's book is known for the excoriating review and subsequent debate it generated in the Parisian journal *Les Temps Modernes*, which Jean-Paul Sartre edited, and for the rift that ensued between Sartre and Camus, who had earlier been allied as intellectual friends both committed, as was the journal itself, to finding a third way between communism and capitalism. As Ronald Aronson demonstrates, the conflict that developed between the two men embodied a far greater ideological conflict of the period, with the central issues being how one imagines and approaches the fact of violence, how one addresses the question of means and ends, and what position one takes toward the possibility of redemption on Earth.[23] Sartre's turn toward Marxism and his reluctance to break with the Soviet Union were combined with a rejection of what was seen as Camus's fastidious idealism, his moralism, and his elevation of the individual over a commitment to an assumed historical trajectory and ultimate redemption.

The Rebel has elements in common with the forms of thought that characterize the bleak liberals of the interwar and early cold war era. It ultimately argues for moderation (*mesure*), or a form of aspiration that understands limits. In this sense it is close to the more pragmatic liberal critiques of radical thought, but it departs from them in its existential solidarity with the human aspiration behind rebellion—the fundamental discontent with what one is. ("Man is the only creature," Camus reminds us in the book's introduction, "who refuses to be what he is.")[24] In the end, Camus privileges rebellion over revolution, faulting the latter for its dedication to wholesale transformation rather than finding a way to accept where we live and the constraints we face. For Camus, revolutionary thought, in its abstraction and its dedication to a planned world, is linked to dictatorship, authoritarianism, and fascism. He combines a principled idealism—which lies behind his nonviolence and his internationalism—with a pragmatic insistence on limits: in this way he too is very much like the noncommunist liberals across the Atlantic. The situation of his reception during and after his life has been complicated by his stance on Algeria (his notion that it would be possible to protect French rights while advancing Algerian interests, and his dismissal, and critique, of Algerian nationalism). But beyond this troubling aspect of his thought, it seems his existential liberalism helped to put him in the same neglected archive—from the standpoint of theory's self-anthologizing—as the bleak liberals in the United States.

In Camus's account, art involves the same protest against reality that rebellion does, and the novel as an art form is exemplary both for its expression of a desired freedom (or different world) and for a need to work within limits:

> By the treatment that the artist imposes on reality, he declares the intensity of his rejection. But what he retains of reality in the universe he creates reveals the degree of consent that he gives to at least one part of reality—which he draws from the shadows of evolution to bring to the light of creation. In the final analysis, if the rejection is total, reality is then completely banished and the result is a purely formal work. If, on the other hand, the artist chooses, for reasons often unconnected with art, to exalt crude reality, the result is then realism. (268)

For Camus, literary art "can neither totally consent to reality nor turn aside from it completely" (269).

The aesthetic orientations canvassed here all can be, and have been, characterized as coterminous with the lamentable ideology of liberalism itself. As Wald argues:

> In various forms most of the . . . New York intellectuals also came to embrace the very supraclass theories they had once rejected. They did so by reorganizing their thought around a cluster of key terms that began to appear increasingly in their writing: "modulation," "variousness," "skeptical realism," "moral realism," "the imagination of disaster," "the end of ideology," and, in the arena of political polemic, "liberal anticommunism" and "anti-anticommunism. All of these coinages were utilized to convince the intellectuals as well as their audiences that they had moved forward rather than backward. . . . [T]he particular political programs they espoused for the reform of capitalism scarcely went beyond the reforms of the New Deal that they had long been accustomed to criticize from the left.[25]

It should be clear by now, however, that this type of analysis fails to capture the dynamic elements within the discursive formation I have been elucidating. It does so by making a number of dubious conceptual moves. First, it reinforces the trend-line argument I identified earlier, imagining that that all these various formulations are expressive of a conservative ideological turn. Second, it converts terms that were meant to focus on forms of experience typically captured most fully in literature or art into evidence of outright political positions that are seen as ideologically blind in their claim to a place beyond ideology. Many of these terms were used precisely to designate the form of an engagement with politics, not a mere escape from it. Third, and perhaps most contentious, it inserts into the list Daniel Bell's term and thesis "the end of ideology." There is a very specific problem with Bell, who himself manifests both the tragic and the pragmatic modes of the cold war liberal temper. The problem, one inherited and repeated by Francis Fukuyama in his "end of history" thesis, is the casting of a political philosophical position as a trend already achieved—as a sociological and historical fact, not a position. What most of the terms denoting complexity and forms of realism or pragmatism are meant to convey is the interrelation between an apprehension of the challenging existential conditions of both life and politics and the commitment to a reformist politics that engages and affirms existing democratic institutions and structures. This does not mean this particular form of liberalism has vanquished—or should or could vanquish—all other political positions and modes of political engagement and practice.

As I have suggested, I believe it is illuminating to consider the moment of cold war liberalism as less a departure from a fully established progressive liberal optimism than a continuation of a line of thinking that typically includes sobering outlooks on sociological trends, psychological tendencies, and the political efficacy of argument and ideals. We already see this in the nineteenth century; the tendency for the twentieth-century liberals to proclaim that the era of Victorian optimism had ended was already an attempt to historicize a philosophical tension within liberalism that runs deeper and finds its expression not only in liberal philosophy but also in the literature of the period, particularly the realist novel. This is not to say that the moment of cold war liberalism was not itself an experience marked with special political and existential density. But simply to consider Mill, who was especially interested by the sociological insights of Tocqueville, is to realize that the so-called optimistic liberalism of the nineteenth century was already marked by a tension between skepticism and hope and, moreover, was seen as an acute existential challenge. And if we consider more recent liberal thinkers such as Habermas, we can see a strong dose of cautionary pessimism about sociological and political counterforces (though one could also argue that Habermas's thought is itself profoundly marked by the crises of World War II and its aftermath).[26]

By way of illustration, I will briefly consider two nineteenth-century precursors, Mill and Hobhouse; the latter might be seen to represent a progressive optimism out of sync with the bleak tradition I am identifying. In the introduction, I adduced Mill's *On Liberty* as illustrative of what historian John Burrow has identified as the characteristic double vision of the modern social thinkers — their combination of a certain sociological realism and a moral aspiration. But of course the story of Mill's philosophical and personal development, narrated in his *Autobiography* and evident in his intellectual itinerary, adds further texture to our understanding of his liberalism. The account of his mental breakdown and recovery in his *Autobiography* may seem a highly anomalous story, unlikely to have general relevance given its unusual context, but it dovetails with a range of responses in the mid-nineteenth century to the excesses of overweening rationalism, and in this sense it resonates with the twentieth-century liberal formation I have been tracing. Moreover, Mill's own story seems to repeat some of the major themes and characterizations in the nineteenth-century industrial novel, most notably Dickens's *Hard Times*, which famously depicts the effects of a utilitarian upbringing on the emotional and imaginative life. As I will show in chapter 3, the industrial novel is particularly committed to correcting the excesses of rational systems of reform, typically by appeal to the forces of sympathy and imagination. The lived relation to ideas — in both negative and positive forms — is of central importance to both Mill and those fiction writers who sought to promote liberal attitudes and liberal reform. In both Mill and Dickens, traditional utilitarianism is shown to be deleterious and productive of pathology because it attempts to rationalize existence, to deny motives and orientations that cannot be reduced to self-interest, and because it deprives individuals of enriching forms of emotional and imaginative life. It also routinizes thinking itself rather than allowing for an expansive, reflective, and living relation to belief.

In *On Liberty*, his major statement on the doctrine of liberalism, Mill makes the central argument very clear, elaborating the two maxims that most people associate with the doctrine of liberty, or with liberalism in its pure form. These maxims specify that one is free to act as one wishes assuming that no harm is done to others, and that if one does in fact harm others, one is subject to "social or legal punishment."[27] But in a way one could say that Mill's strongest forms of attention settle elsewhere, and at some distance from the no-harm principle. Mill is concerned with those practices that most conduce to a life well lived, and in particular, to the furtherance of the examined life, a life in which beliefs are deeply held and animated by ongoing argument with others. Theories of democracy in the twentieth century often emphasize forms of deliberative debate as vital to democratic culture, but interestingly *On Liberty* does not link the ideal of discussion to the procedural forms of representative democracy. A fuller exposition of the ways argument and public debate might inform representative government is contained in *Considerations on Representative Government*, where Mill is concerned to suggest policies that might diminish the overwhelming force of sectarian interests in parliamentary debate. *On Liberty* emphasizes the importance of reflection and argument to the development of individuals and their relation to the truth, and the importance of reflection and argument to the quality of public debate and intellectual well-being in society as a whole, not merely political society. This ideal of informed discussion of those ideas most vital to the self-understanding of society and the individual is utterly central to liberalism as a philosophy, and it appears in different forms in later liberal thought—including Habermas's theory of communicative action and its connection to the practices that animate democratic institutions. As will become clear when I discuss the political novel, this feature of liberalism has major implications for understanding liberal aesthetic form.

Mill's relevance to the broad tradition of bleak liberalism is also evident in his approach to the specific commitments of liberalism. His notion of human dignity centers on the importance of both freedom and self-actualization, and his conceptions of progress are trained in particular on eliminating coercion and creating conditions that will conduce to equality of opportunity. He conveys a sense of hopeful progressivism in many ways that we commonly associate with the liberal mind-set, asserting in *The Subjection of Women* that the great achievement of modern life is to have replaced the long-standing "law of force" with "moral law."[28] In *On Liberty*, he claims that through the strength of discussion, extreme views become modulated over time. And more generally, he believed that modern societies were equal to the challenge of replacing entrenched customs and traditions with a dedication to universal norms and enlightened practices of liberty. Yet his aspirations are everywhere subtended by doubt, sociological and psychological. Concerns about conformity, "the magical influence of custom," and "social tyranny" are memorably expressed.[29] And he is highly sensitive to the effects of ingrained forms of power across several sociological categories, as the following statement in *On Liberty* makes clear:

> Wherever there is an ascendant class, a large portion of the morality of the country emanates from its class interests, and its feelings of class superiority. The morality between Spartans and Helots, between planters and negroes, between princes and subjects, between nobles and roturiers, between men and women, has been for the most part the creation of these class interests and feelings. (45)

Beyond this, Mill singles out religion as a case where it is especially difficult for people to relinquish their intolerance, subtly noting that "in the minds of almost all religious persons, even in the most tolerant countries, the duty of toleration is admitted with tacit reserves" (47). The analysis of gender subordination in *The Subjection of Women* is similarly sophisticated in its understanding of power dynamics where each subject of the dominated class lives in political isolation, as it were, with a member of the dominating class, "with no means of combining against him" and "with the strongest motives for seeking his favor and avoiding to give him offence."[30] While Mill's psychological assumptions about an individual's capacity to own and actualize character may seem naive from a post-Freudian standpoint, his awareness of social psychology, intimate coercion, and soft power is acute, as is his understanding of the corrosive effects of a reason-driven life. These are precisely the sorts of apprehension that twentieth-century liberals emphasize, filtered through the more immediate context of experiences of authoritarianism and world war. Such continuities give the lie to any notion that liberalism fails to confront the darker realities of human and social existence.

The tradition of New Liberalism represented by L. T. Hobhouse and others of the late nineteenth and early twentieth centuries in some respects appears to represent the most confidently progressive form of liberalism, owing to its emphasis on organic development, harmony, and teleology. Linked closely to some of the key tenets of T. H. Green's Hegelian liberalism, most centrally the notion of the common good, the New Liberalism importantly advocates for forms of state intervention and regulation in the service of public welfare, while also maintaining the importance of individual self-actualization, the rule of law, and civic principles.[31] Hobhouse's thought is notable for its moral holism and its argument on behalf of an organicism that reconciles self-actualization and values pursued in common, in contrast to Herbert Spencer's influential valorization of competition, struggle, and self-interest. In general, as I stated at the outset of the chapter, the New Liberalism inaugurates a line of thinking that leads up to John Dewey and other communitarian liberals such as Michael Walzer who stress social cooperation and organic notions of community and democratic life. This tradition of liberalism does not manifest the more pronounced forms of bleakness that are the main object of my analysis, but it does build on interacting perspectives of critique and aspiration that are relevant to the broader economies of liberal thought as well as its aesthetic formations. At the start of his important book *Liberalism*, Hobhouse identifies liberalism's historical emergence with a critical spirit that is sometimes "destructive and revolutionary" and whose "negative aspect is for centuries foremost."[32] And this critical element is linked directly to literature and art: "It would not be difficult, if space allowed, to illustrate its influence in literature and art, to describe the war with convention, insincerity, and patronage, and the struggle for free self-expression, for reality, for the artist's soul. Liberalism is an all-penetrating element of the life-structure of the modern world" (22). Hobhouse here interestingly combines the individualism valorized in writings on the liberal imagination with the forms of principled and combative critique that contribute to the more richly dimensional formal experiments this book investigates. Beyond this, Hobhouse is especially attuned to human violence in war as a force ever threatening the aims of progressive liberals, noting that there are both blatant and more "subtle" forms "in which the military spirit eats into free institutions and absorbs the public resources which might go to the advancement of civilization" (21).[33]

As I hope this discussion of Mill and Hobhouse suggests, it is through understanding the later forms of bleak liberalism that one can begin to notice, and to appreciate, the acute negative insights that have fueled the liberal commitment throughout its history. In the chapter that follows, I will begin to draw out how the writers of the nineteenth century advanced forms of liberal understanding and critique, often in ways that are far more complex and subtle than either the proponents or the critics of liberalism have acknowledged. Before turning to the literary sphere, however, I will consider one further set of challenges to the reconstruction of liberalism advanced by this book: the emergence of neoliberalism as a concept and a diagnosed form of governance. Indeed, recent interest among scholars and theorists in what is perceived as the hegemony of neoliberalism might be seen to pose a unique challenge to the project I am pursuing, raising the question whether the liberalism I am exploring, even supposing it to have the complexities and resonances I am ascribing to it, is effectively disempowered at present, having been eclipsed by the increasing dominance of neoliberalism and its infiltration into multiple spheres of life. This question requires a separate discussion, and I include it here so as to clarify and in fact underscore the book's claims. As I indicated in the introduction, the very dominance of neoliberalism as a concept and diagnostic term for the contemporary condition has contributed to the occlusion of existing liberalisms. Interestingly, the rhetorical and political effects of the term's use within the humanities — as shorthand for the powerful extension of market power within a global capitalist system — do not properly reflect more considered analyses of the idea and reality of neoliberalism. Indeed, it is possible to say that neoliberalism itself has prompted forms of bleak liberal response not unlike the catastrophe-infused thinking of the middle of the twentieth century.

"Neoliberalism" is generally taken to denote a resurgent economic liberalism that aims to extend market logic throughout society and to diminish programs associated with the welfare state, redistributive tax structures, and those regulatory mechanisms that prevent corporate and financial institutions from acting freely to secure and multiply profits at whatever cost. It is important to recognize that neoliberalism is entirely distinct from, and incompatible with, the long traditions of political liberalism and social democracy that challenged narrow forms of classical economic liberalism of the sort associated with John Locke and Adam Smith. Indeed, something of a bell-curve irony is reflected in the historical itinerary of liberalism narrated by many of those who identify neoliberalism as not only a powerfully held theory and aspiration in play since the mid-twentieth century, but also an increasingly dominant systemic reality since the 1970s. By this account, a robust new liberalism came into force beginning in the late nineteenth century, one that laid the groundwork for the social democratic policies animating the rise of the welfare state. This liberalism was most significantly consolidated in the era following World War II, when strong government programs sought to promote equality of opportunity and protection from various forms of disadvantage, poverty, or illness. A minority position from the 1940s through the 1970s, represented by Friedrich Hayek, Milton Friedman, and their followers, neoliberalism manages to gain ascendance amid the economic and political malaise of the 1970s, then slowly undercuts the animating legal and institutional frameworks of political liberalism as well as the established gains of the welfare state and Keynesian economics more generally. A secondary irony is that establishing neoliberal policies required considerable state and judicial activism, giving the lie to the notion of neoliberal anti-statism. But the key feature is the argument that economic liberalism prevails in a way that destroys the gains and the promise of political liberalism.

Beyond considering the merits of this story of neoliberalism's ascendance and contemporary dominance, it is worth looking more closely at some influential accounts of neoliberalism in the broad field of cultural studies and political theory. Foucault's analyses of neoliberalism in *The Birth of Biopolitics* occupy an interesting position in the larger field of debate, since the original seminars were given in the late seventies and not published until 2004 (translated into English in 2008) and therefore had a belated effect on most of the Left cultural analysis of the term within the Anglo-American academy. Foucault's lectures begin with a discussion of the emergence of liberalism in the eighteenth century as a form of "critical governmental rationality" based not on law or rights but on "effects," on forms of success and failure defined in economic terms.[34] This distinction, original to economic liberalism, will be the point of return for the neoliberals of the postwar period in Europe and America.

Foucault's lectures on twentieth-century neoliberalism first analyze German neoliberalism of the postwar era, then consider the distinctive formations to be found in France and America as well. German neoliberalism, or "ordoliberalism," is motivated in part by a determination to avoid conditions that would allow for any return of totalitarianism (103). The ordoliberals believed the state should be founded narrowly upon the economy and should work in the service of economic freedom, in distinction to those liberals and radicals who believed the state should correct for or supplement the effects of the economy via social policies and regulatory mechanisms. One key feature of neoliberalism is therefore its paradoxical state activism in promoting certain economic conditions, particularly competition and the general extension of the enterprise form. Its activist and interventionist features exist in tension with a broad "state phobia" or "paranoic" conception of the state (187, 188). Gathered together in this "paranoic" conception are authoritarian and expansionist forms of the state, whether fascist, totalitarian, bureaucratic, welfare centered, or extensively administrative (187).

German neoliberalism emphasizes policies that promote efficiency; it is strategic, pragmatic, and impersonal, and though it is informed by a larger theory, it is fundamentally oriented toward enacting and enforcing policies that will serve the market's competitive operation. In its stress on negative freedom, moreover, it lacks the disciplinary character of those forms of modern state power that are dominantly bureaucratic, social democratic, or administrative. It is thin rather than thick, less ideological than strategic, though it certainly can become embedded ideologically given the right conditions and a period of time to achieve the status of common sense. But as a narrow economic liberalism, it lacks the forms of positive freedom that have fueled more substantive notions of political belonging and commitment. Indeed, this lack has been identified as a key sociopolitical problem for neoliberalism since its inception (a subject I will return to).

By contrast, American neoliberalism connects more fundamentally to the cultural and institutional surround insofar as it is linked to principles and practices that informed the founding and subsequent development of the nation. In the United States as opposed to the European countries, neoliberalism constitutes "a whole way of being and thinking" (218). While still distinguished from disciplinary forms of power, neoliberalism in the United States is closer in form to the infiltrating techniques we associate with *Discipline and Punish* and volume 1 of *The History of Sexuality*. American neoliberalism "generalizes the economic form of the market . . . throughout the social body" (243); it replaces "*homo œconomicus* as partner of exchange with a *homo œconomicus* as entrepreneur of himself" (226). Foucault stresses that it is precisely as *homo economicus* that the individual becomes "eminently governable," yet he also states that this is not a normalizing operation: it is "an environmental type of intervention instead of the internal subjugation of individuals" (270, 260).

It is not a simple matter to identify Foucault's precise relation to neoliberalism, given the exploratory nature of the lectures and the range of national case studies he addresses. His attitude toward neoliberalism has been variously interpreted as negative, positive, and neutral, which gives some indication of the complexity of the evidence involved. Owing to the anti-statism of neoliberalism and the less intrusive forms of governmentality it employs relative to disciplinary power, commentators such as Daniel Zemora and Michael Behrent have argued that Foucault favors neoliberalism as producing forms of freedom that are not ideologically manipulative in the manner of modern liberalism.[35] By contrast, influential work by Wendy Brown assumes that Foucault presciently identifies the emergent forms of power that will systematically undermine and eclipse an already uneven liberal achievement in the United States and elsewhere.[36] The assumption here is that his writings are in the service of a critical-diagnostic project that seeks to understand the corrosive forms of power that characterize the contemporary global condition. In one key passage in *The Birth of Biopolitics*, Foucault stresses his own evaluative neutrality. Having just identified the broad tendency toward the reduction of the state, and having further differentiated two forms of such reduction (party governmentality, characteristic of totalitarianism, and liberal governmentality, characteristic of neoliberal forms), he states, "I add straightaway that in saying this I am not trying to make a value judgment" (191). He then goes on to make a somewhat more subtle point, that those invested in the significance of their own denunciations of state power should recognize the connection between such a stance and emergent forms of state reductionism. The net effect is to render his position less neutral than undecidable, less genealogically bracketed than ambiguous. The very fact that Foucault describes neoliberalism as holding a "paranoic" conception of the state should alert us to the interpretive knot in play. Foucault's earlier work on disciplinarity itself held a dark view of the state's capacity to infiltrate, and even constitute, the private and subjective lives of its citizens. The use of pathologizing terms ("state phobia," "paranoic") indicates a diagnostic distance from neoliberalism, yet one wonders why Foucault would pathologize an attitude he himself arguably has participated in holding. And his ultimate views on minimizing state power are hard to discern: the achievement of liberal governmentality, especially relative to the impasse of socialism, is notable, but its values and effects must be explored. An open mind is needed, he implies, about what neoliberal government might mean relative to other forms of power.

Thus, part of the trouble with adapting Foucault's analysis to current discussions of neoliberalism is that neoliberalism's status, especially in relation to whether and how it has embedded itself culturally or subjectively, remains uncertain in his account. It is true that the account of American neoliberalism underscores a distinctive meshing of preexisting cultural values and formations with neoliberal orientations. But in a way the distance between the accounts of German and American neoliberalism could be said to reflect an ongoing ambiguity about whether we can think of neoliberalism as a lived ideology. Many influential accounts of neoliberalism stress that it cannot adequately supply the forms of ideological or moral support that any successfully hegemonic worldview requires. In such accounts, this form of support typically comes from elsewhere: from the moral frameworks of traditional liberalism, or from neoconservatism, or from religion. Wendy Brown underscores the idea, apparent in Foucault's analysis, that neoliberalism needs to appropriate more embedded belief frameworks, such as liberal democracy, in order to forward its legitimacy.[37] This need exists in part because it is an emergent form of governmentality, but the problem is not only a temporal one: neoliberalism is fundamentally amoral and strategic, however much it may wish to claim that its policies will ensure freedom. As David Harvey stresses in *A Brief History of Neoliberalism,* neoliberalism is unevenly and only ever partially achieved: "The degree to which neoliberalism has become integral to common-sense understandings among the populace at large has varied greatly depending on the strength of belief in the power of social solidarities and the importance of traditions of collective social responsibility and provision."[38]

For Harvey, neoconservatism is one means by which the "inherent instability of the neoliberal state" is steadied, in that it makes up for the moral deficit that contributes to its instability (82). Similarly, William Connolly's characterization of what he terms "the evangelical-neoliberal resonance machine" rests on the claim that without "an embedded cultural ethos" of the sort religion provides, systems of power cannot maintain themselves.[39] Neoliberalism itself cannot provide the moral and ideological support it needs if it is to achieve its transformative restructuring of the state and the economy. This support is even more urgently needed where the transformations are working not for the common good but for the benefit of the privileged classes. Even though it can be hard to see how the tenets of neoconservatism or evangelicalism could possibly dovetail in an ideologically coherent way with neoliberalism, the key point made in these analyses is that neoliberalism creates a moral vacuum, or it fails to speak to the hearts and minds of the populace, or it actively dispossesses individuals and groups of the forms of life that provide cultural and social cohesion: in these instances something comes in to supply the connections and affiliations that people need and desire.

Ironically, while the general effect of widespread casual references to neoliberalism contributes to a climate in which the entire tradition of liberalism seems suspect, many of the more considered analyses of neoliberal theory and practice actually invoke forms of liberalism as a counter-ideal, a currently diminished or eroded political force whose historical achievements have been notable, corrective, or even exemplary. For example, Wendy Brown emphasizes that neoliberalism not only has borrowed traditional liberal frameworks as an ideological cloak for its starkly economic agenda but has collapsed what hitherto had been an "exploitable" space "between liberal democratic ideals and lived realities."[40] Brown avows her ambivalence and fundamental wariness toward the liberal tradition and her stronger allegiance to radical aims and agendas, but her understanding of neoliberalism is informed by its distinct difference from, and damage to, the tradition of political liberalism that has emphasized civil liberties, the rule of law, and the importance of freedom and equality.

An even stronger endorsement of liberalism is to be found in David

Harvey. The story Harvey tells about the rise of neoliberalism, echoed in many other accounts, is that it essentially undercut and destroyed the gains of the postwar period, which was characterized by the expansion of the democratic promise via a mixed economy, international institutions, and the welfare state. This set of achievements Harvey captures under the term "embedded liberalism," thereby emphasizing its broad integration into frames of understanding linked to ongoing political orientations and practices.[41] In the final chapter of his book he invokes Franklin D. Roosevelt's vision and policies as an exemplary form of expansive liberal response to the need for social and economic justice within democratic parameters. In contrast, the neoliberal agenda is narrowly economic and geared to benefit a privileged class. It lacks the moral commitment that informed the liberalism of the New Deal era. Harvey claims that the neoliberal promise of strengthening capitalism and the freedoms it supposedly offers cannot be met through the policies and agendas being pursued, precisely because neoliberalism is, by his account, not a coherent and principled theoretical position but rather a strategic effort to concentrate power and wealth within a specific class and thereby increase inequality. And, according to Harvey, this will not foster greater economic health and growth: "Paradoxically, a strong and powerful social democratic and working class movement is in a better position to redeem capitalism than is capitalist class power itself" (153).

In notable ways, then, the accounts of neoliberalism manifest the forms of bleak liberal response that characterize the postwar era itself. They are highly alert to the forms of power that threaten the liberal aspiration and promise, both in its more strictly political dimensions (having to do with democratic institutions, the rule of law, and civil liberties) and in its redistributive and market-correcting forms (via welfare, regulatory practices, and progressive tax structures). Interestingly, the debates around neoliberalism also circle back to the question of character and lived commitment that marks the humanistic orientation toward political ideologies more broadly, with which I opened this chapter. In some ways the amorality of neoliberalism derives from its status as a policy orientation or theoretical position that is fundamentally instrumental, aiming to secure economic agendas and advantages. But there are also notable moral effects from this very amorality and impersonality. First, as Foucault observes and many others echo, neoliberalism aims to constitute various agents, both individual and collective, as fundamentally entrepreneurial. In this sense one could say it presupposes a certain type of subject, as narrowly motivated as it may be. Second, within a neoliberal framework, moral offenses are seen through a lens that reduces them simply to errors of calculation. As Brown points out, scandals in the neoliberal era become stories of miscalculation and misjudgment, not of misdeeds and wrongs done.[42] And third, the eviscerating effects of market rationality constitute workers and employees as replaceable and depersonalized, negating their identity as people with layered lives and characters.[43] All this is to say that the critiques of neoliberalism's deprivations and distortions presuppose the significance of a developed sense of moral commitment linked, on the one hand, to one's social and political vision, and, on the other, to a sense of one's own self-actualization and guiding values. The liberal ideal is alive and well in the very diagnosis of neoliberalism's assault on the achievements of traditional political liberalism.

I hope I have shown in this chapter that liberalism has a more complex history than the critique of liberalism assumes. Most important, liberalism as a body of thought cannot be said to be engaged in a disavowal of those psychological, sociological, and political forces that work against its aims and commitments. Given this fact, a guiding axiom of much radical theoretical work has to be called into question. That axiom is that liberalism, in that it disavows its own ideological complicity with the status quo, is a bankrupt mode of critical political thought, since it does not seriously confront the question of violence and the fact of its own interests. Reconstructing liberalism as a felt response to a manifold set of conditions and experiences allows one to see its internal complexity, particularly the aspirations and doubts that accompany its development and some of its most defining historical moments, including its ostensible eclipse by a new neoliberal order. By bringing to the fore—and treating as significant—those attitudes and modes that give liberalism its characterological and existential depth, we can better understand liberalism as a fully serious ideological commitment. This understanding in turn will allow us to perceive a literary history more complex and various in its political imaginings than many of the dominant frameworks admit.

CHAPTER TWO

Liberalism in the Age of High Realism

Now that we have reconstructed the philosophical complexity and existential challenges of liberalism, we can better access a rich tradition of liberal aesthetics. This chapter begins the process of reconsidering the liberal
aesthetic through an exploration of high realist engagements with liberal
thought. In large part, such a consideration contributes to an established
body of inquiry into the relation between literary form and the conditions
of modernity, since the rise of liberalism is a distinct element within what is
variously called philosophical or political modernity. But it is important to
note some limiting assumptions that have attended this form of inquiry and
that bear directly on reconstructing the literary dimensions of a liberalism
that encompasses both its doubts and its aspirations, its diagnostic critiques
and its political ideals.

A number of accounts of the rise of the novel have stressed the genre's
importance as a distinctly modern form giving voice to distinctly modern
questions. Such questions often address emergent forms of social and economic life, new political dynamics attending the broadening of the franchise and the growth of the urban industrial class, challenges to traditional
forms of authority and its claims to truth, and transformed understandings
of selfhood and the relation of private to public life. Well-known examples
include Ian Watt's argument correlating the rise of the novel with the rise
of modern individualism and empiricism, Georg Lukács's account of the
novel as expressing the desire for totality in a world where totality is no
longer directly given, Raymond Williams's discussion of the English novel's
concern with an orienting value of community during the nineteenth cen-

tury's social dislocations and political challenges, and Nancy Armstrong's account of the novel as constituting an irreducibly gendered form of modern individualism.[1]

Modernity is a broader concept than liberalism, but ideas and principles associated with liberalism animate scholarly accounts that stress the novel's close connection to modern conditions and values. Such accounts often adopt a distinctly evaluative stance, construing the novel's relation to modernity either as positive (in the service of progressive ideals) or as negative (in the service of expanding forms of power or control). An example of the former is Robert Pippin's account of the significance of the concept of autonomy, and the broader Hegelian dialectic of dependence and independence, to the modern novel's expression of philosophical modernity.[2] An example of the latter is D. A. Miller's Foucauldian analysis of the representation of private interiority as freedom in the novel's portrayal of, and disciplinary address to, modern liberal subjects.[3] Many accounts are less easy to classify or are mixed in their assessments, such as Lionel Trilling's account of the role of both sincerity and authenticity in the development of literary and philosophical life in the modern era broadly construed (I will return to Trilling later in the chapter).[4] Yet despite the rich range of existing scholarship and the suggestive relation between conceptions of modernity and some of the core elements of liberal thought, there remain continuing barriers to recognizing the full extent to which liberal questions and liberal commitments have been expressed in literary projects.

Scholarship on realism in particular has been disproportionately influenced by strong versions of ideology critique that target both the imagined epistemological claims of realist projects and the ideological forms, bourgeois or liberal, they are seen to express: in such accounts, a restrictive ideological alliance between liberalism and realism is asserted, one in which the consolidation of liberal power and the development of the realist novel are coterminous.[5] Interestingly, while the influence of such accounts on the critical field is waning, there remains a residual bias against liberalism itself, a widespread default use of "liberal" to signal benighted, ideological, or normative elements of thought or art. This has not prevented the emergence of a body of critical literature that reconsiders the significance of liberalism, but it tends to place such literature in a defensive position.

In the introduction, I characterized the various reconsiderations of liberalism within the literary field, including studies concentrating on the public sphere, analyses of the state and its institutions, and appreciations of the liberal temperament in its ethical and political features. All of these approaches have set the stage for a renewed understanding of what we might call literary liberalism, and they have all to some degree inspired the present book. However, in some sense one might say these approaches have failed to capture the dynamic relation between liberalism's focus on systemic inequities and its investment in the achievements of temperament and character. In some instances, moreover, this relation can be shown to take the form of a more charged tension in which the limits of a politics of individualism or an ethics of sympathy are actively registered.

This chapter will reconsider three major realist texts of the nineteenth century—*Bleak House, Middlemarch,* and *The Way We Live Now*—showing how they engage the complexities of liberal thought both formally and conceptually. These novels all aim to show a representative social totality at a particular historical moment, focusing on the ways emergent conditions of modernity are affecting psychological, moral, and social life. They characterize the conditions of modernity in disparate ways—variously emphasizing institutional, economic, and political elements—but each reflects and assesses to some degree emergent liberal forces and principles. In what follows, I aim to capture the internal relation between what may look to be opposing tendencies of progressive aspiration and bleak diagnosis. This will involve special attention to the role literary character plays in the formal dynamics of literary texts that are engaging distinctly liberal concepts and ideas. As I will show, character is a key site for elaborating aspirational ideals and for mediating between differing values or perspectives in the text. Yet many of the writers simultaneously show the appeal and the inadequacy of a character-based approach to liberal political challenges, emphasizing instead the significance of third-person or systemic perspectives, transpersonal communication, or forms of political effort and practice that refuse mystifying forms of personality, tact, or charisma. It is in the valuing and devaluing of exemplary character that we see some of the more interesting dimensions of the realist engagement with liberal thought and practice.

DICKENS'S *BLEAK HOUSE*

Charles Dickens's *Bleak House* famously interleaves a third-person omniscient narration with a first-person narration by a female character, Esther Summerson, who is otherwise one of the characters in the storyworld of the novel (though she is rarely mentioned in the third-person narrative and appears in it only late in the novel). In many ways this novel appears to conform with unusual formal and thematic fidelity to the very tension between liberalism's sobering sociological viewpoint and its aspirational moral viewpoint. The focus on the Byzantine bureaucratic stagnation afflicting the Court of Chancery, England's ancient probate court, and the concomitant critique of English society's negligent disregard of worsening conditions of urban poverty and disease, trains the reader's attention simultaneously on two systemic problems: entrenched, inefficient institutions and intensifying social inequities and challenges. Counterposed to this diagnosis, and advanced via the first-person narration by the female ward of a benevolent philanthropist, is an ideal of vocational self-actualization and general moral responsiveness to suffering as well as a reflective commitment to expanding circles of affiliation.

The third-person narrative engages in a broad critique of established power and its attendant social and psychological effects, including inertia, selfishness, secrecy, suspicion, deprived affections, and thwarted desires. Written in the simple present and focused on questions of power and knowledge—who knows what, who suspects whom of what—the third-person narrative gives the effect of an airless world ruled by ever-present forms of diffuse power effects, strategic rationality, and corrosive self-interest. For example, the relationship between Tulkinghorn and Lady Dedlock, a key narrative interest, is presented as a kind of poker game. This is of course not the only form of relationship presented; there is also a disclosing of positive secrets such as Sir Leicester's affection for Lady Dedlock. But throughout the third-person narrative attention settles on relations of power as well as on the atmospheric effects of constraining social systems. While the form of narration—impersonal, present tense, almost but not exclusively third-person—seems to reinforce the sense that there is no escape from the general conditions of power under diagnosis, occasional interruptions occur: moments of heightened moral condemnation of the system, voiced indignantly and via a suddenly embodied first- or second-person mode. In such moments we are made to understand the principles and forms of life that are thwarted or denied by the prevailing system: legal and social justice, unperverted childhood, individual self-development, and moral openness. These moments of critical intervention are a comment on the system otherwise being described in totalizing terms—they light up the informing evaluative perspective of the broader systemic critique.

Esther's narrative, by contrast, produces a distinctive vision that, in its most enlarged view, allows for the effects of systems on individuals but ultimately emphasizes the importance of moral agency based on love's insight ("my comprehension is brightened when my affection is").[6] Thematically,

Esther's narrative foregrounds exemplary moments of affection, understanding, and sympathy and advances an oblique critique of those who
neglect home duties (Mrs. Jellyby) or are too invested in systematic philanthropy (Mrs. Pardiggle, the "inexorable moral Policeman" [132]). Additionally, a certain ennobling avoidance of suspicion is rendered in comic form
in the character of Jarndyce and the fiction of the east wind that he uses to
avoid blaming any individual or disparaging anyone (Ada and Esther view
this device as a mark of his "eccentric gentleness" [102]).

A range of political viewpoints have been ascribed to the world of Dickens's novels. The later novels—those published in the late 1840s and beyond—have been singled out by the Marxist critics Terry Eagleton and
Raymond Williams for their "systemic" understanding and their ability to
"dramatise those social institutions and consequences which are not ac-
cessible to ordinary physical observation."[7] Others have identified Dickens
as a liberal or reformist writer, drawing in part on an assumed continuity
between his novels and his reform activities and writings in the fields of
education, crime, prostitution, and public health. Beyond this, some have
drawn arguments directly from the novels to support a liberal reading of his
politics—citing the importance of moral autonomy and individual freedom,
the desirability of a sympathetic response to suffering, and the acknowledgment of the impact the environment and faulty institutions have on the life
outcomes of individuals.[8] Most interesting for my purpose, however, are
those who highlight what they take to be an arrested or relentlessly negative
style of critique accompanying the more sentimental or moralizing modes
that govern depictions of idealized characters or the moment of plot closure.
Walter Bagehot argues that Dickens engages in a "sentimental radicalism,"
describing evils extensively, hinting that they are "removable," yet refusing
to reveal by what means.[9] George Orwell, writing from a different political
perspective entirely, makes a similar complaint: Dickens engages in ongoing criticism of society, "attacking everything in sight," but the orientation
remains "almost exclusively moral" in that he offers no structural alternative and implies that the solution is simply for people to behave decently.[10]
And more recently Lauren Goodlad has suggested that while Dickens
criticizes forms of entrenched and emergent self-interest, he "persistently
undermines the modern agencies that might unsettle pernicious deadlock,"
instead favoring heroic agency, charisma, and domestic life.[11]

Many of these readings see the turn to local response or individual
agency as itself fundamentally liberal in character, and herein lies one of
the impasses in cultural criticism's understanding of liberalism: any em-

phasis on the individual over against the system is seen as fundamentally playing into liberal ideology, and liberalism itself is seen as always likely to tilt toward an overvaluation of negative freedom, of freedom from interference or systemic constraints. But such an approach remains unable to see that the critical diagnosis and the emphasis on local response or individual agency form a complex whole and together constitute the very kind of liberalism this project aims to reconstruct. The modest approach to reform indicted by liberalism's critics is importantly subtended by a sometimes searing systemic critique whose exposures negatively express informing values, thereby prompting forms of understanding integrally related to what counts as morally meaningful local action.

The dynamic between the two narratives in *Bleak House* helps to disclose this complex interrelation. The effect is achieved in the first instance by interleaving the two narratives into an implied complementary relation in which Esther's narrative expresses the voice of moral aspiration while the third-person narrative presents a world dominated by negative psychological and sociological conditions. But the narratives are not mere complements, and indeed the separation between the two is not absolute. There is a range of mediations between them, both formal (having to do with character and plot) and rhetorical (having to do with narrative voice). There are implicit and explicit critiques of Chancery, of the educational system, and of systematic philanthropy in the Esther narrative, and there are positive values represented in the third-person narrative: the domestic life of the Bagnets, the exemplary form of professional caretaking and navigation of urban space represented by Allan Woodcourt, and the meritocratic challenge of the Rouncewells to the imperious assumptions of Sir Dedlock. Some figures, moreover, are at home in both narratives, such as Woodcourt and the detective Bucket, and other characters move consequentially from one to the other (Richard, Jo, Esther). As I will show, Woodcourt not only appears in both narratives but can mediate effectively between the forms of knowledge and access associated with the third-person narrative and the values and modes associated with Esther's narrative. This mediation contrasts with the unidirectional slide represented by Richard, who is slowly destroyed, morally and physically, by his entry into the world of the third-person narrative. His decline coincides with his abandonment of a search for vocation and his alliance with professional lawyers who consider self-interest a paramount, driving motive and wariness the appropriate stance toward the actions of others. Overtaken by suspicions that Jarndyce is not to be trusted because Jarndyce's interests in the Chancery suit do not converge with his own, Richard becomes dedicated to guarding and advancing his own claims (hiring Vholes to do so for him). The lawyer is of course the prime exhibit within *Bleak House* of a degraded professional dedicated to a negative view of motive and human nature.

The doctor Woodcourt, by contrast, represents the possible agential mediation between the two worlds, via a range of capacities that include informed understanding of human and social conditions and a practical form of care. Interestingly, when Woodcourt first appears, at the death of Nemo and within the third-person narrative, he is unidentified. Described as a dark young man who mysteriously observes from the other side of the bed, he displays a form of interest different from others', preeminently Tulkinghorn's:

> During this dialogue Mr. Tulkinghorn has stood aloof by the old portmanteau, with his hands behind him, equally removed, to all appearance, from all three kinds of interest exhibited near the bed—from the young surgeon's professional interest in death, noticeable as being quite apart from his remarks on the deceased as an individual; from the old man's unction; and the little crazy woman's awe. (168)

In this passage we get a sense that Woodcourt, even while acting in a fundamentally professional capacity, has an important ability to treat others in a humane way, to recognize their individuality. For the lawyer Tulkinghorn, by contrast, no distinction is made between his professional suspicion and his assumptions about others and their motives. Woodcourt thus seems to represent the possibility that an individual could move effectively between the personal and impersonal perspectives housed by the larger narrative that is *Bleak House*.[12]

Late in the novel, it is Woodcourt who is able to navigate Tom's All-Alone and find Jo. The details of the narrator's description are striking:

> A brown sunburnt gentleman, who appears in some inaptitude for sleep to be wandering abroad rather than counting the hours on a restless pillow, strolls hitherward at this quiet time. Attracted by curiosity, he often pauses and looks about him, up and down the miserable by-ways. Nor is he merely curious, for in his bright dark eye there is compassionate interest; and as he looks here and there, he seems to understand such wretchedness, and to have studied it before. (710-11)

Again Woodcourt is characterized as combining two attitudes, but here the professional attitude is broadened and more fully synthesized with the sympathetic forms of feeling promoted in Esther's narrative. He thus embodies a morally charged sociology that can understand and respond to wretchedness, in contrast to the often cold assessments of the third-person narration, trained on complex games of power or larger social dynamics. Interestingly, an unnamed figure (we have not yet been told this is Woodcourt) associated with observation and inaptitude for sleep could also be surmised to be a narrator figure, perhaps one capable of writing the dual narration.[13] A sunburn is also a notable feature in a novel where one character symbolically associated with Chancery spontaneously combusts and where many others catch infections, both physical and moral. A sunburn is a sort of protective layer accreted by one who travels out in the open and is only inoculated by the system, not destroyed or infected.

As the scene progresses, we see that Woodcourt has a special aptitude for engaging the poor without condescension. This aptitude immediately sets him apart from those philanthropists in the text who are depicted unsympathetically and places him in line with the quieter forms of philanthropy praised by Jarndyce. But he also has a practical knowledge of the system and of the streets, a rare capacity in this novel. He thus approaches the challenge of what to do about Jo practically and compassionately. He rejects the institutional options of the hospital and the workhouse and instead takes Jo to Mr. George's in the hope of securing him "any poor lodging kept by decent people" (723). As he says to Mr. George:

> I am unwilling to place him in a hospital, even if I could procure him immediate admission, because I foresee that he would not stay there many hours, if he could be so much as got there. The same objection applies to a workhouse; supposing I had the patience to be evaded and shirked, and handed about from post to pillar in trying to get him into one—which is a system that I don't take kindly to. (722)

In light of this statement, one might argue that even to the more practically minded Woodcourt, institutional solutions pose all sorts of barriers and problems. Insofar as such solutions are considered and rejected in favor of private charity, one therefore might be tempted to conclude that Woodcourt hardly seems to advance a program of liberal reform. But this overlooks key elements in the novel, including Woodcourt's own informed sociological and critical viewpoint (he is critical of the way certain institutions are working, not against them in principle) and his sensitive focus on Jo's individual psychological state (which is likely to make him run away from a hospital or workhouse, since he equates these sites with the omnipresent eye of Bucket). Moreover, it is important to note that Woodcourt ultimately marries Esther and becomes a "medical attendant on the poor" in Yorkshire, a community that dynamically encompasses both rural and urban forms of life, including "streams and streets, town and country, mill and moor" (919). Importantly, then, he does not withdraw to a rural enclave and become a doctor known for his charity; rather, he actively participates in local medical administration in a changing community. It is not persuasive, in this context, to assert that Woodcourt represents an anti-institutional form of moral response expressive of Dickens's retreat to the realm of the private and the domestic.[14]

A reading focused on this broader interpretation of Woodcourt still might be impelled to conclude that Dickens resolves the gap introduced by the dual narration via characterological mediation. Presenting the reader with an exemplary individual able to access and combine the sociological and the moral perspectives, Dickens is able to make the case for modest progressive reform as an appropriate response to the challenges of modern England. But what I have referred to as the novel's rhetorical mediations complicate the interpretive situation, as does the way Woodcourt himself might be seen as a narrator figure and not simply a situated agent. Both of these features seem to insist that the novel's larger vision—at once moral and sociological, aspirational and bleak—is best captured through aesthetic methods that both employ and exceed traditional models of ideal or heroic character.

The most striking of the novel's rhetorical mediations, and arguably the crux of the book, is the passage where the narrator attempts to understand what it is like to be illiterate, to be like the street sweeper Jo:

> It must be a strange state to be like Jo! To shuffle through the streets, unfamiliar with the shapes, and in utter darkness as to the meaning, of those mysterious symbols, so abundant over the shops, and at the corners of streets, and on the doors, and in the windows! To see people read, and to see people write, and to see the postmen deliver letters, and not to have the least idea of all that language—to be, to every scrap of it, stone blind and dumb! It must be very puzzling, to see the good company going to the churches on Sundays, with their books in their hands, and to think (for perhaps Jo *does* think, at odd times) what does it all mean, and if it means anything to anybody, how comes it that it means nothing to me? To be hustled, and jostled, and moved on; and really to feel that it would appear to be perfectly true that I have no business, here, or there, or anywhere; and yet to be perplexed by the consideration that I *am* here somehow, too, and everybody overlooked me until I became the creature that I am! It must be a strange state, not merely to be told that I am scarcely

human (as in the case of my offering myself for a witness), but to feel it of my own knowledge all my life! To see the horses, dogs, and cattle, go by me, and to know that in ignorance I belong to them, and not to the superior beings in my shape, whose delicacy I offend! Jo's ideas of a Criminal Trial, or a Judge, or a Bishop, or a Government, or that inestimable jewel to him (if he only knew it) the Constitution, should be strange! His whole material and immaterial life is wonderfully strange; his death, the strangest thing of all. (257–58)

It is noteworthy that the third-person narrator is able to do a number of things that Esther cannot. He can place Jo within a broader frame of references — to multiple modes of being, multiple systems of communication, and a broader institutional structure including the courts, the government, and the church. Interestingly, too, the narrator actively seeks to inhabit Jo's perspective, even attempting a kind of meld with Jo's consciousness by using the first-person singular, the "I." What is most alien about this passage, especially in contrast to the world of Esther's narrative, is the sociological extremeness of what the narrator is attempting to capture here: he is essentially describing social death. The narrator describes this state externally, then imagines it from an internal perspective, to insist, it seems, that sympathy with such a condition is crucial to an understanding of it. The passage thus works to insist on common humanity even as it shows extreme social marginality. But the passage is also linked to a critique of society that the narrator is capable of given his comprehensive view of urban geography, social classes, and institutions. And it moves sharply to a satirical mode, with its excoriating view of the jewel of the constitution and the offended delicacies of those who are repelled by Jo and his like. It is also worth noting that the narrator is asking the reader, through language, to consider the situation of those who cannot read the very book he is writing, a book that includes a complex linguistic representation of the illiterate condition. The narrator is thus asking the reader to recognize the great gulf between those who can read and those who cannot, and the even greater gulf between those who can read a complex narrative like *Bleak House* and those who cannot read at all.

This crucial passage does something else: it forces the reader to break out of the comfort of being moved by represented scenes of sympathy between characters in the novel and instead to contemplate the effects of reading about the lives of those who are profoundly socially marginalized. One might compare this passage with the moments in Esther's narrative that highlight sympathetic exchange, as when Ada, on a charity visit, comforts the wife of one of the brick-makers after the death of her baby. Esther writes, "Such compassion, such gentleness, as that with which she bent down weeping, and put her hand upon the mother's, might have softened any mother's heart that ever beat. The woman at first gazed at her [Ada] in astonishment, then burst into tears" (134). This passage, which sets up a chain of humanizing equivalences via the term mother and climaxes in a sentimental release, is a far cry from the Jo passage, which insists on the mediating function of the narrative and profoundly alters the conditions for sympathy, keeping a volatilized sense of the systemic conditions, and the radical condition of illiteracy, as interruptive pressures against the very possibility of easy universality. Rather than simply seeing the third-person narrative as capturing the conditions of pervasive power, then, we can understand the novel as a complex formal enactment of the estranging but also enabling moral consequences of attempting to think the moral and the sociological perspective in relation to one another. The novel uses the informing tension between first- and third-person perspectives to help promote such thinking, and it indirectly makes the case for enlisting narrative's formal resources as a way to move beyond limiting conceptual approaches to poverty and social injustice. It therefore makes a claim for literary art as a power that can further moral and social understanding not only through characterological mediation, but also through significant breaching of the structuring gap between sociological and moral perspectives. Given the dynamic relation between these perspectives within the history of liberalism, it is important to assess the formal achievement and innovation of Dickens's novel as a distinctly liberal aesthetic.

TROLLOPE'S *THE WAY WE LIVE NOW*

In Anthony Trollope we again encounter the primacy and the limits of characterology as a formal site for elaborating liberal ideals. As I have stressed, individual character, and in particular exemplary character, is often seen as the natural ally of an emergent liberal ideology. Indeed, as I have pointed out, the rise of the novel has been read as a primary vehicle for the development of conceptions of individual interiority and self-actualization within conditions of assumed liberty. And yet within the novel character is also often viewed in terms of older aristocratic or traditional frameworks in which ideal manners are associated with clearly defined roles and tacit understandings of rank, responsibility, and deference. As we will see, it is precisely in the dynamic between competing notions of character and virtue that Trollope's encounter with liberal modernity is staged.

There is no question that character is of central moral and aesthetic interest to Trollope. In his *Autobiography* he writes, "I think the highest merit which a novel can have consists in perfect delineation of character, rather than in plot, or humour, or pathos."[15] In the same text, he also makes what looks to be a rather fundamental claim for the moral transparency of his writings, one based on the legibility of virtue and vice. His aim in writing, he states, is to "[impregnate] the mind of the novel-reader with a feeling that honesty is the best policy; that truth prevails while falsehood fails; that a girl will be loved as she is pure, and sweet, and unselfish; that a man will be honoured as he is true, and honest, and brave of heart; that things meanly done are ugly and odious, and things nobly done beautiful and gracious" (145).

This statement may capture a desire on Trollope's part that his writing will directly impart moral teaching, but the novels consistently show both character and virtue to be complex concepts, especially when viewed within the changing conditions of modern life. Habitual modes of comportment associated with settled character, for example, are subject to extraordinary pressure when traditional, taken-for-granted forms of life are challenged. In such a situation, psychological reactivity can seem to interrupt or re-inflect established moral traits. For example, in *Barchester Towers*, the diminished powers of gentlemanly tact in the glare of the press renders Harding mute and passive; the intuitive stream of mannered life has been indefinitely suspended by the forces of transparency and reform. Similarly, Archdeacon Grantly's anger at being asked to justify his doctrine and the customs of his parish fatally disrupts his seamless authority; he begins to sputter and rage where he once ruled implicitly.

For Trollope, "the perfect delineation of character" thus often includes not only settled comportments, but also reactive postures issuing from a sense of entitlement sorely tested by direct challenges from others who are exposing entrenched privileges and forms of hypocrisy. Within this complex mix, honesty emerges as the crux virtue, precisely because it is at once a traditional individual virtue (it quintessentially defines the "gentleman") and a form of truth-telling or critique aligned with both the evaluative diagnoses of the narrator and specific challenges by characters within the story to the doxa of those traditional communities Trollope often seems to affirm.

Trollope's treatment of honesty can profitably be viewed through the lens of Lionel Trilling's analysis of sincerity and authenticity as two key ideas in modern social and moral life.[16] In Trilling's account, sincerity is linked to the emergence of the concepts of society and the public, and it refers above all to one's self-presentation in public in accordance with prevailing norms. But the principle of sincerity extends further than this notion of personal integrity through social role. For Trollope, sincerity also comprehends principles of moral integrity, civic virtue, and social critique. In this sense it is intimately connected to what Jürgen Habermas has identified as the emergence of the public sphere in Enlightenment Europe, a condition in which critique, argument, and debate inform developing political practices and institutions. Sincerity is thus double-edged: it is tied to negative values of conformity and self-discipline yet also linked to the positive, progressive values of critique, transparency, and civic virtue. This has direct bearing on Trollope's dual conception of honesty as an embedded, fundamentally socialized virtue, on the one hand, and a critical function, on the other. The personal virtues of honesty and sincerity, central as they are to the ethos of gentlemanliness, in Trollope are often assumed in an uninterrogated way to be of primary value.[17] But the critical form of sincerity, whether narratorial or characterological, takes reflective distance and subjects the assumptions of the gentlemanly ethos to a fundamentally liberal critique.

In contrast to sincerity, authenticity in Trilling's account refuses to accept the social as a final limit on human development and self-expression. Authenticity looks beneath or beyond the surface of convention to access meaningful funds of human experience—nature, the unconscious, creative transgressive possibilities. Expressing itself through the aesthetic, and in particular via irony and the sublime, authenticity seeks a way beyond both social and moral convention. In Trilling's genealogy, authenticity comes to eclipse sincerity in the modern era and is most strongly associated with the emergence of modernist aesthetics, especially with the writings of Oscar Wilde and Friedrich Nietzsche.

Trilling tends to associate the British nineteenth-century realists with a pre-modernist emphasis on sincerity, but of course, as we have seen, Trollope's interest in psychology, and in the tension between psychological pressures and moral postures, could certainly be seen to introduce elements Trilling associates with authenticity.[18] But even more interesting is Trollope's vivid presentation of a dynamic that remains subdued and underexplored in Trilling: that between sincerity as socialized morality and sincerity as critique. This is especially noteworthy because throughout his career Trollope remains invested in embedded ethos as the medium in which solid moral character, particularly the breeding of gentlemen, is most reliably able to occur. The discussion of his opposition to competitive civil service examinations in the *Autobiography* is a particularly explicit and well-known example of this view, but it continually crops up in the fiction as well, sometimes as an ambivalently or nostalgically held view, but as a strong sentiment nonetheless.[19] The general tension in his work between nostalgic communitarianism and progressive liberalism helps to explain his famously elusive statement in the *Autobiography*, that he is "an advanced, but still a conservative Liberal" (291). A crucial and insufficiently studied element of Trollope's novelistic project, critical sincerity does not rise to the level of a settled and firm value in his work, both because of his divided investments and because he is so keenly aware of all the forces, psychological and otherwise, that irreducibly mediate it. But it is an unmistakable feature of his novelistic world, and without due acknowledgment of it any interpretive account of that world remains incomplete.

Beyond moments of situated critique, enacted either through characters or through the narrator, a larger critical ambition discernibly animates Trollope's intention, across his opus, to give us a comprehensive grasp of the social totality. Whether it be the relatively bounded world of the Barsetshire series or the more cosmopolitan reach of the Palliser novels, Trollope aims to represent the social and political world in its complexity, no matter at what seductively long-winded length he may telescope down to questions of psychology and ethics. And of course individual novels also aspire to something like sociology, most strikingly, perhaps, *The Way We Live Now*, which announces its systemic ambition in its title. Trollope's remarks about the book in his *Autobiography* capture his sociological vision while also asserting the primacy of its moral dimensions and consequences: "[A] certain class of dishonesty, dishonesty magnificent in its proportions, and climbing into high places, has become at the same time so rampant and so splendid that there seems to be reason for fearing that men and women will be taught to feel that dishonesty, if it can become splendid, will cease to be abominable" (354–55).

Yet even as Trollope seems to understand dishonesty as both an impersonal force and a personal trait, there is a recognition sprinkled throughout his writings that systemic dishonesty can't adequately be answered by, or reformed as, characterological honesty. An acknowledgment of the difficulty inheres in a conversation between one of *The Way We Live Now*'s most modern characters, the American Mrs. Hurtle, and Paul Montague, who is himself pulled between the traditional values of Roger Carbury and the excitement of the racy Mrs. Hurtle, whose relation to the vertiginous speed of modern life is reflected in her name. In a conversation about Melmotte, the great speculator who serves as the novel's representative of grandiose dishonesty, Mrs. Hurtle states that "such a man rises above honesty as a great general rises above humanity when he sacrifices an army to conquer a nation. Such greatness is incompatible with small scruples."[20] While this is not a view of the matter that Trollope condones (as, among other things, plot developments make clear), it reflects the novel's apprehension that a too circumscribed or blinkered idea of honesty or character cannot answer to systemic forces. Paul Montague's response to Mrs. Hurtle, "Personally, I do not like him," seems to swallow itself as an utterance; it is a particularly impotent response to Mrs. Hurtle's eloquent appeal to Melmotte's capacity to rise above conventional morality and exploit the commercial practices of the age (205).[21]

The complexity of Trollope's vision in this novel has invited readings that stress how his seeming ideals are always compromised by the inescapable negative forces that pervade all social behavior; thus dishonesty defines even the so-called respectable spheres of life, which all rely on ambitious self-interest and misrepresentation.[22] There is no world apart from the "way we live now" that can represent the way some exemplary subset of us still manages to live. Trollope's own admission in his *Autobiography* that as satirist he cannot fully separate himself from the dishonest practices of the age, the suggestion that there may be no vantage point of pure honesty from which to wage a crusade against an impure age, seems to play directly into the spirit of these readings, which themselves extend a line of criticism whereby Trollope is understood to be more complex, modern, or relativist than had been assumed by more traditional understandings of his guiding moral framework.[23]

The picture changes, however, if one recognizes how far Trollope's critique of systemic dishonesty in *The Way We Live Now* is complemented by moments that foreground a liberal and communicative principle of honesty. Because these moments project integrity even as they register complexities of power and psychology, it is hard to incorporate them into an interpretation of Trollope as fundamentally negative or relativistic in his worldview. Indeed, Trollope manifests a distinctive version of the tension, explored throughout this book, between negative assessment (in this case satiric) and liberal aspiration. Interestingly, while the aspiration is typically housed in individual characters who challenge the reigning doxa — often for personal reasons — Trollope takes some pains to mark liberal critique as importantly transpersonal in its reach, linked to principled challenges that transcend the pressure of unreflective custom and associated also, as we shall see, with an imagined transparency of writing as opposed to forms of embodied ethos.

The world of *The Way We Live Now* is very different from the world of Trollope's earlier novels, particularly the chronicles of Barsetshire. By the time of *The Way We Live Now*, the forces of modernity have infiltrated all aspects of life in what is depicted as a pervasively commercial, speculative, cosmopolitan society. There are certainly representatives of the traditionalist ethos, but they are marginal rather than central and therefore more fully on the defensive. And the liberal challenge to modernity is also handled differently, as a brief comparison between *Barchester Towers* and *The Way We Live Now* reveals.

In *Barchester Towers*, an embedded way of life is suddenly challenged by a group of churchmen who mount their offensive most effectively by demanding debate and transparency. The Proudie party, and in particular Mr. Slope, target a series of practices associated with mystified forms of religious power that thwart the possibilities for individual reflection and observance. Mr. Slope insists on rendering explicit those principles that animate his own doctrine and argues against the reliance on ritual and rule by authority in the High Church. Although Slope is described as odious and ungentlemanly, as manipulative and power-hungry, the challenge he poses to the Barsetshire Tory High Church is one that is, in a key respect, liberal and democratic, insofar as it demands accountability and transparency. In this context, it is no accident that Slope is strongly connected to members of the press, and that he both believes in the press and uses it to advance his aims.

One member of the Grantly party, Eleanor Bold, makes a point of defending Slope, precisely on liberal principles. She in fact takes over the position initially voiced by her father, Mr. Harding, when the clergy meet in crisis to discuss what to do about Slope's public sermon challenging the Barsetshire church to abandon the mediated, shrouded, and affective modes of the High Church and move instead toward intelligible services that will speak to the parishioners' reflective powers. At this meeting, Mr. Harding questions why Slope should be silenced at all, to which Mr. Grantly replies, "It is not because his opinion on church matters may be different from ours—with that one would not quarrel. It is because he has purposely insulted us."[24] The Grantly party consistently appeals to manner over substance, as is evinced by a subsequent conversation in which Mr. Harding plays Grantly to Eleanor's Mr. Harding. Eleanor suggests to her father that Mr. Slope may well have thought it his duty to express his dissenting opinion, to which Mr. Harding replies that it cannot be Slope's duty to be discourteous to his elders. Here Mr. Harding verges on the notion that Slope is necessarily wrong because his convictions insult church authorities. In this socioreligious conception, doctrine is subordinate to the way it is mediated, whether in church ritual or social conversation, and any bald challenge to authority delegitimates itself for this very reason.

At this point the defense of Slope shifts entirely to Eleanor, for whom a liberal posture on the Slope question becomes, we are told, "an habitual course of argument" (180). While she claims to share the antipathy to Slope's person that others foreground in every discussion of him, she insists on separating "acts" from persons ("I judge people by their acts" [270]) and laments the tribalism of her social group. Interestingly, we hear these views from Eleanor not only in challenging conversations with the Grantlys and Harding, but also in more lighthearted conversations with Mr. Arabin, the High Church member who is brought to the community by Archbishop Grantly as a counterweight to Mr. Slope. A reserved, Oxford-educated vicar who is known for his strong formal debating style, Arabin has battled Slope in print without ever having met him. The most salient fact about his function in the novel is that, once in Barsetshire, he does not debate Slope or confront him in any way in the social and religious world they cohabit, nor is any debate between them directly represented anywhere in the story itself.

Eleanor and Mr. Arabin, however, whose engagement closes off the plot of the novel, themselves take part in a series of arguments about argument. When Eleanor complains of the infighting among the clergy, Arabin counters by stressing the importance of ongoing debate over doctrine as a deterrence against authoritative decree. Arabin believes in the value of "moderate schism," which lies in its capacity to promote the reflective endorsement of religious matters; in this sense Arabin is a muted, tactful version of what Slope so loudly and tactlessly and instrumentally calls for (169). He represents the perfect dovetailing of ethos and (muted) argument in doctrinal matters; his is the ideal characterological form to express an allegiance to the High Church and a recognition of the need for modest justificatory debate, for disagreement without disagreeableness.

If Arabin's dedication to argument is subdued by characterological dignity, Eleanor's critical challenge is actively defused by the narrative, diverted into an erotic/romantic channel. It is true that when her social group wrongly reads her championing of Slope as romantic interest, she is outraged. Yet when she discovers that Slope wishes to marry her, she collapses into forms of self-recrimination. And notably, there is absolutely no dialogue, and no formal assent, in the proposal scene between Arabin and Eleanor: Arabin simply claims Eleanor ("Eleanor, my own Eleanor, my own, my wife!" [466]), who speechlessly yields. In a parallel way, Arabin is depicted at the end of the narrative as studious and silent, producing the same articles anew.

In *Barchester Towers* the liberal critic (Eleanor) is ultimately chastened and absorbed via the romance plot; by contrast, *The Way We Live Now* presents a memorable liberal critic within a minor subplot about a failed courtship (that between Brehgert, a successful Jewish banker, and Georgiana Longestaffe, the daughter of a country squire). In its presentation of the corrupt financier Melmotte, *The Way We Live Now* makes it clear that the surrounding society associates Jewishness with moral corruption and rootless cosmopolitan finance. But the inclusion of Brehgert within the narrative underscores that Trollope does not share in this prejudice against Jewishness.[25] Brehgert is depicted as honest and forthright: he steadily confronts Mr. Longestaffe's objections to the proposed marriage, and the narrator emphasizes his integrity in dealing with Georgiana, who is exposed as unequal to recognizing his worth. This is an instance, in other words, where Trollope's liberal bent is markedly in evidence: he makes clear that there is no necessary connection between forms of life, sociocultural identity, and character. In the drama of this situation, moreover, the limits of the gentlemanly ethos are forcefully challenged. It is also noteworthy that here, in contrast to *Barchester Towers*, the challenge to tacit custom exposes assumptions underlying the ideology of courtship and marriage, whereas in the earlier novel the courtship plot is used to contain and lighten such challenges.

Trollope emphasizes these informing liberal principles through the content and effects of a letter Brehgert sends to Georgiana after her father has tried to forbid the match. Brehgert reports the three objections her father stated to him: that he is in trade, that he is older and already has a family, and that he is a Jew. He takes up each of these objections in turn, disputing their merit in the case, then concludes by stating he understands that Georgiana nonetheless may not wish to alienate herself from her family, and that while he thinks her father is wrong and himself desires the marriage for all the reasons that motivated him to ask her in the first place, he will not hold her to her promise if she is moved to change her mind. He then discloses that an impending financial loss will affect his ability to maintain two establishments (there will be no house in London) but beyond that should not affect his providing for her.

The letter is very long, and the chapter it appears in announces its

importance in the title ("The Brehgert Correspondence"). A key section of
the letter addresses Mr. Brehgert's Jewishness:

> "As to my religion, I acknowledge the force of what your father says — though I
> think that a gentleman brought up with fewer prejudices would have expressed
> himself in language less likely to give offence. However I am a man not easily
> offended; and on this occasion I am ready to take what he has said in good part.
> I can easily conceive that there should be those who think that the husband and
> wife should agree in religion. I am indifferent to it myself. I shall not interfere
> with you if you make me happy by becoming my wife, nor, I suppose, will you
> with me. Should you have a daughter or daughters I am quite willing that they
> should be brought up subject to your influence." *There was a plain-speaking in
> this which made Georgiana look round the room as though to see whether any one
> was watching her as she read it.* "But no doubt your father objects to me specially
> because I am a Jew. If I were an atheist he might, perhaps, say nothing on the
> subject of religion. On this matter as well as on others it seems to me that your
> father has hardly kept pace with the movements of the age. Fifty years ago
> whatever claim a Jew might have to be as well considered as a Christian, he
> certainly was not so considered. Society was closed against him, except under
> special circumstances, and so were all the privileges of high position. But that
> has been altered. Your father does not admit the change; but I think he is blind
> to it, because he does not wish to see." (603-4; my emphasis)

In addition to the single interjection that Trollope places in the midst of the
letter, describing Georgiana's reaction, he also elaborates on her response
to the letter as a whole:

> This very long letter puzzled Georgey a good deal, and left her, at the time of
> reading it, very much in doubt as to what she would do. She could understand
> that it was a plain-spoken and truth-telling letter. Not that she, to herself, gave
> it praise for those virtues; but that it imbued her unconsciously with a thorough
> belief. She was apt to suspect deceit in other people — but it did not occur to her
> that Mr. Brehgert had written a single word with an attempt to deceive her. But
> the single-minded genuine honesty of the letter was altogether thrown away
> upon her. She never said to herself, as she read it, that she might safely trust
> herself to this man, though he were a Jew, though greasy and like a butcher,
> though over fifty and with a family, because he was an honest man. (605-6)

Georgiana reacts more immediately to the absence of romance in the letter, the allusions to her own age, and the disclosure that Brehgert will find
it impossible to maintain a London residence. When she writes to ask for
reassurance on the last point, Brehgert states that he can provide none and
concludes the engagement. But what is particularly striking is the impor-

tance and effect of Brehgert's epistolary communication, especially viewed in relation to the larger theme of honesty and dishonesty in the novel. First there is the fact that its most exemplary effects, in the narrator's view, are so fully a function of its status as disembodied communication. As a kind of speech that escapes the pressures of Brehgert's all too palpably embodied Jewishness ("though he were a Jew, though greasy and like a butcher"), the letter actualizes a kind of truthful communication that is not only inherently efficacious ("it imbued her unconsciously with a thorough belief") but also productive of a kind of social consciousness ("There was a plain-speaking in this which made Georgiana look round the room as though to see whether any one was watching her as she read it"). Trollope makes it clear that this communicative scenario can't fully actualize what it gestures toward, emphasizing that Georgiana is not equal to it, but it stands as a liberal moment that relies not only on Brehgert's characterological sincerity, but on the possibilities of a communicative practice that at once disarms prejudice and privileges the principles of autonomy and respect. Interestingly, it is not clear that Georgiana's sudden awareness of audience should be read narrowly in terms of gender ideology, as prompted only by the reference to a future sexual relation. And that is because it remains unclear whether this moment is attended by any real sense of shame or constraint: there is, tellingly, no mention of a blush. This is not to deny the sexual and gendered aspect of the communication, but rather to say that "plain-speaking" is operating more broadly here as a form of respect, as is indicated by the repetition of the word in the more general description of the letter ("it was a plain-spoken and truth-telling letter"). Trollope may tend to circle back to the importance of character ("because he was an honest man"), but his liberalism introduces an ideal of honesty whose principles and effects are as transpersonal as the dishonesty that defines "the way we live now."

The implications of the Brehgert correspondence are underscored if we compare it with another moment in the novel where the relative efficaciousness of epistolary and embodied communication is brought into play. As Paul Montague prepares to confess his history with Mrs. Hurtle to Hetta Carbury, whom he hopes to marry, the narrator considers the soundness of Paul's decision to convey the news in person: "The soft falsehoods which would be as sweet as the scent of violets in a personal interview, would stand in danger of being denounced as deceit added to deceit, if sent in a letter. I think therefore that Paul Montague did quite right in hurrying up to London" (581). This passage affirms the idea that disembodied communication holds out the promise of a kind of transparency (in this case dishonesty will out). Thus, whereas elsewhere in Trollope embodied manner seems so crucially to define the ethos of the gentleman, manner here promises (but also crucially threatens) to muffle and distort the truth. This interesting reversal in Trollope is connected to the tension between his appeal to the importance of embedded ways of life and his interest in the corrective powers of liberal critique. For Trollope there appears to be a persistent concern that disembodied communication will fail to capture the elusive elements of manner that constitute ethos and character. But in the case of the Brehgert correspondence, and negatively in Paul's refusal to commit words to paper, writing transcends embedded ethos in a critical way.[26]

I do not mean to suggest that Trollope imagines depersonalized communicative practices in the service of critique to have entirely broken free of character, to be simply enacting a transcendental criterion of truthfulness in speech. Sincerity as critique, as I mentioned earlier, is always placed in relation to a notion of characterological integrity. The Brehgert episode thus comprehends both characterological honesty and a communicative practice that appeals to respect and reciprocity. It insists, moreover, on bringing these principles to light, over against what stands as unexamined prejudice and mystified appeals to common understanding. Indeed, a future conversation on monetary matters between Mr. Longestaffe and Brehgert, who have been brought together briefly over losses sustained by Melmotte, drives this point home. In discussing the Melmotte affair, Brehgert refers to his earlier anticipation of financial loss in the letter to his daughter, and Mr. Longestaffe is horrified that Brehgert dares to recur to this episode, dares to be so indelicate in a matter—the proposed marriage—that he always regarded as "impossible" (677). Brehgert refuses to honor Mr. Longestaffe's claim that the subject is "painful," and he is firm in the face of Mr. Longestaffe's attempt to retreat by aphoristically invoking a code of tactful silence: "Perhaps on so delicate a subject the less said the soonest mended" (677).

This is a powerfully interesting moment, one that shows up the competing emphases of Trollope's ideal of sincerity. On the one hand, honesty and sincerity are assumed to be continuous with an ideal of gentlemanliness relying on an unspoken code of conduct that seeks to navigate differences through a delicate balancing of recognition and tact. On the other hand, honesty and sincerity are powerfully associated with those forms of critique, often advanced by socially marginal characters, that challenge the very hierarchies the code preserves. Brehgert's response to Longestaffe illustrates this latter tendency: "I've nothing more to say, and I've nothing at all to mend" (677). Insisting that he rejects the terms of Longestaffe's delicacy, which is in this instance a cover for invidious religious and racial distinctions, Brehgert also insists that he hardly wants to return to any dynamic that requires he silently endure the status quo in the service of some asymmetrical cordiality. Longestaffe may himself be presented as ridiculously prejudiced, but there is a larger set of concerns in play here that affect the core of Trollope's project: honesty must break through the blinkered constraints of the ethos of delicacy or gentlemanliness in order to effectively and candidly diagnose the dishonesty of the age. Saying that Melmotte or Slope is not a gentleman is hardly adequate to the task at hand. Many of Trollope's characters are reduced to inarticulate impotence when those around them fail to conform to the tacit rules of conduct that define their moral world (among these would be Longestaffe, Roger Carbury, Archdeacon Grantly). As Shirley Letwin points out, this situation means that those who inhabit the traditional gentlemanly ethos, which is certainly being challenged by new forms of mobility and by encounters with new forms of social and cultural difference, are suddenly forced to defend their way of life.[27] Such a defense requires actually describing and justifying it, an activity itself performatively at odds with the emphasis on unspoken rules that are ingrained over time and best fostered in a stable community underwritten by landed property. "Least said, soonest mended" is the half-lit awareness of this problem, a reactive and psychologically strained attempt to quickly appease the demands of justification.

In light of this complex treatment of sincerity, it becomes clear that simple notions of honest character are put under pressure not only by the larger negative forces of modernity, but also by the principled demands of progressive liberalism itself. There's a moment in a conversation between Paul Montague and Roger Carbury where Carbury, hearing of Paul's misgivings about the railway scheme, advises Paul to take Ramsbottom's advice: "You have to bind your character to another man's character; and that other man's character, if it be good, will carry you through" (303). This is the desperate position of a man whose way of life is under siege and who cannot bear to relinquish the gentlemanly ideal that participates in its mystifications. The fact is that in moments like the Brehgert correspondence Trollope imagines an alternative ideal where familiar practices and enclosed communities are placed under the lamp of liberal principle.[28] It is also of interest that Trollope's liberalism is a sober one: it locates strong voices of resistant critique among those who have either suffered prejudice or endured the disenchantments of mercenary courtship scenarios.[29]

It certainly cannot be claimed that Trollope unequivocally supports a liberal ideal; there is a genuine tension between his liberalism and his persistent valuing of traditional forms of life in the face of what for him are the negative dimensions of modernity. But there are compelling features, at once conceptual and formal, at play in Trollope's engagement with liberal ideas. The most striking is the double role played by sincerity, which as we have seen functions as both a characterological virtue and a critical ideal. This duality finds expression not only in narratorial satire and character interaction, but also in the novel's own theme of the significance of writing, which is held up as the medium of a kind of sincerity that can achieve forms of transparency and unaffected candor that remain clouded in a manners-suffused world.

ELIOT'S *MIDDLEMARCH*

Like Trollope, George Eliot is concerned with the conditions and challenges of modernity. She is especially interested in the demands and opportunities presented by a view of religion from the anthropological, Feuerbachian perspective: if we are no longer surrounded by a "coherent social faith and order" that can provide a clear framework for the morally purposeful life, then we are left to devise our own self-authorized modes of engagement with the world.[30] In such a situation, self-actualization becomes a prime value, as does reflective endorsement of various principles and frameworks for action.

Of course this is only half the story, since Eliot is a discernible gradualist when it comes to the political sphere, and she can often appear conservative. This general conservatism is evident not only in "The Natural History of German Life" and "Address to Working Men, by Felix Holt" but also across the novels. It is especially noteworthy that one can find evidence for these views in *Felix Holt* and *Middlemarch*, the two novels most directly engaged with political reform and the widening of the franchise and democratic access in Britain. Complementing the explicit and implicit cautions against mob action and accelerated transformations, moreover, throughout the novels there is a subtending endorsement of traditional communities and the moral grounding they provide. Yet such emphases must always be set against the modern dimensions of Eliot's project. As Suzanne Graver has so persuasively shown in *George Eliot and Community*, a dialectical interplay of gemeinschaft and gesellschaft values informs Eliot's work, by means of which modern principles of autonomy and individualism are balanced against the claims of community and tradition.[31] One recurring formation involves the main protagonist's reflective endorsement of long-standing relations or defining identities, as in Maggie Tulliver's chastened reaffirmation of her ties to Lucy Deane and to her brother Tom, or Daniel Deronda's commitment to his newly discovered Jewish heritage. Another takes the form of a commitment to self-actualization as opposed to the strictures of society, particularly in the case of women, but also for others unfairly limited in their opportunities. Last, and increasingly as her work progresses, there is an investment in deliberative self-understanding through dialogical engagement, typically between aspiring idealists and more doctrinaire figures (the key examples here would be Romola and Savonarola, and Deronda and Mordecai, though the relations between Esther Lyon and Felix Holt and between Gwendolen and Deronda are also relevant). These relationships foreground the difficulty of living a morally examined life, and they stress the importance of argumentative dialogue, a key liberal practice, as a form of self-examination and self-transformation.

As I have argued elsewhere, the staging of relations between aspiring idealists and doctrinaire figures reflects an informing tension between theory and existence, one that also often maps onto the distinction between the narratorial perspective, which engages in philosophical statements about the best way to live, and the perspective of situated characters who find it hard to meet the exacting demands of the novel's informing moral doctrines. This is especially true with respect to the law of consequences, which requires extraordinary vigilance lest one's actions set up a train of harmful effects.[32] While the law of consequences may appear to be in sync with liberalism's no-harm principle, the informing assumption is rather that actions are so enmeshed with circumstances, and our lives are so intertwined, that action without some negative consequences for others is essentially impossible.[33] This is why the attempt to live the doctrine is so fraught with a sense of inevitable failure. The doctrine is in essence a critique of the ideal of negative liberty underlying liberalism.

Middlemarch stands out in that it lacks the type of productive tutelary relationship that aims to express and work through an aspiring idealism. The novel also is of interest to the present discussion because it is set in the time directly before the First Reform Bill and contains a character, Will Ladislaw, who becomes a member of Parliament working on behalf of reform. Will is unusual both within the character system of the novel itself and within the larger character system of Eliot's novels. As we saw in the discussions of Trollope and Dickens, character may seem to be the key formal element in those novels that seek to promote a liberal orientation toward modern life, yet the novelists often push beyond traditional conceptions of character, especially of moral exemplarity, as they seek to conceive of political forms appropriate to the current challenges. In Dickens, the interaction between third- and first-person perspectives promotes a more sociologically informed liberal sympathy than the cushioned scenes of sympathy between characters can provoke. In Trollope, similarly, forms of transpersonal critique help to dislodge traditional conceptions of gentlemanliness and the stable, embedded character it was taken to represent. In Eliot, as we shall see, Will Ladislaw's story poses a fundamental challenge to the notion that individual moral character should underwrite large-scale aspiration of the type that would inform a project of political reform.

Will is a notably mercurial character within a novelistic oeuvre in which such a trait is elsewhere associated with lack of integrity and with a form of protean political maneuvering fundamentally amoral in nature, as in the case of *Romola*'s Tito Melema. Moreover, Will's choice of vocation is associated with an indicting arbitrariness: he falls into the role of journalist for the cause of reform only because he wishes to stay in Middlemarch near Dorothea and is willing to work for the wayward Mr. Brooke.[34] Before this he was drawn to the artistic life, but in that venture he was a mere dilettante, lacking vocational purpose. A comparison with *Daniel Deronda* is illuminating. Deronda's wayward detachment and free-floating sympathy are in need of correction through a form of partiality based on primary affiliation, not situational opportunity, as in the case of Ladislaw. Within the world of Middlemarch, moreover, Will stands out: he differs significantly from Lydgate, who despite his consequential failings—weakness in the case of women and financial imprudence born of a sense of entitlement—has a clear sense of what he hopes to accomplish vocationally. Lydgate importantly combines an interest in science with a desire to help others and forward the cause of medical reform through his discoveries. Medicine as a vocation offers "the most perfect interchange between science and art" and "the most direct alliance between intellectual conquest and the social good."[35]

Lydgate has extraordinary promise, but he is caught up in petty political conflicts as well as trouble around love and money. His is a tragic tale of aspiration thwarted by a mix of circumstance and character weakness. One casualty of his failure is the cause of reform within the medical profession which he had hoped to forward. Will, by contrast, becomes an active reformer by means of a practical accommodation to limiting circumstances, and he himself espouses a pragmatic understanding of political opportunity. Indeed, one of the central political principles Will affirms, what he calls "the wisdom of balancing claims," is asserted precisely against the demand for moral and characterological integrity in political agents. It is no accident that the assertion takes place in a conversation with Lydgate, who has been faulting Will's focus on the interim progress of franchise reform as "crying up a measure as if it were a universal cure, and crying up men who are a part of the very disease that wants curing" (465). Lydgate goes on to state a position reminiscent of that advanced in *Felix Holt*: "You go against rottenness, and there is nothing more thoroughly rotten than making people believe that society can be cured by a political hocus-pocus" (465). In response, Will makes a key distinction between individual moral merit and the importance of responding to larger social wrongs: "Wait for wisdom and conscience in public agents—fiddlestick! The only conscience we can trust to is the massive sense of wrong in a class, and the best wisdom that will work is the wisdom of balancing claims. That's my text—which side is injured? I support the man who supports their claims; not the virtuous upholder of the wrong" (465–66). Will then goes on to press Lydgate toward the realization that he himself has used an alliance with a less than ideal agent (Bulstrode) to forward his own plans for medical reform.[36]

This exchange introduces a very different evaluative approach to political life and practice than we see elsewhere in Eliot, where such bald instrumentalism and the subordination of moral to political principles is cast in an unambiguously negative light. For example, not only does *Felix Holt* caution against political mobilization on behalf of reform, but, as Henry Staten has pointed out, it contains a discredited union man who voices the same practical approach as Will does, arguing that the workers should support a liberal aristocrat if he will advance their cause.[37]

Middlemarch thus invites the question whether the very project of liberal reform that Will pursues calls for a different understanding of action and commitment than is typically associated with Eliot or characteristic of the main storylines of Lydgate and Dorothea, which emphasize failed idealist striving. In the case of Dorothea, the novel makes the case for chastened accommodation to forms of ordinary betterment over grand scale actualization or reform of the type associated with Saint Teresa. Dorothea is at once associated with Will—annexed to and supportive of his efforts—and dissociated from him in her more diffuse and affective modes of moral and social engagement. She is seen as vitally connected to a larger force for good in the world that is essentially moral rather than political, spiritual rather than practical: "The effect of her being on those around her was incalculably diffusive: the growing good of the world is partly dependent on unhistoric acts; and that things are not so ill with you and me as they might have been, is half owing to the number who lived faithfully a hidden life, and rest in unvisited tombs" (838).

In an influential reading of the novel, D. A. Miller argues that *Middlemarch* houses a tension between what he designates as the community's narrative, which he associates with the genre of realism, and the protagonists' scripts or aspirations, which belong to utopian fiction. Interestingly, Miller observes, the text manifests a "double ambivalence," in which community is "achieved but discredited" while the utopian scripts are "valorized but dismantled."[38] Attributing a frustrated idealism to the novel's resolution, Miller argues that the emphasis on failure is essentially a way of paying tribute to the thwarted ideals of the main protagonists: "The original project (what Lydgate meant to do, what Dorothea might have done, if she had been better and known better) may be frustrated, but it still insistently governs the perception of disarray. . . . Defining itself as the negative image of successful transcendence, failure is a bottom line strategy of paying homage to it" (144–45).

Will occupies an anomalous and not very satisfactory place in Miller's account. Miller states that he chooses the one career that is impossible in Middlemarch, that of reformer, since the normative power of the community makes that career choice quixotic (and ultimately mandates that he leave the community to pursue it). Miller includes Will among those who are diminished over the course of the novel: in turning from a life of art and freedom to a life defined by Dorothea and reform, Will too is involved in the frustration of an original ideal. The marriage settlement governing the novel's resolution means that Will and Dorothea's union is also a form of failure—it is a traditional settlement in place of the transcendence originally sought. Thus, in Miller's schema political reform is assimilated precisely to the realm of the diminished ordinary. But this fails to notice how unassimilable political reform actually is to Eliot's larger value system. Even were one to grant Miller's point that the ending of the novel is governed by a frustrated idealism—I would contest this point myself—Will's situation is in no way equivalent to that of Dorothea and Lydgate.[39] Will did not start out with a quixotic ideal; he chose to work for reform because the opportunity presented itself and he saw it as a worthy cause. It is true that reformist aspiration is itself seen as destined to fall short of the aim, but neither Will's relation to the project of reform, nor political work as Will defines it, can be viewed as parallel to the thwarted idealism of Dorothea and Lydgate. Consider this statement from the finale: "Will became an ardent public man, working well in those times when reforms were begun with a young hopefulness of immediate good which has been much checked in our days."[40] This may look like a statement that can be easily folded into Miller's schema, but Will can hardly be assimilated to the "young hopefulness of immediate good," given what we know about his sober realism. And perhaps most important, even if ardency is a valued quality in a public man, in the sphere of politics moral character is simply not the salient force—we are not told anything about the "effect of [Will's] being" on those around him; we are told that he "worked well" in the sphere of politics during a period of hopeful beginnings whose hopes were not borne out. This hardly strikes one as the language of thwarted transcendence or the forms of spiritual personality that, for Eliot, underwrite it; the terms are different, as is the form of accommodation required.

A further consideration of the presentation of Dorothea's character illuminates how we might begin to understand this difference and its implications for the novel's conception of political as opposed to ethical life. Dorothea's journey involves grappling with the desire to fuse life and doctrine, to find "a binding theory which could bring her own life and doctrine into strict connection with [the] amazing past, and give the remotest sources of knowledge some bearing on her actions" (86). Early on we see indications that this desire for fusion is misguided: there are clear signs that her ardent aspirations have elements of blindness, and of course this fact is underscored in her fateful acceptance of marriage with Casaubon, which for her promises a life at once "rational and ardent" (86). We are invited to notice in the moment of her receiving Casaubon's epistolary proposal that Dorothea's response to him is merely a channel for her character-defining struggle toward "an ideal life," and that her precipitous embrace of the unconventional life offered in the Casuabon marriage is in part driven by "her discontent with the actual conditions of her life" (45). These comments on Dorothea reveal that what is required is not a fusion of "life" and "doctrine" but a mediation between them.

The problem with Dorothea's idealism when it takes the form of intellectual aspiration is fairly clear, and it can be judged against the representation of more concrete vocational purpose in the case of Lydgate, who at the very least clearly differentiates between the spheres of social good and intellectual aim, who likes medicine because it conjoins the two, not because it collapses them. But Dorothea's character is also defined through its more immediately expressed and felt moral nature. There are many instances when Dorothea's tenderness and generosity are emphasized, and

these features of her character seem to carry the narrative's full endorsement (rather than serving as objects of ironic comment or knowing judgment). In a number of key moments of crisis, for example, we are reminded
of Dorothea's natural impulse toward moral repair: "Permanent rebellion,
the disorder of a life without some loving reverent resolve, was not possible
to her"; "however just her indignation might be, her ideal was not to claim
justice, but to give tenderness"; "she disliked this cautious weighing of consequences, instead of an ardent faith in efforts of justice and mercy, which
would conquer by their emotional force" (194, 202, 733). And we are told
elsewhere of her "gentle loving manifestations" in the face of Casaubon's
persistent suspicions; her "impetuous generosity," her "generous sympathy" (418, 733, 763).

This moral impulse does not seem to require the same adjustment as the
original desire to fuse life and doctrine, especially since it is endorsed in
the narrative's final sentences about Dorothea's effect in a time lacking the
possibility for fully enacted moral heroism. This aspect of Dorothea also
becomes a form of moral inspiration for others: "that simplicity of hers,
holding up an ideal for others in her believing conception of them, was
one of the great powers of her womanhood" (772). In this respect Eliot's
ideal of sympathy includes a powerful element of recognition that prompts
self-actualization.

The emphasis on situated moral response that we see in the endorsement of Dorothea's ethical being is in line with the adjustment in scale that
marks her existential itinerary in the novel. In learning to relinquish her
desire for an immediate and far-reaching actualization of the ideal, Dorothea engages in local and limited interventions rather than in any organized
philanthropy such as that represented in her early idea for new cottages on
the Brooke estate or her later idea of a workers' colony (after Casaubon's
death). Instead, Dorothea focuses on doing the good that lies to hand—
helping Lydgate restore his reputation so that he may continue his medical
work, and helping Lydgate and Rosamond in their marriage conflict. We
are told in the finale that such an orientation toward ethical life will add to
the good of the world, even as it necessarily works on only a small scale.

The example set by Dorothea, and the novel's ongoing endorsement of
her moral nature, has led to the long-standing sense that Eliot's most privileged register is the ethical one—that what matters is precisely the effect of
one's ethical being on those around one. This is what defines the good, this
is what contributes to the good. Such an emphasis, along with Eliot's investment in the importance of community and existing ties, has led many to

find the political dimensions of Eliot's work implicitly or explicitly conservative. But the character of Will, and the values he represents, complicates such a view. He certainly has qualities that can be recruited to the ideal of sympathy: his impressibility (388), his ability to enter into others' feelings (496), and his indifference to conventional forms of self-interest mark him out as a person with significant moral potential. In addition, there is something in the nature of his response to Dorothea that affirms her being in a powerfully enabling way: it is not so much the form of "believing conception" that we see in Dorothea's response to others as simple acceptance and acknowledgment, a letting-be that powerfully counteracts the starving nonrecognition from Casaubon. But despite these qualities, we cannot really connect Will's character directly to his vocation. He tells Lydgate directly that he wishes to work on behalf of whichever side is injured, and the finale states that "Dorothea could have liked nothing better, since wrongs existed, than that her husband should be in the thick of a struggle against them" (836). Will, it seems, is precisely elevating principles of justice and right over moral force of the sort that Dorothea embodies. Moreover, he is working not on behalf of individuals or even of utopian community (as Dorothea would in the case of the cottages or the imagined colony), but rather on behalf of a class of people who are experiencing injury or wrong. Which is to say, simply, that his aim is distinctly political, and in a way very different from that of Deronda, whose nationalist commitment centrally involves a desire for community at a higher level.[41] Will does not privilege the stability of community, and therefore his commitments can be connected to the forms of resistance associated with liberal reform directed toward inequity internal to the community. There are other moments in the novel when we are reminded of these internal divisions: the conversation between Brooke and Dagley, the reaction to Brooke on the hustings, and the encounter between Caleb Garth and the laborers who are confronting the railway surveyors. In each of these moments, as Staten has ably shown, Eliot is by no means simply on the side of established interests; she is highlighting the problem of vested interests, political blindness, and entrenched inequities.[42]

Eliot thus marks a difference between ethics and politics, and she does so through Will's story. The question is how we are meant to interpret and weight the political life Will represents. On one hand it seems to be an intensified version of the problem of modern vocation: if we do not have unifying frameworks of meaning and faith, then politics is itself a deficient or partial activity. Rather than taking place within a clearly defined structure of meaning, it is simply reactive, responding to the negative conditions of injury and wrong, not building an encompassing institutional world. There is no positive principle of equality invoked, and indeed there is more emphasis in the novel on corruption or "rottenness" than on the aspiration to democracy via the franchise. Now, of course one could say that such a negative diagnosis presupposes an ideal or healthy state, that the very identification of the wrong indicates what an uninjured existence would look like. In this sense the discourse around politics might be argued to mirror the tone in which failure of individual self-actualization is lamented in the text: it harbors a frustrated ideal.

And yet it might be more interesting and fruitful to consider the ways political life does not fit the novel's centrally dramatized experience of ethico-spiritual life. This approach would allow a different way of understanding the history of dissatisfaction with the character of Will Ladislaw, the sense that he is unworthy of Dorothea, or not satisfactorily drawn as a character, or simply, as Henry James puts it, "a failure."[43] From this perspective one could interpret the sense that Will lacks substance, or that Dorothea's marriage to him is a disappointing settlement for the novel's close, as reflecting the gap between ethico-spiritual life, as represented by Dorothea, and political life as represented by Will. For Eliot one can't positively and immediately exemplify politics in the way one can positively and immediately exemplify an ethos. This may go some way toward explaining why Will's life as a public man is not really brought before us or detailed in any way. Given the importance to Eliot of a form of commitment expressed through character, or brought to bear on the development of character, what we have in the novel is something of a compromise: an ethical endorsement of political purpose through Dorothea's commitment to Will and his political aims.[44] The most interesting aspect of the novel's settlement is precisely that the typical sign of unity and reconciliation — marriage — only lights up a key discrepancy between ethics and politics; and it shows how liberal politics, in its aim to alter conditions so as to expand the possibilities for realizing individual life aims, involves not simply accommodation to actual conditions, but a fundamental insistence on eliminating wrongs that reach beyond the individual case. Rather than a reparative sympathy that responds to pain and suffering and individual injury, liberalism of the sort Will is aligned with requires a claim for recognition of, and participation by, a class of people. Ultimately, the frustration voiced about the character of Will may be a symptom of the unsettled apprehension that politics must cultivate a certain indifference to the seduction of exemplary character if it is to remain focused on its distinctive, and fundamentally impersonal, aspirations.

Interestingly, in Eliot politics is at once more bleak and less bleak than ethics. More bleak because it cannot be consoled by the radiating effects of ethical being, less bleak because it is more impersonal and pragmatic, less driven by an idealizing aspiration. Like *Bleak House*'s move to supplement characterological mediation and familiar scenes of sympathetic exchange with an estranging and challenging moral-sociological synthesis enacted by the third-person narration, and like *The Way We Live Now*'s emphasis on impersonal communication via writing as a check to the mystifying effects of tact and ethos, *Middlemarch*'s representation of a political challenge to the primacy of exemplary character lights up the complexities that liberal concepts and principles can generate within literary form.

CHAPTER THREE

Revisiting the Political Novel

In the previous chapter I explored distinctive features of the realist engagement with liberal thought, analyzing three major nineteenth-century British novels. Focusing in particular on the formal mediation of liberalism's struggle with the limits of character as a site of value, I showed how Dickens, Trollope, and Eliot each acknowledge the significance of individual moral exemplarity while insisting on the importance of perspectives and practices—sociological, impersonal, and political—that exceed the domain of the individual. It is precisely the interplay between first-person and third-person perspectives, between embodied presence and impersonal critique, between ethics and politics, that characterizes the liberal project as it develops in the nineteenth-century novel. We are so accustomed to thinking that the realist novel simply presents to us the figure of the liberal individual, fundamentally reinforcing liberalism in its staging of the struggles of the heroic protagonist, that we fail to see the dynamic interrelation of character and critique in the evolving experiments of those writers for whom liberal ideas were generative and challenging and not simply assumed or ideologically channeled.

In this chapter I turn to the subgenre of the political novel to further develop the formal dimensions of the liberal aesthetic. I begin my discussion with examples drawn from the well-known canon of nineteenth-century political novels, then turn in the final section to a discussion of E. M. Forster's *Howards End*, which allows for an exploration of the role of argument within the tradition of the novel of manners, thereby setting the stage for a reading of Lionel Trilling's ideological novel of manners *The Middle of the*

Journey in the chapter that follows. As will become clear, the present chapter seeks to establish the centrality and significance of argument as a formal mode in the political novel (typically enacted through political or ideological discussions between characters) as well as political novelists' common interest in depicting a lived relation to political commitment or belief. This latter element may seem too obvious to note, but its importance will emerge as I proceed. Both these features are key to understanding to what extent certain political novels are distinctly liberal in their orientation and effects, in that liberalism privileges deliberative debate as well as acknowledgment of the conditions and limits within which political life is waged.

Typically identified as the industrial novel, the social-problem novel, or simply the political novel, the nineteenth-century political novel has proved difficult to characterize and to classify.[1] Generally novels are placed in this category when they centrally treat conditions and crises occasioned by the Industrial Revolution in Britain, including the discontent and misery of the working classes; the negative effects of a world increasingly dominated by machinery, alienated labor, and the profit motive; and, not least, the impact of worker uprisings, strikes, and violence (with the example of the French Revolution always in the background). Beyond this orienting set of concerns, there is one other key feature of the mid-nineteenth-century political novel in England: it tends to position itself as an intervention. In addressing the problems they expose, that is, these novels proffer some sort of solution, even if that solution is only the reading of the novel itself (which thereby allows for insight into under-recognized problems, or prompts sympathy for suffering, or otherwise effects a transformation in the reader that might enable a constructive approach to the problems depicted).

While recognition of an aim to intervene in a social problem certainly enfolds the idea that the novel makes an argument or claim, the standard characterizations of the industrial novel don't foreground the significance of argument form within the novel, nor do they isolate the centrality of the lived experience of political belief or commitment. Moreover, established tendencies within the literary field have made these distinctive features of the political novel difficult to recognize, let alone assess. To begin with, most political accounts of the history of the novel diminish the distance between those novels that explicitly position themselves as political novels and the genre of the novel as a whole. The major accounts of the novel as a political form commonly tell a story about the novel's rise in relation to the emergence and consolidation of modern power or ideological formations.[2] In such accounts the political is understood quite capaciously: it infiltrates all aspects of experience and therefore all aspects of the novel's storyworld. Those spheres of life within the novel or the larger culture that define themselves against the political, or wish to place themselves beyond its limit, are typically shown to be part of the general political system—either because power or ideology always necessarily resides within them or because, as deceptive sites of freedom, they merely consolidate a liberal regime. Thus, appeals to realms that are imagined to exceed the political—extending to art, to romance, to private experience or private morality—are viewed as mystified or evasive. One consequence of this tendency is a failure to sufficiently acknowledge and analyze the specificity of politics as a delimited practice in its own right, with a multiplicity of liberal democratic and radical forms, from argument and voting to strike and revolution. Beyond this lies the larger problem I have alluded to: the inability to take seriously a politics that acknowledges its own limits.

A disinclination to assign distinctive political significance to emergent experiments with argument form in the novel can be seen with instructive force in Jacques Rancière's *The Politics of Literature,* which tells a story about the rise of literature and its relation to democracy. Rancière reads the emergence of modernism, represented in Flaubert's style, as democratizing in its uniform attention to all manner of subjects and objects: in his succinct assertion, "the absolutization of style was the literary formula for the democratic principle of equality."[3] For Rancière, this development involves a deliberate move away from the democratic political stage and hence justifies a diminished attention to formal politics. By his account, modernism as a new form of literary democracy rejects an earlier regime, classical in origin, that privileges rhetoric and oration or the power of speech in action associated with drama and an elitist heroism.

Rancière thus reverses the political valence of Sartre's critique of Flaubert. For Sartre, a writer who champions prose as engagement and action, the process of moving words away from debate and political struggle is a nihilistic strategy. For Rancière, by contrast, not simply Flaubert but literature itself "pits a different politics against this democratic mise en scène," both by its democratizing style, which rescues ordinary life in its abandonment of heroic, speech-oriented political action, and by its exposure of the darker realities and forms of negative experience that society hides beneath its surface. In this account literature "quit[s] the state of speech carried by sonorous voices in order to decipher the testimonies that society itself offers for us to read, to disinter those society unwittingly and unintentionally deposits in its dark underground shoals. The noisy stage of the orators is opposed by the journey through the subterranean passages that hold its hidden truth" (20).[4]

There are notable similarities between Rancière's argument in *The Politics of Literature* and the work of Adorno on politics and aesthetics. Adorno too lays emphasis on the importance of modernist literary registrations of diminished life under capitalism, claiming that "it is now virtually in art alone that suffering can still find its own voice, consolation, without immediately being betrayed by it."[5] Similarly in Adorno, we find an opposition between a more authentic registration of the experience of life under a debasing system and traditional political speech, which focuses on the problem of making one's commitment explicit: "The notion of a 'message' in art, even when politically radical, already contains an accommodation to the world: the stance of the lecturer conceals a clandestine entente with the listeners, who could only be rescued from deception by refusing it" (193). While Rancière's writings on politics more generally differ from Adorno's approach in their stress on the active and direct contestation of inequality, *The Politics of Literature*'s theory of what we might call literary redistributions of the sensible certainly seems to reproduce the logic whereby art is accorded special political potency and forms of committed art are seen as part of a power-laden system.

These frameworks make it difficult to assess the formal and conceptual work done by forms of argument, and by the explicit engagement with ideas and ideology, within the political novel. In contrast, I will seek to establish the narratological significance of political discussion between and among characters. Insofar as philosophical and ideological discussion is a feature of the broader genre of the novel of ideas, the approach I advance here would be relevant to analysis of that genre, of which the political novel is arguably a subset or special instance. It should also be noted at the outset that political argument in the novel is not limited to character-character dialogue but also can inhere in narratorial discourse as well as in mediations between narratorial discourse and character speech.[6] But for my present purposes I will explore the unique features of character-character dialogue.

Another practice within the critical field prevents recognition not of the argument form but rather of the active writerly imagining of a lived relation to commitment and belief. Less self-conscious and less elaborated than the literary histories described above, this ingrained critical habit involves the assumption that specific authors and texts are reliably identifiable within a political spectrum extending from left to right. Often a reflexive move among politically minded critics, sometimes merely nonce-descriptive, this tendency can also lend support to or significantly underpin the forms of grand theory animating ambitious political literary histories. For example, texts adduced as evidence within larger histories are often characterized as fundamentally conservative or liberal in nature: they are either resisting change to the status quo or uncritically supporting an emergent liberal ideology. In this approach, whole genres can be assigned to ideological positions, and in fact the industrial political novel of nineteenth-century Britain has been treated in just this way. Criticism of this genre remains strongly influenced by Raymond Williams's claim that these novels characteristically give voice to conservative anxieties about unrest or change and seek to evade politics by redirecting attention to the sphere of moral concern, with its more reassuring scale of aspiration and practice (enacted through self-transformation and sympathy).[7] By contrast, texts, authors, and movements designated as radical are typically defined in opposition to the general ideological or normative framework of the culture; they tend to constitute a minority or exception, often a heroic or aggrandized one.[8]

This critical propensity, insofar as it secures interpretive closure by reference to the power of ideology and class interest in the last instance, refuses at some level to take seriously the writers' own beliefs and convictions about the conditions of political life as represented in the work. Even in a critic as capacious as Williams, whose concept of "structures of feeling" recognizes ambivalent investments and thus honors a notion of lived experience, there is still a move to read the nineteenth-century industrial novel symptomatically, to see it as undermined or deflected by fears fundamentally ideological in nature. It is not that one has to read works entirely with the grain, but new elements emerge if one takes seriously their own representation of a lived relation to political commitment. And as I will show, political novels tend to situate the experience of political commitment or political practice within a broader context of forces and conditions, many of which often directly challenge or complicate political life. As Irving Howe stresses in *Politics and the Novel,* any noteworthy aesthetic engagement with politics — whatever the discernible political orientations of a text or an author might be — will not express political commitment in any simple way; rather, this commitment will be exercised by the complexity and difficulty of trying to live or enact or promote the political ideals it engages.[9]

Ironically, this aspect of the political novel has been neglected in part because of discomfort with an aesthetics of "commitment" or concerns about message-driven art. I say ironically because of the significant distance between directly avowed commitment and the mediated understanding of a lived relation to political commitment that we find in the novelistic genre under consideration here. But even sophisticated literary treatments of commitment are often seen to belong to a lesser aesthetic tradition, largely because of the continuing effects of Adorno's thought. Adorno's critique of the existentialists in the essay "Commitment," and his well-known critique of Lukács, makes it clear that he maintains skepticism toward any art that seeks to represent and give heroic centrality to the drama of engaged political consciousness. And more generally, as I noted earlier, a too-explicit political message is seen by Adorno to collapse the distance between art and reality, evacuating art of its power to negatively redeem a damaged world. In contrast, Adorno favors those forms of modernist literary art, exemplified by the works of Kafka and Beckett, that convey the suffering and thinned-out experience of an administered life. Adorno's discussion of these artists has certainly established the distinctive formal and experiential power instantiated in their works, and his aesthetic theory more generally has opened up a broad array of critical work that moves beyond the antinomies of Marxist aesthetics, particularly its valorization of forms of realism. But there also exist powerful novelistic projects, both realist and modernist, that more directly depict active political life, exploring reflective relations to belief and the mediation of belief through practice. An interpretive project dedicated only to tracking forms of diminished experience under modern political systems will fail to recognize these projects, and it will also fail to capture some of the key formal features used to express and complicate the lived relation to ideology, including liberal ideology.

In line with the critical tendencies mapped here, nineteenth-century political novels are praised precisely for their depictions of misery, alienation, and discontent, and they are faulted for ideological mystification when they redirect attention toward nonpolitical values or highlight sincere scenarios of communicative action, either narratorial or dramatic. There is a well-established body of criticism, for example, tracking the conceptual and formal economies of the industrial novel in relation to the deflection of political concern. One consistent feature of such criticism, evident in and beyond the work of Williams, is the tendency to see competing narrative foci as indicative of a political evasion that is fundamentally conservative. Most commonly, romantic storylines in industrial novels are seen to draw attention away from the political plot and to enforce a sense of resolution and stability through marriage. Similarly, inconsistencies of mode—among them melodrama, tragedy, political argument, documentary realism, and religious discourse—are often read as indications of ideologically conditioned impasses.[10] Viewed from a different angle, however, these plot tensions and shifting modes can be seen to stage the specific challenges of politics and to register forces that exceed its realm. Indeed, in many cases the novels are presenting political questions or challenges in relation to complex and fluid conditions of human existence. In a related way, if we shift our attention to the mode of argument in these works, we can disclose forms of productive critique that are overlooked in the dominant ideological readings. To that end, I will consider character-character argument a narratological element in its own right, one that cannot simply be subsumed under traditional understandings of dialogue.

Charles Dickens's 1854 novel *Hard Times* demonstrates the significance of the two features of the political novel advanced here. The peculiar force of the novel lies in its charged registration of both the power and the limits of ideology. From one perspective, Dickens's novel delivers a strong negative verdict on the attempt to live ideology, as the project to enact utilitarianism fails disastrously. Dickens's novel is therefore anti-ideological in a stronger sense than other industrial novels, such as Elizabeth Gaskell's *North and South*, that stress the complexity of life over the poverty of theory. In its own way, *Hard Times* is as innovative as *Bleak House*; its estranging formal features suggest that established novelistic conventions cannot accommodate self-conscious critique of ideology. As critics have noted, most notably F. R. Leavis and David Lodge, *Hard Times* stands out for its taut and compressed quality, its likeness to moral fable rather than realistic narrative and, perhaps most strikingly, its lack of any typical hero or heroine (rather, we are presented with a symbolic configuration of characters, some of whom are morally privileged, and set pieces in which they figure).[11] And, significantly, this novel does not end in a marriage, a feature I will discuss presently.

In exposing the deleterious effects of a utilitarian mentality that imagines it can manufacture human subjects according to a scientific understanding of material facts, *Hard Times* mounts a critique of any system that seeks to deprive human experience of those life-giving immaterial forces—imagination, feeling, desire—that cannot be captured by rational means. The individual Gradgrind children who are raised in such a milieu are the prime victims on display in the novel, but the narrator also makes evident the ramifying effects on institutions such as the factory, the school, and Parliament. The novel thus underscores the practical power of the ideology that is nonetheless being discredited: it is potent yet fraudulent. Utilitarianism purports to comprehend the whole of existence, yet its inadequacies and failures materialize as strained efforts and unnatural effects. In the description of Coketown, for example, we see the power of the governing ideology, its constituting force within the social and institutional realms, as well as its necessary limits, given its denial of underlying humanity:

> Fact, fact, fact, everywhere in the material aspect of the town; fact, fact, fact everywhere in the immaterial. The M'Choakumchild school was all fact, and the school of design was all fact, and the relations between master and men were all fact, and everything was fact between the lying-in hospital and the cemetery, and what you couldn't state in figures, or show to be purchaseable in the cheapest market and saleable in the dearest, was not, and never should be, world without end, Amen.[12]

The novel's positive values take several distinct forms. It is often assumed that the life of the imagination and the life of feelings constitute the informing values of the novel's critique. But other elements at play indicate the quality of this novel's liberal response to the discredited radical politics of utilitarianism.[13] First the novel isolates specific moral exemplars within the character system. This element is important because it counters the threat of a world in which agents of power, from the family to the school and beyond, are perpetrating utilitarianism on a vulnerable population, distorting and maiming them.[14] That certain individuals manage to elude this power is crucial, demonstrating that Dickens takes a strong stand for persons against either theories or institutions. Through his treatment of Stephen Blackpool's relationship with Rachel, and several characters' relationships with Sissy Jupe, Dickens implies that one should orient oneself morally not toward principles or theories, but toward an exemplar, a moral hero. (It is no accident that the novel is dedicated to Thomas Carlyle, who advocates heroic exemplarity as a response to the deadening effects of mechanical thinking and industrial life.) Indeed, in the case of Stephen's promising Rachel that he will not be involved in the labor union, explanation is entirely eschewed: all position taking, and ideology itself, becomes moot. He made a promise to her, and he will keep it. The reader does not learn why he made this promise; we are only reminded that he sees Rachel as infallible, as capable of saving his soul. Similarly, Sissy's influence helps to prepare Mr. Gradgrind for conversion, and she serves as an orienting moral beacon after Louisa's crisis.

There is more at play than a simple contest of values, however. In keeping with the political novel generally, Hard Times insists on ineluctable facts of existence, facts that cannot be contained or controlled by human will or reason. Two elements of the novel, both expressive of a kind of inexorable fate, stand out in this regard: the intense mental suffering of Louisa Gradgrind, one of the children on whom the father's utilitarian experiment is performed, and the trials, and eventual death, of the worker Stephen Blackpool. We might be tempted to read Louisa's mental suffering simply as the outcome of a utilitarian upbringing, but such a reading would fail to fully capture her function in the novel. Louisa represents what exceeds the reach of fact and reason: her tendency to stare into the fire represents inaccessible interiority and an unmet (and possibly combustible) desire. Arguably, it is the novel's commitment to this volatilized desire that precludes conventional romantic closure or a standard marriage plot. Separated from Bounderby and fundamentally unsettled, Louisa remains a live interest at the novel's close, in contrast to Stephen Blackpool, whose death in an abandoned mine shaft evokes not so much industrial negligence as the larger force of universal fate. As Stephen says to Rachel when he lies dying, "When it [the mine] were in work, it killed wi'out need; when 'tis let alone, it kills wi'out need. See how we die an no need, one way an another—in a muddle—every day!" (203). This statement is closer to the vision of Thomas Hardy than to anything else: the naturalism of Blackpool's story, and the irresolvability of Louisa's, shows with special power the impersonal forces that thwart the moral and political ambitions of individuals. The critique of political ideology is thus also centrally about what lies beyond the horizon of any political or sociological framework.

The novel's emphasis on the limits of politics is thus made powerfully clear. However, the critique of utilitarianism does not cover the whole of the novel's treatment of the sphere of politics itself. *Hard Times* has been directly criticized for its negative representation of the trade unions and for idealizing Stephen Blackpool, the worker who refuses to join the union.[15] But there is also an emphasis on reform in this novel, which often fails to attract notice and is linked to the formal feature I have suggested is critical to the political novel: character-character dialogue. One of the more interesting features in this fable-like novel is the use of intermittent dramatic dialogues, which David Lodge has likened to Brechtian interludes.[16] These conversations perform a certain kind of political critique and exposure in that they involve challenges to authority, sometimes oblique, sometimes frontal. More important, the work done in these dialogues creates a critical effect that exceeds both the individual character and the narrative voice, one not reducible to simple ironic comment or the usual devices of dialogic effect. There are several such scenes, but I will isolate one in particular,

when the worker Stephen Blackpool comes to question Bounderby about
the marriage law, trying to find out whether there might be some way to
divorce his dissolute, drunken wife and marry the angelic Rachel. Stephen
tells Bounderby he has read in the paper that rich people can get divorced,
and he wants to know if this will be possible for him. It is a very long
dialogue, with much back and forth, that exposes the social and material
consequences of an economic bias in the divorce law. A key portion reads
as follows:

"Now, a' God's name," said Stephen Blackpool, "show me the law to help me!"

"Hem! There's a sanctity in this relation of life," said Mr. Bounderby,
"and—and—it must be kept up."

"No no, dunnot say that, sir. 'Tan't kep' up that way. Not that way. 'Tis kep'
down that way. I'm a weaver, I were in a fact'ry when a chilt, but I ha' got-
ten een to see wi' and eern to year wi'. I read in th' papers every 'Sizes, every
Sessions-and you read too-I know it!-with dismay-how th' supposed unpos-
sibility o' ever getting unchained from one another, at any price, on any terms,
brings blood upon this land, and brings many common married fok to battle,
murder, and sudden death. Let us ha' this, right understood. Mine's a grievous
case, an' I want-if yo will be so good-t' know the law that helps me."

"Now, I tell you what!" said Mr. Bounderby, putting his hands in his pock-
ets. "There is such a law."

Stephen, subsiding into his quiet manner, and never wandering in his attention, gave a nod.

"But it's not for you at all. It costs money. It costs a mint of money."

"How much might that be?" Stephen calmly asked.

"Why, you'd have to go to Doctors' Commons with a suit, and you'd have
to go to a court of Common Law with a suit, and you'd have to go to the House
of Lords with a suit, and you'd have to get an Act of Parliament to enable you
to marry again, and it would cost you (if it was a case of very plain sailing),
I suppose from a thousand to fifteen hundred pound," said Mr. Bounderby.
"Perhaps twice the money."

"There's no other law?"

"Certainly not."

"Why then, sir," said Stephen, turning white, and motioning with that right
hand of his, as if he gave everything to the four winds, "'tis a muddle. 'Tis just
a muddle a'toogether, an' the sooner I am dead, the better."

(Mrs. Sparsit again dejected by the impiety of the people.)

"Pooh, pooh! Don't you talk nonsense, my good fellow," said Mr. Bounderby, "about things you don't understand; and don't you call the Institutions
of your country a muddle, or you'll get yourself into a real muddle one of these
fine mornings. The institutions of your country are not your piece-work, and

the only thing you have got to do, is, to mind your piece-work. You didn't take your wife for fast and for loose; but for better for worse. If she has turned out worse—why, all we have got to say is, she might have turned out better."

"'Tis a muddle," said Stephen, shaking his head as he moved to the door. "'Tis a' a muddle!" (60–61)

This type of dialogue advances a critique by indirection and could also be said to perform narration by other means. Unlike the more basic device whereby dialogue helps disclose key elements of plot or character, dialogue functions here to convey a critique of the class-based double standard operative in the marriage law. Stephen's "a' a muddle" in this instance is very different from the one that, in the final coal pit scene, registers the inexorability of an extrasocial violence and fate. Here it serves as a code utterance for "what you are telling me is incoherent from the standpoint of justice" and "I'm not going to budge from this judgment." In a sense it is meant for the reader but it also conveys its own impact of "speaking truth to power." One might imagine, of course, that this is an anomalous sympathetic treatment of the working class in a novel that is otherwise legibly against trade unions and strikes. But it is one in a series of moments that work to cast doubt on, or considerably complicate, the novel's presentation of agitators and union activity more generally. Such moments include Bounderby's false accusation that Stephen has been influenced by the union agitators in his views on marriage injustice; a longer conversation in which Stephen gives voice to the felt injustice of the workers' lives as well as the exacerbating effects of indifference and authoritarian imposition by those in power; and a conversation between Miss Sparsit and Bitzer (112–17, 88–89). In the last of these, Miss Sparsit makes a cold inquiry about what the trade unionists (whom she dubs "restless wretches") are doing and receives from Bitzer the following response: "Merely going on in the old way, ma'am. Uniting, and leaguing, and engaging to stand by one another" (88). Although Bitzer has his own self-interested motives and calculations, the interchange ironically discloses sincere and laudable motives among the workers while exposing bias among the upper classes. The thought-provoking challenge of the exchange—the tension between exposed blindness and punctual insight—functions as a critique that transcends the characterological specificity of those within the dialogue, instead suggesting that a form of noble solidarity characterizes the unionists' activity and that the conspiratorial view of it (the claim that they are "leaguing") is precisely a defended view from those who wish to hold on to their privilege and power. The effect is similar to that produced in dramatic monologues, where speech discloses certain truths that are out of the reach of the speakers themselves: here the effect has to be read, in some sense, between the lines spoken. If assessments of the political novel were to give more attention to character-character dialogue[17]—which as I indicated tends be discounted relative to the narrator, the character system, the plot, and the ending—one could recognize a significant form of liberal critique.[18]

Two points about form are in order here. The first is that there is an effect at play in such character-character dialogue, familiar in both political novels and the novel of ideas, that transcends mere situated dialogue and begins to set itself in relation to the formal narration, or to compete with it, or even, for a moment, to constitute the formal narration. As is well known, the narratological model of Seymour Chatman makes a distinction between story and discourse: the story is what is told, the discourse is how it is told.[19] Thus the chronological events and the characters involved make up the story, while the discourse consists of all the elements that structure and inflect the telling of the story. Adapting an important critique of Chatman that has been offered by James Phelan, I suggest that these moments of dialogue and argument in the political novel are functioning simultaneously as story and discourse. Phelan emphasizes the ethical dimension of dialogue within narrative, arguing that a broad class of novelistic dialogues not only operate as events in the story, but also do significant "mediated telling."[20] In the case of much dialogue in the political novel, I am contending, a distinct version of such mediated telling appears, effecting moments of provocation and critique that count as a part of the larger political and communicative effect of the novel. As Phelan stresses, that Chatman's influential communicative model

real author → implied author → narrator → narratee → implied reader → real reader

does not include characters is a consequential problem, because it restricts character narration or speech to the storyworld, when in fact it can simultaneously function as a version of narration. Such character speech includes a series of features that need to be interpretively considered, including the characters who are speaking, the effect and content of the dialogue as a whole, the place of the dialogue in the overall structure, and the relation of its content to the general narrative perspective and plot structure. In a political novel, such dialogue is particularly heightened given the genre's tendency to foreground ideas and ideology and to mediate those elements through character. The industrial novels of Elizabeth Gaskell also centrally employ argu-

ment, through both narratorial intervention and character-character discussion. This aspect of her work has not received the attention it merits, in
large part because of the prevailing judgment that the novels seek to miti-
gate class tension through appeasement and advocacy for limited reform.
Rather than truly confront problems of urban industrialism, the criticism
claims, Gaskell appeals to an ethic of sympathy that ultimately upholds the
status quo and enforces the power of the middle class. Even though she is
credited with interesting formal innovations and a commitment to portray-
ing working-class culture and life, there is a sense that the novels disap-
point, both in their failure to proffer solutions adequate to the problems
depicted and in their tendency to allow romantic plots to eclipse the political substance.

Marks of class-based unease are certainly discernible in Gaskell's novels,
especially in *Mary Barton*, where the narrator seems particularly anxious to
contextualize and explain the violence of the workers, on the one hand, and
the immovability of the masters, on the other. But Gaskell's fiction also represents a powerful working through of the challenges attending emergent
democratic modernity. Her industrial novels are key precursors to the novel
of ideas and are pathbreaking in their presentation of ideological and philosophical positions. Much of this work is done through the mode of (embedded) argument. Gaskell is interestingly self-conscious about this, even going
so far as to show how inhospitable the traditional novel is to argument
about matters political. One central example here would be the scene, in
Mary Barton's eighth chapter, in which the romance plot is ambushed by
the political plot. Jem Wilson, an industrious and apolitical young worker,
has come to visit his love interest, Mary Barton. The chapter frames the
scene through Jem's eyes: he is anxious and distracted as Mary's father,
John Barton, holds forth on economic and political issues, promoting the
workers' cause. But the chapter performs an interesting *volte face*, forcing
the reader, by way of a long narratorial intervention that interrupts the
chapter's focalization through Jem, to pay attention to the issues John had
been discussing. This tactic self-consciously reframes formal conventions so
as to redirect audiences toward a new form of novelistic, readerly scrutiny
of social and political problems.[21]

More interesting still is Gaskell's use, in *North and South*, of a mode of
argumentative dialogue to forward romantic and political plots simultaneously. Abandoning her use of a moderating, appeasing narrator, Gaskell
places the substance of ideological disagreement in dialogues between Margaret Hale and Mr. Thornton and between the worker Mr. Higgins and

members of the middle class. In their discussions of the strains industrial life produces in the relations between the classes, Margaret and Mr. Thornton argue over the relative merits of, on the one hand, Christian responsibility and managerial transparency about key labor decisions (endorsed by Margaret) and, on the other hand, a stringent economic liberalism that stresses principles of property, contract, and management's rightful authority to act without explanation (endorsed by Thornton). One of the striking things about these conversations is that both Margaret's and Thornton's speeches can sound like context-transcending narratorial speech, which is to say they partake of the sincerity and the larger moral emphases we associate with the narratorial voice more generally. Not every moment of the exchanges works this way, of course, but it is interesting that we cannot simply judge the narrative to be endorsing Margaret over Thornton, though it may tend that way at times. Consider the following exchange in the novel's key debate, early on, among Mr. Hale, Margaret, and Mr. Thornton:

"You must grant me this one point. Given a strong feeling of independence in every Darkshire man, have I any right to obtrude my views, of the manner in which he shall act, upon another (hating it as I should do most vehemently myself), merely because he has labour to sell and I capital to buy?"

"Not in the least," said Margaret, determined just to say this one thing; "not in the least because of your labour and capital positions, whatever they are, but because you are a man, dealing with a set of men over whom you have, whether you reject the use of it or not, immense power, just because your lives and your welfare are so constantly and intimately interwoven. God has made us so that we must be mutually dependent. We may ignore our own dependence, or refuse to acknowledge that others depend upon us in more respects than the payment of weekly wages; but the thing must be, nevertheless. Neither you nor any other master can help yourselves. The most proudly independent man depends on those around him for their insensible influence on his character—his life. And the most isolated of your Darkshire Egos has dependents clinging to him on all sides; he cannot shake them off, any more than the great rock he resembles can shake off—"

"Pray don't go into similes, Margaret; you have led us off once already," said her father smiling, yet uneasy at the thought that they were detaining Mr. Thornton against his will, which was a mistake; for he rather liked it, as long as Margaret would talk, although what she said only irritated him.

"Just tell me, Miss Hale, are you yourself ever influenced—no, that is not a fair way of putting it;—but if you are ever conscious of being influenced by others, and not by circumstances, have those others been working directly or indirectly? Have they been labouring to exhort, to enjoin, to act rightly for the sake of example, or have they been simple, true men, taking up their duty, and doing it unflinchingly, without a thought of how their actions were to make this man industrious, that man saving? Why, if I were a workman, I should be twenty times more impressed by the knowledge that my master was honest, punctual, quick, resolute in all his doings (and hands are keener spies even than valets), than by any amount of interference, however kindly meant, with my ways of going on out of work-hours. I do not choose to think too closely on what I am myself; but, I believe, I rely on the straightforward honesty of my hands, and the open nature of their opposition, in contra-distinction to the way in which the turn-out will be managed in some mills, just because they know I scorn to take a single dishonourable advantage, or do an underhand thing myself. It goes farther than a whole course of lectures on 'Honesty is the Best Policy'—life diluted into words. No, no! What the master is, that will the men be, without over-much taking thought on his part."[22]

In a character-character debate such as this, we find ourselves serially within different argumentative positions, each with a kind of integrity, and each taking on its own authority via what we might call a mode of narrative argument that functions as mediated telling. In this case the juxtaposition of vying claims makes the effect more than simply the combination of positions—it creates in the reader the experience of hearing contrasting beliefs that are sincerely held and strongly argued, both of them meant to compel a certain acknowledgment and respect, insofar as they resonate with moral values the novel endorses. That Margaret swerves into simile and Thornton insists on characterological exemplarity beyond message-driven discourse creates another layer of complexity, as central aspects of the novel's own literary art are invoked by the debaters.

Interestingly, what emerges as the guiding value at the end of the novel is precisely the need for ongoing dialogue, a position Thornton elaborates in some detail in conversation with a member of Parliament during a party in London:

"I have arrived at the conviction that no mere institutions, however wise, and however much thought may be required to organise and arrange them, can attach class to class as they should be attached, unless the working out of such institutions bring the individuals of the different classes into actual personal contact. Such intercourse is the very breath of life." (391)

Thornton goes on to stress how important ongoing interaction is to the vitality and success of any reform undertaken by the members of different classes, warning that such projects will fail if they do not enable people to become "acquainted with each other's characters and persons, even tricks of temper and modes of speech" (391). The ideal proposed here, evocative of the novel's own world making, is modeled in the formal dimensions of character-character argument that recur throughout the narrative, involving at once the exchange of ideas and accreting forms of familiarity among onetime strangers from different walks of life. Those arguments in turn function as mediated telling, with the reader as addressee experiencing claims and counterclaims that are at once situated in the story and, as formal argument, elevated to the special status of what we might call dual (or multiple) narration by other means. While it is certainly true that what prevails ideologically in the mutual understanding of the two main characters is a Christianized liberalism that favors the continued power of the current system refined through modest reforms, it seems important to register the novel's formal and thematic insistence on continuing collective deliberation. This deliberation is a primary component of liberal-democratic practice and crucially counters the sense of closure wrought by the romantic plot and even the stability of the content and reach of proposed reforms. If everything will be decided by ongoing deliberation, as the novel insists, then one cannot freeze the ideological content of the storyworld.

It is worth considering the literary history of this formal feature. Beginning with Jane Austen's *Pride and Prejudice*, a romantically charged form of socially and politically critical dialogue has been a key element of the courtship novel, and it is interesting to note where argument stands at the conclusion of Austen's narrative. While *Pride and Prejudice* legitimates a (reformed) Pemberley, it does so in large part by holding up the relationship between Darcy and Elizabeth as exemplary. And what is the form of that relationship? It is one that privileges direct, extensive, and mutually improving debate founded on the energy of attraction. Argument is important because it keeps critique and self-examination vital. There is no question that the sharpness of Elizabeth's criticism has been softened, but the active air of challenge and debate remains vital at the end of the novel, where we find that Elizabeth's habit of challenging Darcy is instructive to Georgiana, effectively schooling the next half-generation in a mode of lively debate. What is innovative about *North and South* is the insistence that the energy of debate will continue within the institutional sphere of the factory, supported by the forms that were put in play through the "antagonistic friendship" of Margaret and Mr. Thornton (219). To imagine Gaskell's use of a courtship plot as somehow downgrading the role played by argument in revisioning class relations is to read simplistically in terms of plot closure—an all too common tendency in readings of the industrial novel.

At stake in the appeal to ongoing interaction among individuals from different walks of life is the novel's more general investment in the profound importance of everyday familial life. For Gaskell, both in this novel and in *Mary Barton*, loss and change are ineluctable aspects of life, and major loss has the capacity to rend the sustaining fabric of existence, leading to disabling incapacity, reactive violence, or, interestingly, productive moral or political engagement. Those forms of loss and suffering that stem from curable conditions are shown to motivate anger but also well-meaning forms of political action, while other moments of more natural loss can promote connection among those from different parts of society, since the experience of loss is recognized as universal. The emphasis on loss in Gaskell's novels enables both an insistence on forms of experience that exceed the this-worldly orientation of political struggles and also a somewhat radical plea to make collective political effort a way of life, at once grounded in the ongoing present of everyday engagement and future-directed in a way the immediacy of the domestic is not.

The question of how dialogue and debate function formally and politically within the novel has received very little attention, but it is arguably central to an understanding of the relation of liberal democracy and literature. In *Against Democracy: Literary Experience in the Era of Emancipations*, Simon During interestingly isolates what he calls "conversational democracy" as a feature of many novels of the modern era.[23] "Conversational democracy" occurs in moments when a certain communicative equality is represented despite power differentials: this is where characters talk "across ranks," as it were. Drawing examples from Benjamin Disraeli and George Eliot, During reads this feature as a way authors acknowledge or allow certain forms of democracy while remaining fundamentally skeptical of democracy's likely effects on society. He reads it somewhat cynically, that is, even in its stronger "speak truth to power moments" when an actual injustice or inequality is exposed. The larger argument of During's book is something like the photographic negative of Francis Fukuyama's *The End of History* or Daniel Bell's *The End of Ideology*, both of which announce and celebrate the historical triumph of democracy over the counterforce of communism. For During, conversely, democracy is triumphant, and it was destined to succeed since about 1848; but that's *not* a good thing (essentially because of the imbrication of democracy and capitalism). In light of the bleak capitalist democracy he identifies, During ends up supporting what he calls a Left conservatism, linked to the history of literary criticism itself, which has the capacity to criticize capitalist modernity from without, as it were. Beyond this embrace of a specific form of counter-ideology, During is also interested in showing various ways literary writers register moments of democratic experience, some presented as more inspiring and value-laden than moments of conversational democracy. In a reading of *Howards End*, for example, he argues that the end of the novel promotes a form of radical, mystical democracy in the diverse group gathered at the farm, which for During represents an imagined democratic communitarianism based on love, asserted against the encroaching force of social democracy and all it will entail in terms of the administered life and the accommodation to capitalism.

Following the set of analytic claims and interpretive methods advanced in this chapter, however, one might read *Howards End* differently. During favors the representation of immanent and ordinary experience over anything like deliberative democracy, and this predisposition effectively mutes forms of argumentative critique in the novel. Even the term conversational democracy dissolves the critical force of character-character argument: it is to redescribe as a form of democratic manners within the story what can also function as mediated telling. This distinction is consequential for an understanding of *Howards End*, which shows with notable lucidity a certain necessary and productive tension between argument and immanence, a profound and ongoing feature of some key political novels of the twentieth century.

Howards End stages an encounter between the cosmopolitan, argument-oriented world of the Schlegels and the potent Mrs. Wilcox, who by contrast figures the force of place, connection, and nature. The Schlegels are crucially disarmed when Mrs. Wilcox imposes her mute negations on their lively debates, as is evident in the luncheon scene where she seems to stand out so anomalously. The relationship between the Schlegels and Mrs. Wilcox reflects *Howards End*'s complex response to its contemporary milieu. The novel's interest in the displacements occasioned by modern life, and in the loss of an organic relation to others and to the land one inhabits, has a dual focus and a dual system of value. On the one hand, there is an impulse to move beyond words (and the dissension they cause): to simply be with others and embrace both social heterogeneity and the natural world. But on the other hand, there is a recognition that such a move is utterly dependent on the discursive and reflective forms that allow one to recognize the need for calm acceptance. It is only after Margaret has argued a need to overcome divisions that issue from social hierarchy and power, and has forced her disquisition upon Henry, that she can come to embrace what is. Forster's novel is therefore still, quite powerfully, a social problem novel, and it exerts its force by keeping in play the intractable energies of liberal critique, which we might distinguish from the nondiscursive democratic energies that captivate a critic like During. The key instance of such liberal critique comes as Margaret is trying to persuade Henry to allow her sister, who is pregnant with an illegitimate child, to stay at Howards End for the evening. Henry refuses, saying it will desecrate the memory of his wife:

> "You have mentioned Mrs. Wilcox."
>
> "I beg your pardon?"
>
> "A rare occurrence. In reply, may I mention Mrs. Bast?"
>
> "You have not been yourself all day," said Henry, and rose from his seat with face unmoved. Margaret rushed at him and seized both his hands. She was transfigured.
>
> "Not any more of this!" she cried. "You shall see the connection if it kills you, Henry! You have had a mistress—I forgave you. My sister has a lover—you drive her from the house. Do you see the connection? Stupid, hypocritical, cruel—oh, contemptible!—a man who insults his wife when she's alive and cants with her memory when she's dead. A man who ruins a woman for his pleasure, and casts her off to ruin other men. And gives bad financial advice, and then says he is not responsible. These, man, are you. You can't recognize them, because you cannot connect. I've had enough of your unweeded kindness. I've spoilt you long enough. All your life you have been spoiled. Mrs. Wilcox spoiled you. No one has ever told what you are—muddled, criminally muddled. Men like you use repentance as a blind, so don't repent. Only say to yourself, 'What Helen has done, I've done.'"
>
> "The two cases are different," Henry stammered. His real retort was not quite ready. His brain was still in a whirl, and he wanted a little longer.
>
> "In what way different? You have betrayed Mrs. Wilcox, Helen only herself. You remain in society, Helen can't. You have had only pleasure, she may die. You have the insolence to talk to me of differences, Henry?"
>
> Oh, the uselessness of it! Henry's retort came.
>
> "I perceive you are attempting blackmail. It is scarcely a pretty weapon for a wife to use against her husband. My rule through life has been never to pay the least attention to threats, and I can only repeat what I said before: I do not give you and your sister leave to sleep at Howards End."
>
> Margaret loosed his hands. He went into the house, wiping first one and then the other on his handkerchief. For a little she stood looking at the Six Hills, tombs of warriors, breasts of the spring. Then she passed out into what was now the evening.[24]

We are invited to grant Margaret authority because the narrative privileges her through focalization and free indirect discourse. But other elements indirectly endorse her speech: there is an echo of terms that have been used by the narrator, such as the call to connect, and the pedagogical mode that Margaret engages in is one we see elsewhere in the novel. It turns out that this constitutes the end of argument, as far as the novel is concerned. When next we see Mr. Wilcox he is utterly quiescent, a compliant member of the group who make up the community at Howards End—Margaret wins the argument, but in part by moving beyond argument. In the moment of the confrontation, however, character-character argument serves as a crucial moment of mediated telling as well as story event; challenging speech in this instance is linked to liberal or democratic critique and so upends the distinction Rancière makes between heroic speech in action as elitist and democratizing style as egalitarian.

Do we really want to dismiss this moment and hold up the communitarianism of the novel's ending? More interesting is the relation between them. What is at play here, in part, is a clear indication of the limits of argument. Mutual understanding is not achieved; there is an intractable clash of worldviews (though one is distinctly psychologized as defensiveness); and argument cannot be sustained. The glare of exposure and critique harms relationship if continued in this way, and the novel ultimately seems to endorse a nonreflective "being with." But there's a *relationship* between the moment of argument and moving beyond it; the latter requires the former. Fundamentally, critique yields to community, but critique has also enabled community and shown its value. And the energy of the preceding argument hovers over the novel's ending, especially given the passage containing Margaret's own reflection on the significance of her speech: "She would not have altered a word. It had to be uttered once in a life, to adjust the lopsidedness of the world. It was spoken not only to her husband, but to thousands of men like him—a protest against the inner darkness in high places that comes with a commercial age" (235). The adjustment of the world's lopsidedness does not take place only in the moment of utterance, it must be stressed, as it would have if Henry and Margaret had separated. Instead, Helen and her illegitimate child are welcomed into the community of Howards End.

Of course, the quietude of the ending can feel like the abandonment of the political as well, which is what makes During's argument compelling, as he points to another modality of democracy beyond liberal critique. Yet one might rather see the ending as registering the difficulty, even impossibility, of living the examined life in a sustained way, the pressure it puts on individuals and relationships. This existential challenge is not unfamiliar in novels that engage a lived relation to political commitment. If we read the novelistic registration of the limits of politics as the abandonment of politics, or as a fundamentally conservative move, then we are asking literature to be something it isn't, something entirely coterminous with political theory or political action. This is not to say we can't make claims about the ideological positions of texts and authors, but rather to claim that one is applying a blunt mechanism if one sees literary representations of the limits of politics, or of the pressures on politics from other forces—psychological, emotional, natural—as necessarily ideologically conservative.

In isolating these examples, my goal has been to emphasize two literary features in particular—the role of argument in the political novel and the importance of what we might call the existential density of novelistic renderings of political life, which includes registering, in various ways, the limits of politics, including the limits of political argument. As I will show in the chapters that follow, the kind of analysis I have offered here can productively be brought to bear on certain novels of the mid-twentieth century as well, many of them immediately influenced by the intense conflict of ideologies and by existentialism in its various guises. In Lionel Trilling's *The Middle of the Journey*, an ideological novel of manners that is modeled in some ways on *Howards End*, and in Doris Lessing's *The Golden Notebook*, an experimental novel treating communism and feminism in the cold war era, we see staged in different ways the dynamic tension between political argument and broader pressures of existence. In Trilling's novel the pressures have to do with sex, death, illness, and a kind of violence of intimacy (rather than political violence). In Lessing's novel, apart from the great interest its complex experimental form poses, transhistorical forces exert a powerful pressure, particularly those forces of violence and sexual desire that thwart the will's attempts to assert control and order.

CHAPTER FOUR

The Liberal Aesthetic in the Postwar Era: The Case of Trilling and Adorno

In this chapter and the one that follows, I return to the mid-twentieth century as an especially illuminating moment in the history of literary liberalism. Focusing on the postwar era, I examine liberalism's relation to a contemporaneous intellectual formation destined to have an enduring influence on aesthetic and political theory: the Frankfurt school. My more particular aim is to elucidate the thought of Lionel Trilling through comparison with certain features of Theodor Adorno's thought. Both Trilling and Adorno display a governing bleakness of outlook that is best understood as a post-catastrophic response to the war, to fascism, and to disappointment with the Soviet experiment. This convergence brings to light certain under-recognized elements of the liberal tradition, while the differences between the two underscore the complexity of postwar aesthetics and help disclose what is distinctive about Trilling's literary liberalism. After describing the broader context of postwar political thinking as well as the divergent aesthetic values of Adorno and Trilling, I will turn to Trilling's 1947 novel *The Middle of the Journey* to show how he adapts the novel of manners to explore the social life of political affiliation. Trilling's thinking about liberalism prompted an understanding of the modern novel trained on the lived relation to ideas, in both its social and its existential dimensions. In this sense his book is very much in line with the tradition of the political novel discussed in the previous chapter and in fact can be seen as a distinctive adaptation and extension of E. M. Forster's novelistic art.

A deeper consideration of the relation of liberal and radical thought in the mid-twentieth century is also useful in that it illuminates recurrent impulses and dynamics in the critique of liberalism. Not only is the work of the Frankfurt school incorporated into later consolidations of the critique of liberalism, but it in fact presages the aggregating moves that characterize the academic Left's critiques of reason and liberalism in the latter half of the twentieth century. To begin with, the Frankfurt school in the United States advances the idea that liberalism is continuous with fascism, making the economic argument that monopoly capitalism promotes the development of totalitarianism and the cultural argument that fascism was enabled through a vitalist and romantic reaction to liberalism's limiting modes of self-understanding.[1] These critical orientations—the view that capitalism fundamentally defines and corrupts liberalism and that liberalism promotes not freedom but conformism or violence—share affinities with the influential Foucauldian critique of liberalism as masked power always multiplying its forms of dominance, and they are reprised in Giorgio Agamben's account of the modern politicization of life, where liberalism is once again directly linked with totalitarianism.[2] The political critiques also end up dovetailing with the general poststructuralist critique of the Enlightenment and the autonomous, unified subject (which Adorno also anticipated). Of course, for many theorists this entire tradition of critique from the Frankfurt school forward persuasively captures the workings of capitalism, modern power, and problematic forms of thinking. But if liberalism is a term and concept assumed always to signal ideological manipulation or blindness, it becomes impossible to recognize the lived reality of liberal thinking and liberal commitment within historical moments or, more precisely, impossible to recognize them as other than false consciousness or a ruse of power.[3]

As I have argued throughout this book, the tendency to associate liberalism with ideological enforcement has foreclosed recognition of the formal and conceptual dimensions of active literary engagements with liberal thought. While there have been significant departures from the strong forms of Foucauldian and Marxist literary analysis that link literature to the consolidation of existing or emergent powers, we have yet to reconstruct the full range of aesthetic enactments of liberal thinking, in part because literary studies has a fairly limited and generally negative understanding of what liberal thinking is. Most of the more considered debates on liberal theory have taken place within political philosophy and particularly within the liberal-communitarian debates of the 1980s and beyond, which involved little or no discussion of aesthetic concerns. As I mentioned in the introduction, the debate-defining theories of Jürgen Habermas and John Rawls are famously inattentive to aesthetics, and it has been difficult to bridge the tem peramental and conceptual divide between the philosophical and literary approaches to liberal thought. Exploring the hybrid literary-philosophical formations common among the postwar liberals and the Frankfurt school may prove fruitful in thinking past the divide. It is arguable that throughout its history liberalism has had a richer relation to literary culture than more recent disciplinary trends would lead one to think.[4]

As I demonstrated in chapter 1, the liberalism of the early postwar era was marked by a chastened rationalism and a caution against progressive optimism. While my focus in this chapter is on Trilling, this frame of mind was shared by a number of avowedly liberal thinkers of the era, including Arthur Schlesinger, Daniel Bell, and Reinhold Niebuhr in the United States, Albert Camus and Raymond Aron in France, and Isaiah Berlin in Britain. Given the tendency to assimilate these thinkers and writers to the trend leading from liberal anticommunism to neoconservatism and reactive resistance to the New Left, their full significance has been lost to view. What is noteworthy about these thinkers is their apprehension of reason's limits and their interest in the role the aesthetic might play in registering the complexities of political and moral life. In the political sphere they tended to advocate piecemeal reform based on social democratic principles. Their political mood expressed itself as a form of restraint or skepticism, though there were other liberals of the era—notably John Dewey and Sidney Hook—who were committed to pragmatic scientism and therefore to the possibilities of more ambitious social and technological transformations.

Trilling is an interesting figure to single out, because he is at once representative in his attention to the limits and dangers of progressive rationalism and distinctive in his aesthetic valuations and overall style of thought. Given his carefully modulated formulations and the shifts in his thinking over time, his work has prompted an unusual range of responses and characterizations. Some hold Trilling up as the type of public intellectual and broadly humanist critic sorely lacking in today's academic culture; others dismiss the general culture of the New York intellectuals as insufficiently rigorous and as limited in its relevance to contemporary theory.[5] In some cases Trilling's ambiguities are resolved by plotting them onto genealogical narratives: either his thinking is in keeping with a model of conservative liberalism reaching back to Arnoldian elevations of culture over the perceived dangers of political action or, like the cold war liberals generally, he represents an emergent conservatism that helps to entrench liberal anticommunism and sets the stage for the rise of neoconservatism.[6] To others there is something bracing and productive about his dialectical suspensions and his ongoing "dissent from the orthodoxies of dissent."[7] And to others still, the emphasis on style and self-cultivation, either through a "politics of the self" or through a regimen of "existentially engaged" reading, provides an exemplary and timely model for literary practice.[8] To further complicate matters, these vying perspectives on Trilling's work can coexist within a single reading; Trilling's complexity draws many critics into an unresolved analysis not unlike his own, or at the very least it provokes concessions about those aspects of his work that may carry implications different from the ones they are stressing.

I will return to the elusive nature of Trilling's complexity in the final pages of this chapter, after an analysis of his own experiment with the literary form of the political novel. But first I want to reframe the analysis of his work by situating it within the climate of mid-twentieth-century political thought in Europe and the United States. It is especially pertinent to consider the Frankfurt school in relation to the US liberalism of this era, given that the Frankfurt school was in New York at this time (though notably there was very little interaction between the two groups).[9] If the liberalism of the era is a bleak liberalism, the Frankfurt school's midcentury work is a bleak radicalism. It encompasses a disparate range of thinkers and projects, to be sure, but some of its features in the forties and beyond are noteworthy when considered in relation to both the liberalism of the era and its influence on future theoretical work in the humanities. Such features include an intensifying pessimism about the possibility of social and political transformation through Marxist revolution, accompanied by an increasing emphasis on theory over praxis; an interest in the psychosocial formations that characterize contemporary society; a movement away from a historically specific account of violence in the capitalist era to a *longue durée* account of the domination of nature by instrumental reason; and a belief in the utopian and critical possibilities of the aesthetic (as against the political), built on a critique of mass culture and the idea that successful art "expresses the idea of harmony negatively."[10]

For the most part the Frankfurt school actively opposed liberalism, not only as an ideology and a framework of governance, but also as a reformist politics that ultimately secures the status quo.[11] But the question raised by a comparison of the Frankfurt school with postwar liberalism is whether the liberalism that serves as the defining other for the Frankfurt school and subsequent theorists accurately reflects the existing liberalism of the same era in which these theoretical formations were produced. A somewhat different picture emerges if one views both theoretical formations as a response to

catastrophe: in this respect they share key features, and the ways they differ are illuminating for intellectual and political history and for a renewed
consideration of liberal aesthetics.

The most striking resonance between the liberal and radical formations,
apart from their bleak tenor, lies in their negative assessment of specific
forms of reason involving the imposition of power, mastery, or domination. The precise emphases diverge: the liberal thinkers tend to see ideological thinking as itself a danger, whereas the radicals are more concerned
with the category of instrumental reason. But the attempt to move beyond
the limits of specific forms of rationality will be of central importance in
the turn to aesthetics undertaken by both forms of political thought. The
case of Trilling and Adorno is particularly revealing because the resonances
extend further, and the differences are instructive. Beyond their interest in
destructive forms of rationality, both concern themselves with the psychosocial dimensions of political life, and both appreciate the ways Sigmund
Freud's theories challenge stabilizing concepts of humanity. In Adorno's
case Freud's stress on biology disrupts identity thinking and his differentiated understanding of psychological power dynamics helps explain social psychology under damaging systems. In Trilling's case Freud allows
for a more complex, because appropriately tragic, conception of human
endeavor, one that disables the progressive optimism he associates with an
inadequate liberalism. Over time, Trilling moves from this conception of
Freud's relevance—a moral relevance linked to the need to relinquish the
pleasure principle in favor of the reality principle—to a greater insistence
on biology as a fundamental fact of existence to be maintained against attempts to subordinate identity to ideology or to deny the relevance of bio-
logical being.[12] Interestingly, there is a way Trilling too privileges thinking
over praxis. One might see this as reconstructed Arnoldianism, but it aligns
more fundamentally with Trilling's wariness of twentieth-century rational
progressivism. As we will see when I turn to Trilling's novel *The Middle of
the Journey*, his most valued form of thinking is a practice of negative capability that ideally complements an openness to the experience of embodied
being. Last and most crucial, both Trilling and Adorno advance a strong
claim for aesthetics as a response to the limits and dangers of formal politics. Here, however, we see an instructive divergence in the form of aesthetics that is promoted and valued.

Adorno's conception of aesthetics was negatively defined in more than
one way. Not only does he believe in art's potential to indicate harmony
negatively, but he defines his position in part by opposing specific aesthetic

attitudes and forms. He rejects any attempt to convey explicit political mes-
sages in art and also mounts a critique of the less blunt literature of commitment associated with Jean-Paul Sartre. Insofar as Sartre asks literature to
"awaken the free choice of the agent which makes authentic existence possible," his approach is fundamentally misguided, since "within a predeter-
mined reality," which is to say an administered world, "freedom becomes
an empty claim."[13] Adorno also attacks literary realism, which naturalizes
the damaged system and fails to capture modern experience under capitalism. Certain forms of modernist literature, by contrast, powerfully convey
this experience:

> Kafka's prose and Beckett's plays, or the truly monstrous novel *The Unname-
> able*, have an effect by comparison with which officially committed works look
> like pantomimes. Franz Kafka and Samuel Beckett arouse the fear which exis-
> tentialism merely talks about. By dismantling appearance, they explode from
> within the art which committed proclamation subjugates from without, and
> hence only in appearance. The inescapability of their work compels the change
> of attitude which committed works merely demand. He over whom Kafka's
> wheels have passed, has lost for ever any peace with the world and any chance
> of consoling himself with the judgment that the way of the world is bad; the
> element of ratification which lurks in resigned admission of the dominance of
> evil is burnt away. (191)

The contempt for the existentialists is important, since it brings us to the
heart of the difference between Adorno and Trilling on the matter of aesthetics. Trilling was certainly alive to the potentialities of modernist art, but
on the matter of political literature he tended to indicate strongest appreciation for what we might call existential realism.[14] While for Adorno modernist art involved a negative utopianism in its representation of the forms
of suffering, damage, and thinned-out experience in the modern capitalist
order, for Trilling the most relevant literary art shows individuals actively
living their moral and political lives within conditions that always exceed
the realm of ideology. Others among the New York intellectuals shared
this view. As I mentioned in chapter 3, Irving Howe, argues in *Politics and
the Novel* that compelling political novels stress above all the lived relation
to political commitment.[15] And *Partisan Review* editor Philip Rahv argues
against the deficiencies or excesses of American literature by calling for a
more differentiated understanding of the relation between ideas and experience—a more differentiated understanding of the way ideas are held.[16]

It is instructive, moreover, to see the number of times European existentialist novelists are adduced: André Malraux and Ignazio Silone hold

a special place in the discursive network, repeatedly appearing as positive counterexamples or exemplars. What determines their significance is a perceived ability to imagine the lived relation to ideology or ideas and the ability to complicate the portrayal of political life through reference to forms of experience that exceed or trouble political frameworks. Rahv writes, "A comparison of European and American left-wing writing of the same period will at once show that whereas Europeans like Malraux and Silone enter deeply into the meaning of political ideas and beliefs, Americans touch only superficially on such matters."[17] Similarly, Trilling singles out Malraux's *Man's Fate* and Silone's *Bread and Wine* as exceptions to the general failure among political novelists to deal adequately with the problem of moral judgment.[18] These works, and the aesthetic they represent for those who reference them, cannot be reduced to the literature of commitment rejected by Adorno, but they do accord significance to forms of heroic aspiration and tragic consciousness that would not sit well with Adorno. *Bread and Wine*, for example, which treats the political resistance to Italian fascism, values a form of reconciliation or balance between persistent political aspiration and practical morality attentive to embedded ways of being, both individual and communal. Similarly, *Man's Fate* provides a constellation of individual ways of confronting the burdens of existence, politically, ethically, and interpersonally. In the context of a chance encounter between a pastor and the revolutionary actor Ch'en on his way to the attempted bombing of Chiang Kai-shek, the narrator writes, "Like Ch'en, this man *lived* his idea: he was something more than a restless bundle of flesh" (emphasis in the original).[19] As elsewhere in the novel, the frames of understanding are not commensurate but the felt existential intensities are. The core interest is in exploring consciously held beliefs and their relation to both embodied existence and situated ethical and political judgment.

A key question to consider in thinking about the relation of the bleak radicals and bleak liberals is whence the bleakness derives, philosophically speaking.[20] In the radical view generally, damage radiates out from, or is caused by, the capitalist system, whose negative effects derive in turn from forms of labor, production, and exchange. For Trilling and other bleak liberals, by contrast, there is a chastened recognition of the limits of human aspiration, not only natural limits such as illness and death, but the fact of aggression and violence, what in Reinhold Niebuhr takes the form of sin. Thus there is a divergence between an anthropological approach that sees in human life conditions that must be accepted and tendencies that must be guarded against and a sociological approach that sees such negative force within society as it has developed historically.[21] And yet in

the case of Adorno and Trilling the line cannot be drawn so simply, given
the movement in Adorno's thought toward a more universal conception
of domination, one that presents as a generalized feature of human life or
consciousness. Conceptually elusive, and hard to describe in clear relation
to his accounts of the larger social order, domination is variously characterized as a persistent tendency within human ways of thinking, as a form of
psychological response or process, or as a mode of approach to the natural
world.[22] It is challenging to consider why this current of thought blended
into later radical political and aesthetic theory while similar emphases in
the bleak liberals did not seem to alter conceptions of liberalism in the theoretical field.

In Adorno's aesthetic discussions, the bleak conditions enforced by the
social order come to the fore and show, by contrast, what is at stake in Trilling's approach to the art of moral and political life. For Adorno, art must reject any stance of accommodation toward the existing world, which means
it must subvert traditional realism in order to capture salient elements of
contemporary sociohistorical life, above all its reduced and blunted forms
of human experience and interaction. A richly detailed traditional realism
reinforces the status quo and denies the conditions of estranged subjectivity and abstract relations in late capitalism. The modernist art of Kafka and
Beckett, by contrast, captures the contemporary situation more authenti-
cally, and its distinctive use of form is paramount: "What is socially de-
cisive in artworks is the content [Inhalt] that becomes eloquent through
the work's formal structures. Kafka, in whose work monopoly capitalism
appears only distantly, codifies in the dregs of the administered world what
becomes of people under the total social spell more faithfully and powerfully than do any novels about corrupt industrial trusts."[23]

Adorno's conception of art is very far indeed from an "existential realism" characterized by the active living out of ideological aspiration amid
limiting conditions and by the embrace of a nature presumed to exceed
political and social structures. Such a literary mode seems to represent the
forms of accommodation and resignation that Adorno stringently rejects.
Trilling's own comments on Kafka in his essay on John Keats seem to reinforce this impression, in that Kafka there serves as a negative contrast to
Shakespeare's ability to affirm life even as he acknowledges evil: "Kafka's
knowledge of evil exists without the contradictory knowledge of the self in
its health and validity."[24] For Trilling, the world of Kafka that Adorno ad-
mires for its uncompromising deprivations is a world false to the embedded
particularities of living persons. In Kafka the accused "has been stripped of

all that is becoming to a man except his abstract humanity, which, like his skeleton, never is quite becoming to a man. He is without parents, home, wife, child, commitment, or appetite; he has no connection with power, beauty, love, wit, courage, loyalty, or fame, and the pride that may be taken in these" (38–39). In contrast to such a relentlessly bleak vision, Keats's concept of negative capability affirms the complexity of life and the concrete struggles of selves in the making (Keats is held up for replacing "the vale of tears" with "'the vale of Soul-making'" [44]).

And yet Trilling's views on modern literature and the value of embedded social existence are more layered than this moment of contrastive commentary might suggest. Interestingly, the sentence about Kafka contains the following footnote: "It would, of course, be less than accurate and fair not to remark of Kafka that he had a very intense knowledge of the self through its negation, that his great and terrible point is exactly the horror of the loss of the Shakespearean knowledge of the self" (39). While the repeated use of the word knowledge here implies that Trilling is making a point about intellectual culture rather than capitalist modernity, the acknowledgment of the power of negation is significant, and it resonates with his more general tendency to balance moral critique with dialectical negation and existential struggle. If Trilling at times seems to affirm settled existence against what he sees as the moral irresponsibility of the culture of modernism, he elsewhere insists on the productive force of "spiritual militancy" and on the potential importance, not only to art but to politics, of modernism's antagonism toward the values and simplifications associated with pleasure, especially insofar as an ideal of pleasure—happiness, fulfillment, satisfaction of needs—animates political thinking and individual aims.[25] In "The Fate of Pleasure," the strongest articulation of this argument, Trilling makes the suggestive point that literary engagements with "unpleasure" may need to be taken into account by an as yet unforeseeable politics: "There is developing—conceivably at the behest of literature!—an ideal of the experience of those psychic energies which are linked with unpleasure and which are directed toward self-definition and self-affirmation. Such an ideal makes a demand upon society for its satisfaction: it is a political fact. It surely asks for gratification of a sort which is not within the purview of ordinary democratic progressivism" (85). For Trilling, negativity, unpleasure, and the death drive must be part of any understanding of a livable social order, which is to say a literature that insists on unpleasure doesn't "express the idea of harmony negatively" but rather faults any understanding of politics that imagines it can move beyond negativity.

A close look at Trilling's 1947 novel *The Middle of the Journey* can help to further tease out his enigmatic appeals to the political implications of various forms of literary art. Trilling's novel foregrounds the psychological dynamics of ideological self-positioning and addresses a number of themes at play in his essays, including the inability of the progressive liberal Left to deal with tragic dimensions of life, particularly illness and death. At its most suggestive, Trilling's novel intimates a new form of the novel of ideas, something like an ideological novel of manners, where individuals are differentiated according to their concrete individuality, their relation to ideas, and their placement in the social order. As Trilling writes in *The Liberal Imagination,* "Social class and the conflicts it produces may not be any longer a compelling subject to the novelist, but the organization of society into ideological groups presents a subject scarcely less absorbing. Ideological society has, it seems to me, nearly as full a range of passion and nearly as complex a system of manners as a society based on social class."[26]

Set in the late 1930s but shadowed by the time of its writing ten years later, Trilling's novel takes up the case of the "fellow traveler" relation to communism through a character system built out of mirrored dyads, in which one character's radicalism sustains another's liberalism and vice versa. The central character, John Laskell, is a fellow-traveling liberal who at the opening of the novel is recovering from scarlet fever. While recuperating, he travels to the country to visit his friends, Arthur and Nancy Croom, both of whom share his political sympathies. The key moral crisis of the novel, in some sense, is introduced by a fourth figure, their more radical friend Gifford Maxim (famously based on Whittaker Chambers), who dramatically leaves the Communist Party and becomes obsessed with the conviction that his life is in danger as a result. This conviction, along with what they see as the morally repugnant act of betrayal, offends the sensibilities of the liberals in the novel.

The novel repeatedly asks us to notice that liberals prop their beliefs on those who hold stronger views than theirs, and they do so by means of a concrete relationship or tie.[27] Thus Laskell gets something important out of his relationship with Maxim, which is part of the reason the break is so traumatic for him.

> Certain things were clear between Laskell and Maxim. It was established that Laskell accepted Maxim's extreme commitment to the future. It was understood between them that Laskell did not accept all of Maxim's ideas. At the same time, Laskell did not oppose Maxim's ideas. One could not oppose them without being illiberal, even reactionary. One would have to have something better to offer and Laskell had nothing better. He could not even imagine what

the better ideas would be. He sometimes regretted this but, after all, although he was an intelligent man, he could scarcely set up as an original thinker. He was left very much exposed, not to Maxim's arguments, for Maxim seldom argued, but to Maxim's inner authority. This Laskell did not regret. Maxim never formulated an accusation in words, yet he did make an accusation. He made it by being what he was. This accusation was unlike any other—it was benign. It brought the guilt into the open, the guilt of being what one was, the guilt one shared with others of one's comfortable class. There was a kind of relief in admitting the guilt to this huge dedicated man.[28]

This passage holds in balance a complex of psychological, moral, and political factors. Above all it insists on the force exerted by ways of being: one holds one's political views in a certain way, and in relation to others, whose ways of holding views are likewise always defined differentially, through dynamics that are at once psychological and moral. Trilling seems to imagine we are at a point in history where ideas and ideology, as self-consciously held conceptions, are a fundamental part of the identity of certain individuals and classes of individuals. Similarly, one's relation to one's ideas, and to the ideological stances of others, has moral consequences for both individual and collective life. The novel reflects the notion that a distorted relation to ideas, their perversion into fixed ideologies, defines the threat of radical thought in the twentieth century. But this is not the only way the moral life of ideas is imagined. The liberal is singled out as afflicted with a certain dependence and passivity, which is in part why Maxim's defection hits so hard. As Laskell says to the Crooms:

"Giff knew a great deal and was very deeply committed. That's why he seemed so important to us, isn't it? After all, we've been nothing but liberals and perhaps that's all we'll ever be. That's all right, but it means that we pretty much limit ourselves to ideas—and ideals. When we act, if we can call it action, it's only in a peripheral way." (168)

The stress on relational definition is a core element of Trilling's presentation. But in the case of liberalism, he presses hard on its ideals in a more concentrated way, precisely by foregrounding the limits of argument and logic. For Trilling, argument is absolutely vital to the life of ideas, including political ideas. But it also has crucial limits, and those who engage in it must recognize that communicative practices include elements of aggression and withdrawal and that the intellectual life is not immune to the pressure of what we might call the claims of existence. Through the character of Laskell, Trilling advocates a recalibration of thinking being in the face of an awareness of these limits to argument. One could say this characterization is just a fancy name for the liberal temperament, but that would fail to capture it. Argument is everywhere shown to be driven by antagonism or limited in its relevance to the fundamental moral or existential issue at hand. For example, it is underscored that Maxim's break with the party has nothing to do with doctrinal issues, nothing to do with theory. It is fundamentally an existential moral action and for this reason is open to being classed as an aberration linked to a psychological pathology. In removing Maxim's action from the field of opinion formation and from any liberal notion of commitment or reflective endorsement, the narrative insists that the full spectrum of moral life cannot be captured by such idealized categories. Similarly, certain of Laskell's experiences that take place outside the orbit of ordinary social and political life—his illness, and his affair with Emily Caldwell—allow him to experience forms of certainty that elude logic but carry the force of persuasion. Emily tells Laskell it is all right to desire death, as he did when he was ill, and it is after having sex with her that he experiences the force of her claim: "It was only later, when they were lying precisely side by side, their clasped hands hidden from sight between them, that Laskell felt that he understood not so much the logic as the basis in fact of her argument" (234). The embrace of being that we see here and elsewhere in the novel sits at a distance from the narrative's moral-political anatomizing of ideological positioning.

The novel's complex relation to argument is apparent even in what might seem a straightforward theme-announcing debate scene, the final conversation between Laskell, the Crooms, Maxim Gifford, and the Jeffersonian liberal Kermit Simpson. In that conversation a standoff occurs between Maxim, who promotes his recently affirmed religious framework, and Nancy Croom, who represents a form of doctrinaire liberalism. As Maxim formulates it, "'For you—no responsibility for the individual, but no forgiveness. For me—ultimate, absolute responsibility for the individual, but mercy'" (349). After this, Laskell enters into a meditation over the diminishing force of idealism at the present time and imagines that Maxim represents a certain "swing of the pendulum" (350). What Trilling writes then is instructive:

> This perception, rather than the course of the argument, had been filling Laskell's mind. He was not prepared to answer when Kermit, whom the silence oppressed, said, "John, what is your feeling about this?" To Kermit a difference of opinion was a difference of opinion and showed that liberalism still flourished. Yet Laskell, called upon, had an answer, "Is it really a question, Kermit? I can't see it as a question, not really. An absolute freedom from responsibility—

that much of a child none of us can be. An absolute responsibility—that much of a divine or metaphysical essence none of us is." (350–51)

Laskell's intervention is not well received, and he perceives the group's reaction to him as one of anger at being forced to confront an "idea in modulation" (352). Laskell is here differentiated not only from Maxim but from two political types: the radical or liberal who believes the system and not individuals are to blame, and the liberal who believes in the power of opinion and in argument as the clash and movement of opinion. By contrast, Laskell represents someone who can hold a complex idea in equipoise. This involves a removal from, but also a dependence on, the life of argument. Or perhaps more fundamentally, it internalizes argument, removing it from the realm of conflict so it can function as an orienting flexibility of mind. This is a recognizable liberal formation, but it is situated within an overall novelistic project that, on the one hand, wants to delineate the manners of a sociological group defined fundamentally by its relation to political ideas but, on the other, is interested in the pressures of those elements of life that cannot simply be contained within political thought or aspiration. Part of the way the novel formally puts argument in its place, as it were, is by persistently focalizing through Laskell, who seems in many instances to watch the arguments through glass, and whose convalescent remoteness seems to indict reflective ideological commitment as a misguided distraction from the more immediate demands of embodied life.

Absent from the novel is any substantial or systematic treatment of the larger forces and conditions that prompt ideological commitment in the first place. The novel has a claustral feel, familiar from the novel of manners, even as everyone is talking about politics, including the idea, persistently resisted by Laskell, that society determines what individuals think and do. One notable feature of realist engagements with liberal thought, as I argued in chapter 2, is the form's ability to stage a tension or interplay between third- and first-person perspectives, often by using an omniscient narrator to capture the systems perspective and situated characters to capture the first-person participatory perspective. Charles Dickens's *Bleak House* formally expresses this tension in its dual narration, enacting the bleak view in the third-person narration and the aspirational view in Esther's first-person narration. There are of course many different versions of this dynamic, not always so clearly marked. *The Middle of the Journey*, however, remains focalized through Laskell in ways that prevent the systemic perspective from showing itself except via assertions from other characters, and the insular effect is intensified by the pastoral setting and the convalescent ambience. What *The Middle of the Journey* does emphasize is the elusiveness of causality and hence responsibility. As the final argument shows, giving primacy to the system over the individual problematically moots moral responsibility, but this does not mean that actions and events are not overdetermined by many things, including the social order and its effects. Indeed, around the final tragic incident, the death of the young girl Susan Caldwell, the novel stages both the impulse to assign clear lines of blame and the impossibility of doing so. In general, the novel is most invested in flexibility of mind, acknowledgment of embodied being, and ethical responsiveness to those who share our immediate world. It seems to shy away from political action and systemic critique, seeing both as too dangerously confident. The novel might be seen as a liberalism of retreat, but I believe Trilling views the vision of the novel as the necessary precondition for any renewed or appropriate political engagement.[29]

Trilling's valuing of internalized complexity places him in a curious relation to the New Critics, of whom he writes in *The Liberal Imagination*, "we often feel of them that they make the elucidation of poetic ambiguity or irony a kind of intellectual calisthenic ritual."[30] One might be tempted to dismiss this as the narcissism of minor differences, since Trilling and the New Critics privilege a similar set of terms: ambiguity, complexity, irony, difficulty. But there is a major difference in where the complexity is placed: for the New Critics it is in the text itself, and for Trilling it is in the consciousness and temperament of the critic and the imagined reader. It becomes an ethos and hence reaches back to Arnold and forward to Foucault. This is underscored by the term that Trilling's oeuvre conspicuously adds to the group of terms favored by the New Critics: *tragedy*. For Trilling one must acknowledge complexity but also those conditions that conduce to tragedy, and one must aim to respond to those conditions with moral strenuousness. The forms of suspension or equivocation that mark his moral stance are above all a caution or vigilance in the face of moral dangers associated with instrumental action, especially action based on moral passion (rather than the standard origin, self-interest). When in *The Liberal Imagination* he advocates a literary form ("moral realism") that will reflect an understanding of these dangers, he insists that its significance lies not in "some highflown fineness of feeling," but in its relevance to the consequential fact that the "moral passions are even more willful and imperious and impatient than the self-seeking passions."[31] It is for this reason that Trilling privileges hesitation over commitment, appreciation of complexity over action. Notably, Foucault also produces a mode of intellection and ethics that stresses a delicate suspension, as for example in the call to consider "the techniques of management, and also the ethics, the *ethos*, the practice of self, which would allow . . . games of power to be played with a minimum of domination."[32] As in Trilling, an apprehension about the very use of political power is met by a turn toward a morally heightened attention to the self's relation to the self. The coincidence here touches on our understanding of both Trilling and Foucault. Trilling's ethical sensitivity to violence and domination is indelibly a part of his liberalism and bespeaks a wariness of power effects rather than mere quietism. Foucault's chastened response to the ubiquity of power shares affinities with postwar liberalism, just as his turn to practices of the self privileges the forms of self-actualization and avoidance of harm that liberalism seeks to promote.

Trilling's focus on finely calibrated practices of the self is in keeping with the existentialist dimension of his thought and may seem to place him at a significant remove from Adorno, yet there is a striking connection in the two thinkers' conceptions of the importance of readerly experience. Adorno may not like existentialist assumptions about individual human choice, but his description of Kafka's power inevitably rests on a picture of readerly response that has profound existential consequences. Even as he rejects the importance and centrality of subjective experience, insisting instead on the power of modernist art to disrupt and even assault the reader through its potent objective representations of debased reality, he at the same time necessarily invokes a readerly process and indeed transformation, a formative relation between reader and text, that stands in as the most important critical and ethical event occasioned by art. Such a process disallows standard forms of aesthetic distance such as Laskell enacts, producing instead a violent encounter with the stark conditions of an administered world: "He over whom Kafka's wheels have passed, has lost for ever any peace with the world and any chance of consoling himself with the judgment that the way of the world is bad." In that this situation leaves the reader entirely suspended in the negations enacted by the artwork, it is not entirely different from some of the most politically suggestive moments in Trilling, where a demand based on the unresolved recalcitrance of literary art—either to moral clarity or to interpretive finality—is held up as the best promise of a future politics dedicated to the fullest realization of human nature. Both Adorno and Trilling turn toward art as a kind of dynamic refuge from formal politics, invoking specific aesthetic energies—negative, suspensive, dedicated to difficulty—to reorient moral and political thought. One key difference is this: the implication in Trilling is that any future politics must, like the most powerful literature, embrace the divided nature of human life—its negations and its affirmations and its necessary embeddedness in ongoing conditions. For Adorno, the absolute inescapability of present negations implies a vision, however unreachable, of absolute transformation.

A close study of Trilling's work, and a recognition of its place within a broader pattern of political response in the twentieth century, complicates the notion of the liberal temperament and the liberal imagination, which is to say, both the ethos of liberalism and its aesthetics. As *The Middle of the Journey* demonstrates, literary engagements with liberal thought are often conceptually and formally complex in ways that have not been adequately captured given the specific field conditions in literary and cultural studies. Trilling is an especially interesting case given his own reworking of the novel of manners, which extends the Forsterian project he so admired. As I will show in the chapter that follows, there are modernist novels that engage this topos as well, for example, Ralph Ellison's roughly contemporaneous *Invisible Man* (1952) and Doris Lessing's *The Golden Notebook* (1962), which give expression to the political disenchantment of the era in formally innovative ways.

The more general irony I have tried to underscore is that there is a tradition of liberalism that resonates significantly with the bleak radicalism that has become such an enduring theoretical disposition in our field. Given established tendencies toward conflict between the radical Left and liberal Left, Trilling's own emphasis on the psychology of ideological self-definition, or the tendency for liberals and radicals to define themselves against each other, seems particularly telling. The aim of this chapter has been to disable that tendency somewhat without obliterating the real differences that do exist. The radical Left tradition relies on strong critique, often negative, trained on the economic system viewed in relation to multiple spheres of life. The liberal tradition, by contrast, typically seeks incremental reform of existing democratic institutions and states as well as extensions of principles of justice and access. But as the example of the mid-twentieth century shows us, both traditions seek to come to terms with human suffering and human violence, and in doing so they express in varying ways a bleak view of their own political projects. It is tempting to single out Trilling by saying he provides an internal critique of an otherwise benighted liberalism, and certainly he employs formulations consonant with that view, as when he urges criticism to "recall liberalism to its first essential imagination of variousness and possibility."[33] But I propose a rather different view, one that sees Trilling as exemplifying liberalism's ongoing embrace of difficulty in both politics and art.

CHAPTER FIVE

Bleak Liberalism and the Realism/Modernism Debate: Ellison and Lessing

This final chapter will extend the discussion of the liberal aesthetic to two works of modernism that are known both for their experimentalism and for their stories of disenchantment with communism: Doris Lessing's *The Golden Notebook* and Ralph Ellison's *Invisible Man*. As we saw in the previous chapter, Lionel Trilling's *The Middle of the Journey* remains within the tradition of the novel of manners, even as it adapts that genre by focusing on the "manners" of ideological affiliation rather than class (though class remains pertinent). Trilling's novel also takes up the form of character-character argument drawn from the political novel (as discussed in chapter 3) and central to the history of literary engagements with liberal thought. What is absent from Trilling's text, focalized as it is through the singular liberal temperament of John Laskell, is the broader systems perspective typically captured by third-person narration in the realist novel, an absence that is all the more striking since a view of the system is integral to ideological thinking itself. As demonstrated in the analysis of nineteenth-century realism (chapter 2), it is the third-person perspective that regularly enables a broader critical perspective on the social system, one that then helps to inform an aspirational or experiential orientation grounded in the first-person perspective. The formal dynamic between these two perspectives can express distinctly liberal energies or commitments, but let me emphasize that I am claiming no strict formal determination. While the interplay of first- and third-person perspectives is an identifiable feature of liberal thought more generally (chapter 1), it can also express the moral and sociological orientations of other ideological positions.

Trilling's novel, like his criticism, exemplifies the privileging of individual temperament seen as characteristic of liberalism. As I have argued throughout this book, liberalism's tendency to privilege individual temperament has exacerbated the perception that liberalism involves withdrawal from the demands of systematic politics and has reinforced the divide between liberalism as a political philosophy and liberalism as an aesthetics. A similar charge of retreat from a larger political perspective into isolated consciousness animates one of the defining moments of the realism/modernism debate, in which the Marxist critic Georg Lukács argues that by narrowing its focus to perspectives of subjective interiority, modernism abandons the resources of the realist novel, which was able to represent the social system, evaluate it critically, and situate individual experience within its larger conditions and forces.[1] Theodor Adorno's response, as is well known, was to say that Lukács neglects form in favor of content, imagining that art is a mere reflection of society or, even worse, a kind of social science. For Adorno, modernism is superior because it is able to capture diminished forms of life under capitalism, maintaining art's autonomy and refusing any reconciliation with the real.[2]

Disagreement over the relative merits of realism and modernism animated much of the literary and political intelligentsia in the interwar, war, and cold war period and was heightened by debates on social realism and committed art. A close look at the period shows a mix of engagement with realist and modernist modes and reveals the difficulty of marking clear delineations between them. Recent reappraisals of modernism and realism in light of the larger geopolitical context of the era add further layers of complexity. Joe Cleary, for example, argues that the war and cold war context produced stark positions in the formal debates that are ultimately unhelpful in understanding the literary strategies novelists employed, both in the metropolis and on the periphery.[3]

Cleary's approach introduces questions highly pertinent to the history and theory of the novel. His revisionism, however, reinscribes some of the distortions that have prevented a clear appraisal of liberalism in both its political and its literary manifestations. Cleary begins from the premise that the history of the novel during the nineteenth century and beyond is best viewed in terms of the history of imperialism, with nineteenth-century realism characterized by its repression of imperialism and with modernism reflecting the transition between the old geopolitical world order and the new imperialism forming under the conditions of the cold war. Viewed through such a lens, the twentieth century reveals a complex use of both realism and modernism across different geopolitical contexts. By contrast, what have hitherto served as the seminal treatments of realism's history and modernism's emergence — the accounts of Georg Lukács and Erich Auerbach, above all — have told a story limited in its scope and driven by distorting polarities. Specifically, in viewing realism's eclipse by modernism as "catastrophic," Cleary argues, these accounts act out the crisis mentality and "civilizational distress" at play in the twentieth-century response to fascism, communism, and World War II (257).

While this approach rightly and persuasively argues that it is misleading to map realism and modernism in a polarizing way, it is itself limited in its insistence on imperialism as the determining cause of literary genres and their transformations. In arguing that the key driver in the development of modernism was a world crisis over the demise of the old imperial order, that is, Cleary's account risks reproducing the very antinomies (now refracted through the category of empire) it seeks to dislodge. It also presents a rather narrow understanding of literary political vision. Even if we accept the notion that the nineteenth-century novel only minimally engages the fact of imperialism (and this is an arguable claim), it nonetheless registers, with great intensity, many forms of power and violence, including the "slow violence" of the Industrial Revolution; forms of exclusion practiced by traditional communities; inequality based on laws of inheritance, gender ideology, religion, and race; and the apprehension of forces that exceed human control and challenge the power of human action and understanding. The interplay of formal modes and strategies can be operative with respect to a wide range of forms of human experience, and it is constricting to limit the debate to a single historical condition or narrative. As I argued in chapter 2, nineteenth-century realism powerfully engages the challenges that emergent democratic and liberal commitments pose to traditional communities and beliefs, and it often does so through noteworthy adaptations of established literary conventions.

The claim that debates over realism and modernism in the mid-twentieth century were fundamentally conditioned by the polarizing conditions of the cold war likewise occludes the ways certain writers were thoughtfully engaging those conditions. Indeed, some of the writers who were most responsive to the disappointment of the communist aspiration and the entrenchment of the cold war registered their experiences and convictions through distinctive literary experiments not easily classifiable in terms of the structuring debates over realism and modernism. Through an exploration of two major and significant examples of such literary experiments, this chapter will show the formal and conceptual complexities that arise out of the political disenchantments of the postwar era. Both Lessing and

Ellison retain a strong attachment to progressive aspiration, even as they unflinchingly register the bleak conditions—both psychic and social—that committed individuals face in the mid-twentieth century.

INVISIBILITY BLUES

In its criticism of the dogmatic attitudes and practices within the Communist Party, Ralph Ellison's *Invisible Man* shares features of the liberal anticommunism associated with Trilling and other New York intellectuals such as Daniel Bell, Richard Hofstadter, and Arthur Schlesinger. Yet it would be misleading to associate him too closely with this group, since he reconfigures some of the key elements of this intellectual formation.[4] Moreover, his aesthetic investments are quite distinct and often elaborated in opposition to positions held by others. Like the *Partisan Review* group generally, he favors modernism, but there are nonetheless important specificities to his art that disclose his orienting philosophical and political convictions.

Ellison's views on the strengths and shortcomings of different novelistic forms and writers illuminate both his political views and his aesthetic preferences. Because of his memorable debate with Irving Howe about Howe's essay "Black Boys and Native Sons," it is well known that Ellison was repelled by naturalism's strong deterministic tendencies. He also made a point of underscoring the limitations of the novel of manners, the form Trilling championed. As Ellison writes in "Society, Morality, and the Novel," an essay whose title directly invokes Trilling, the novel of manners "has little value in dealing with our world of chaos and catastrophe."[5] For Trilling, as we saw in the previous chapter, the historical situation in twentieth-century US culture demanded that the novel of manners be adapted to represent relations driven by ideological affiliation rather than class. For Ellison, by contrast, the central cultural and political issue was race, and the defining historical watershed was the Civil War, not the political events of the twentieth century. And it mattered deeply to Ellison how one understood and framed this central experience of race, as his disagreement with Howe reveals. The key caution that Ellison repeatedly sounded was against reifying racial experience or making assumptions about precisely how one's disadvantaged condition was experienced. For Howe, the art of both Ellison and James Baldwin lacked authenticity in that it failed to show the defining force of their sociological experience as Negroes in America, a force that, for Howe, should be registered with "pain and ferocity," as it was in the work of Richard Wright.[6] As his strongly worded response to Howe indicates, Ellison vehemently rejected the forms of fundamentally dehumanizing reduction that characterized Howe's assumption, in Ellison's words, that "un-relieved suffering is the only 'real' Negro experience."[7]

In a way, Ellison plays Trilling to Howe and Howe to Trilling. In the case of his response to Howe, he invokes complexity (a key Trilling term) as well as aesthetic transcendence of conditioned existence. Rejecting the idea that authentic Negro writers will express a sociologically determined suffering and will do so in the mode of at least implicit political protest, Ellison writes:

> He [the Negro] must live [his life] and try consciously to grasp its complexity until he can change it; must live it *as* he changes it. He is no mere product of his socio-political predicament. He is a product of the interaction between his racial predicament, his individual will and the broader American cultural freedom in which he finds his ambiguous existence. (112–13; emphasis in the original)

Like Trilling, Ellison uses the term complexity to counter reductive ideological thinking or art, but he adapts it to focus specifically on the ideology of race. In an interview, he applies the term directly to his differences from Richard Wright, stating, "I think I felt more complexity in life" and "I think I was less interested in an ideological interpretation of Negro experience."[8] There is also a discernible parallel between Ellison's discussion of Wright and Trilling's discussion of Theodore Dreiser in *The Liberal Imagination*. Just as Dreiser represents a certain form of determinism—what Trilling calls "his nearly monolithic materialism"[9]—and just as the reception of Dreiser represents a certain overvaluing by politically minded critics of unrefined expressions of brute reality and power, so too does Wright and his reception by Howe (as the "Northern white liberal version of the white Southern myth of absolute separation of the races") reflect a lack of complexity in the understanding of how experiences of racial oppression can condition and enable transformative "strategies of survival," including forms of art.[10]

In Ellison's relation to Trilling, however, a certain difference emerges in both the content and form of "complexity." As we saw in chapter 1, Trilling consistently sees an emphasis on sociological or group identity as a problematic form of special pleading driven by anxieties about exclusion and destructive of the finer forms of moral differentiation. Ellison, however, insists on the obduracy and internal complexity of the racial question itself, noting its strongly felt intensities of frustration, ambivalence, and aspiration. He is dedicated to the textured representation of the experience of being black and the psychological dynamic between blacks and whites in America. While *The Middle of the Journey* reflects Trilling's interest in the psychological dimensions of ideological relations, in particular the tendency for radicals and liberals to define themselves against one another (both in intimate relations of friendship and in the larger political sphere), Ellison's writing involves a more tense and internally fraught psychic drama involving experiences of guilt, projection, and the struggle for recognition.[11] His sense of the historical centrality of the racial divide to American history produces a social psychology and a literary history attuned to the ramifying effects of an incomplete democracy. Out of that mix arises a modernist aesthetic that combines realist, symbolic, and experimental techniques, so as to capture the disorienting effects of a racially power-laden world and at the same time to assert the specific styles of expression, direct and indirect, adopted by the disenfranchised.

Interestingly, although Ellison develops experimental techniques to convey the psychological intensities of black experience in America, his own view of literary history privileges nineteenth-century realism over what he views as the narrow indulgences of twentieth-century literature. Nineteenth-century literature has for Ellison a moral and political seriousness and depth trained precisely on democratic responsibility. Central to that orientation is not only the writer's understanding of "personal responsibility in the condition of society" but, as in Mark Twain's representation of Jim, a "conception of the Negro as a symbol of Man—the reversal of what he represents in most contemporary thought."[12] In the twentieth century this sense of "tragic responsibility" disappears, and what is left is "intellectual evasion" and the elevation of "personal myth" and "technical perfection," the prime example of this being the writings of Ernest Hemingway (33, 36, 38). The twentieth century ultimately reflects a widespread use of "the Negro stereotype" as "a key figure in a magic rite by which the white American seeks to resolve the dilemma arising between his democratic beliefs and certain antidemocratic practices, between his acceptance of the sacred democratic belief that all men are created equal and his treatment of every tenth man as though he were not" (28).

Ellison's literary aesthetic is meant to capture this psychological dimension of the national imaginary, the projections and hostilities and "magic rites" by which social life is conducted under a riven democracy. And yet, while in some ways *Invisible Man* presents us with a nightmare landscape where disillusionment follows disillusionment and betrayal follows betrayal, there is also a key aspirational dimension of Ellison's project, one that seeks to restore "the full, complex ambiguity of the human" to its central character, the narrator (25). More than that, the ideal of democracy is evoked both negatively and positively, and in this sense Ellison resurrects the moral commitment to liberal democracy that he sees as animating the nineteenth-century works of Twain, Emerson, Thoreau, Whitman, and Melville.

The complex aesthetic animating Ellison's novel involves several interacting elements. The structuring theme of invisibility involves a strong critical diagnosis of the dehumanizing negations at the heart of the nation's entrenched historical racial dynamic as well as a strategic reappropriation of invisibility as power. Alongside this major theme and its unfolding we find an ongoing attention to forms of black cultural expression that acknowledge and work through challenging conditions of existence by means of stylistic enactment, fluid performance, and artistic transcendence. And last, there is a constellation of elements in the novel that deal explicitly with the principles and ideas of liberal democracy. This political aspect of the text is somewhat marginal relative to the grand sweep of serial disillusionment that recurs over several phases of the narrator's life, as well as to the growing momentum of forms of cultural politics in the novel's imagination of resistance and affirmation. But given the emphasis on democratic principle in the epilogue and the disenchantment with communism in the text, it is worth probing this aspect of the work, especially because it has been underexplored in the criticism.

In part the democratic ideals of the text are subject to the pattern of demystification that structures the narrator's journey more generally. After the prologue, the novel presents the narrator's entry into adulthood, marked by expectations of self-actualization through ceremonial public speech and hopeful anticipation of the powerful form of acknowledgment it promises. Instead what ensues is the battle royal, a scene of racial violence in which the narrator is humiliated rather than recognized and his mouth fills with blood instead of words. This initial scene connects with later passages of the narrative in which the narrator invests heavily in the promise of self-actualization through public speech: notably the eviction scene and his selection as a public spokesperson in Harlem for the Brotherhood. In both of these later scenes, the narrator is inspired in the moment to break free of expected scripts. During the eviction scene, even as he experiences powerful ambivalence about the possibility of violence against the marshal, he begins with a call to responsibility meant to halt the escalating anger among those assembled in the streets on behalf of the evicted couple. But as a result of the back-and-forth with others present, his own speech transmutes into a stronger resistance, laced with irony, to the more pervasive forms of dispossession affecting his life and people. He then ends up marshaling a movement of the couple and crowd back into the apartment, against the orders of the police. This moment of active participation in a local political event happens to attract the attention of white activists nearby who belong to the Brotherhood, and they in turn recruit the narrator to work for them.

Notably, the same resistance to a learned script occurs when he is asked to give a speech at a large meeting of the Brotherhood. Blinded by the spotlights at the venue, the narrator finds he cannot summon the information he learned from the training pamphlets he had been studying in preparation for this moment. Instead, he moves forward using rhetorical techniques from his past, both call-and-response and what he calls the "old down-to-earth, I'm-sick-and-tired-of-the-way-they've-been-treating-us approach."[13] Stressing the importance of dispossession and resistance, he then moves into a personal mode and asserts his own sense of feeling "more human" insofar as he has become part of a larger whole, "a militant fraternity" (346). His speech brings the audience to a high pitch, and the result is then debated hotly by the Brotherhood leaders, some of whom feel the narrator has departed dangerously from doctrine in using these tactics to arouse the crowd rather than appropriately educate them. For the narrator the experience is transformative, an epiphany, though he remains somewhat unsettled by the possibility that he is somehow becoming "less a Negro" in experiencing this new affiliation (354).

Even as the narrator finds himself compelled by the universalism of the Brotherhood and inspired to have moved past cultural marginalization as well as the negotiated approach to power disclosed by Bledsoe (and in a different vein, by his grandfather), he is ultimately forced to recognize that the Brotherhood too is corrupted by power and, still worse, views his own people instrumentally, repeating the forms of dehumanization that have recurred throughout the novel's episodes. Stepping aside from the disappointments of the political realm, the narrator then explores forms of freedom and resistance enabled by cultural practices and performed identities—as represented by the zoot-suiters and Rinehart in all his guises. And while Rinehart's protean instability is ultimately not promoted by the novel, it is certainly true that forms of negation (refusal of imposed identities, appropriated invisibility) as well as the general fluid exploration of identity through experience become the conditions of existential protest and advance.[14] In a key epiphany, the narrator realizes it is the sum total of his experiences, most especially the stinging experiences of disillusionment and failure, that precisely define him:

> And now all past humiliations became precious parts of my experience, and for the first time, leaning against that stone wall in the sweltering night, I began to

accept my past and, as I accepted it, I felt memories welling up within me. . . .
They [the past humiliations] were me; they defined me. I was my experiences
and my experiences were me, and no blind men, no matter how powerful they
became, even if they conquered the world, could take that, or change one single
itch, taunt, laugh, cry, scar, ache, rage, or pain of it. (507–8)

Insistence on the experience of humiliation and disillusionment as the
ground of identity points toward the role of art in a world riven by dynamics of power as well as ongoing yearnings for individual self-actualization
in conditions of imperfect justice. This situation is sometimes named by
Ellison as democracy itself, a necessarily incomplete project, and even more
fragile in the twentieth century, as evinced by literary history.[15] Art captures
the difficulty of incomplete democracy as well as the aspirations of individuals struggling against the particularity of their circumstances.

Ellison's novel aims for such transcendence through its experimental
style and the momentum of its prose. His firm belief, moreover, is that powerful literary art serves as a "social action" in a way that the "protest novel"
or the political novel cannot. Here we see the distinctive character of Ellison's liberalism. As he states in "The World and the Jug":

If *Invisible Man* is even "apparently" free from "the ideological and emotional
penalties suffered by Negroes in this country," it is because I tried to the best
of my ability to transform these elements into art. My goal was not to escape,
or hold back, but to work through; to transcend, as the blues transcend the
painful conditions with which they deal. The protest is there, not because I
was helpless before my racial condition, but because I *put* it there. If there is
anything "miraculous" about the book it is the result of hard work undertaken
in the belief that the work of art is important in itself, that it is a social action
in itself. (emphasis in the original)[16]

In a sense, this is an avowedly personalized version of the form of existential realism promoted by Trilling and explored in the previous chapter.
But rather than imagining ideological affiliation or political belief as a form
of "manners," Ellison sees the writer working through the concrete challenges of his particular social and political inheritance (in his case, the race
dynamics set into play by the history of slavery in the United States). What
results is a variation on the bildungsroman chronicling repeated aspiration,
disorientation, disillusionment, and creative response. And, as with Trilling, the understanding achieved through experience is implied to be the
precondition of any deeper or more effective politics, and we are left at
the end of the text with the narrator at once claiming communicative force
for his novel ("Who knows but that, on the lower frequencies, I speak for

you?") and promising that he will eventually emerge from his underground hibernation, since "there's a possibility that even an invisible man has a socially responsible role to play."[17]

But it is important to recognize that for Ellison cultural expression, in this case the novel itself, does not simply replace discredited political experience. There is always a kind of interplay between the cultural and the political. Throughout his nonfiction writings, and particularly in the collection *Shadow and Act*, Ellison emphasizes the way music, and in particular jazz and the blues, captures certain energies and ambitions associated with social struggle and democratic aspiration. Jazz represents for Ellison the dialectic of freedom within constraint and constitutes one among several ineluctable forms of style that constitute "an affirmation of life beyond all question of our difficulties as Negroes."[18] As William Maxwell has shown, in its distinctive practice of expression within limits, jazz can be seen to represent the promise of self-actualization within democracy (he notes in particular the passage in "The Charlie Christian Story" in which Ellison asserts that "true jazz is an art of individual assertion within and against the group").[19] But if jazz formally exemplifies the liberal democratic condition of self-expression within a larger group, it is the blues that best capture (and transcend) the lived experience associated with political and social struggle, as the previous quotation on art as transcendence shows. In an essay on the singer Jimmy Rushing, Ellison characterizes the blues as "an art of ambiguity, an assertion of the irrepressibly human over all circumstances whether created by others or by one's own human failings."[20] Here as elsewhere Ellison aims to combine recognition of the specificity of African American culture with a democratic universalism ("the irrepressibly human"). He goes on to invoke the blues as expressive of a national condition: "They are the only consistent art in the United States which constantly remind[s] us of our limitations while encouraging us to see how far we can actually go" (246). For Ellison, the blues manage to give expression to a uniquely individual experience while also channeling the intense forms of bleak affect issuing out of artistic effort in the midst of limiting conditions, at once concrete and universal. For Ellison, this is what protest is about—it is never simply particular protest, it always connects to the larger human existential condition (here his claims resonate with those of Albert Camus in *The Rebel*).

Beyond its adaptation of the tradition of existential realism exemplified in the political novels of many of his contemporaries, there is within the conceptual economy of *Invisible Man* an engagement with certain principles of liberalism, notably deliberative debate, democratic procedure, and the grounding principle of sincerity in speech and action. These liberal prin-

BLEAK LIBERALISM AND THE REALISM/MODERNISM DEBATE   125

ciples are affirmed primarily in their negation, by their failure to sustain themselves against the pervasive forces of aggression, violence, and deception. There is considerable dialogue in the novel, and much of it involves debating ideas and political positions, a familiar feature from the political novel generally but adapted here to accommodate all sorts of surreal or dreamlike events. Democratic procedure is thematized in one key scene, the union meeting at Liberty Paints, where it is shown to be easily derailed by violence. And sincerity, a significant liberal concept and value, is of course central to the world of *Invisible Man*, again by negation. Many of the key experiences of disillusionment and betrayal involve deception and dishonesty. The most powerful example of this early in the novel occurs when Bledsoe takes his gloves off after the incident with Mr. Norton, the school trustee whom the narrator exposes to elements in the community that Bledsoe would like him shielded from. Believing Bledsoe to be an upright leader of his people, the narrator suddenly discovers that he is fundamentally double, pretending to be deferential to the white supporters of the school while manipulating his self-presentation and his words so as to maintain power in a dishonest way. When the narrator assumes, in the face of Bledsoe's threats and recriminations, that truth can expose the manipulations of power, Bledsoe aggressively asserts that power determines truth, that those in power control what counts as truth:

> You're a black educated fool, son. These white folk have newspapers, magazines, radios, spokesmen to get their ideas across. If they want to tell the world a lie, they can tell it so well that it becomes the truth; and if I tell them that you're lying, they'll tell the world even if you prove you're telling the truth.[21]

A similar eclipsing of principle by power takes place in the union meeting scene. The narrator chances upon the meeting when he leaves the boiler room of the Liberty Paints factory to retrieve his lunch from the locker room, where the meeting is being held. He is immediately suspected by some of the members of being a "fink," of having been sent into the meeting to spy. When he denies the charge, the accusers up the ante and continue to threaten him, disrupting the meeting.

> "Respect the chair!" the chairman shouted. "We're a democratic union here, following democratic—"
> "Never mind, git rid of the fink!"
> "...procedures. It's our task to make friends with all the workers..." (220)

This is a suggestive textual moment. On one hand, there is the bald typographic fact that an aggressive directive interrupts the phrase "democratic procedures." But the dash after "democratic" also constitutes an unfinished phrase and raises the question whether democracy might be defined otherwise than through procedure. As the interaction evolves, democratic procedure becomes distinctly aggressive: first, the chairman insults the narrator even as he puts forward an ostensibly fair-minded motion to investigate formally whether he is a fink. And when the motion is affirmed, the narrator experiences it as an act of violence precisely because he is not given a chance to represent himself: "My face stung as though it had been slapped. They had made their decision without giving me a chance to speak for myself" (223). Procedure in this case is used in a hostile and peremptory manner, and it cannot be cordoned off from the forms of power it is meant to manage or diffuse. Like the moment when Bledsoean power determines truth, this event seems to constitute procedure, the democratic principle in question, as always corrupt in practice, always fundamentally susceptible to the manipulations of power.

Sincerity is the liberal concept most powerfully thwarted in the world of the novel, carrying the strongest charge precisely because of its link to avowed and acknowledged identity within the social field, a primary consideration of the novel forcefully symbolized through the motif of invisibility. To be seen, heard, and recognized is the main aspiration of this novel of identity; and it is also an aspiration up against fundamental barriers of non-acknowledgment, dehumanization, and rigid social hierarchy. The stakes are high and the humiliation is extreme, essentially a form of social death. It is no wonder the allure of embraced invisibility, strategic dissimulation, and the donning of masks is so great. But behind the searing diagnosis and searching acknowledgment of resistant practices resides a powerful ideal: self-expression through speech. In a way the novel itself constitutes a redemptive reworking of that ideal, so often thwarted within the world of the novel itself. Writing becomes the site where the inescapable conditions of power and aggression animating the social field somehow become defused or bracketed, particularly by means of the hermetic strategies of withdrawal into isolated consciousness.[22]

Two cryptically interlinked moments in the text indicate just how strong is the unrealized ideal of sincerity, and how closely it is linked to the entrenched problem of power-laden nonrecognition. Each of these moments occurs in a scene of stinging disillusionment, the first in the narrator's conversation with Bledsoe about the Mr. Norton incident, the second during a meeting with the Brotherhood. In the first conversation, as we have seen, the narrator is subjected to startling revelations about Bledsoe's strategic use of lies. First Bledsoe tells him he should have lied to Mr. Norton to avoid any encounter with Trueblood. Then he has to endure a frontal assault in which Bledsoe accuses him directly of lying when he states that it was no one else's idea to take Mr. Norton to Trueblood's. The narrator swears he is telling the truth.

> "Nigger, this isn't the time to lie. I'm no white man. Tell me the truth!"
> It was as though he'd struck me. I stared across the desk thinking, He called me *that* . . .
> "Answer me, boy!"
> *That*, I thought, noticing the throbbing of a vein that rose between his eyes, thinking, *He called me that.*
> "I wouldn't lie, sir," I said. (139; emphasis in the original)

In this exchange, the accusation of lying is combined with the violence of being called the n-word, which leaves the narrator reeling. In fact it seems as though the latter is a definitively worse event, one that directly dehumanizes the narrator. But the later conversation with the Brotherhood sheds new light on this scene. There Westrum is accusing the narrator of having opportunistically pursued media attention via a magazine interview, when the narrator objects that Westrum's accusation is "a contemptible lie":

> "Who's a lie?"
> "You're a liar and a fat-mouthed scoundrel. You're a liar and no brother of mine."
> "Now he's calling me names. Brothers, you heard him." (402)

The oddity of this exchange, the idea that someone could "be" a lie rather than a liar, raises the possibility that being accused of a lie is a kind of primary indignity, just as is being called the n-word: the two forms of indignity interpenetrate and perform a powerful double knot of negation. And it indicates how central, within the symbolic economy of the novel, honest communication and intersubjective trust are to the animating ideal of social and political life. That this is a frustrated ideal does not evacuate its potent force for the narrator. In the epilogue, he underscores the centrality and difficulty of honest communication, emphasizing that his own writing is an attempt at truth-telling:

> Let me be honest with you—a feat which, by the way, I find of the utmost dif-
> ficulty. When one is invisible he finds such problems as good and evil, honesty
> and dishonesty, of such shifting shapes that he confuses one with the other,
> depending upon who happens to be looking through him at the time. Well,

now I've been trying to look through myself, and there's a risk in it. I was never
more hated than when I tried to be honest. Or when, even as just now I've
tried to articulate exactly what I felt to be the truth. No one was satisfied—not
even I. (572–73)

The narrator also revisits and reinterprets his grandfather's advice ("overcome 'em with yeses, undermine 'em with grins, agree 'em to death and de-
struction"), surmising that he must have meant "that we were to affirm the
principle on which the country was built and not the men, or at least not the
men who did the violence" (16, 574). Here as elsewhere across the literature
that engages liberalism, we see a move to affirm transpersonal principles
that cannot be fully safeguarded by individual acts and actors.

Invisible Man employs the formal strategies and the conceptual frameworks of modernist art, including the idea of protean shape-shifting and
the elevation of style and cultural expression. Yet at its core lies a profound
orientation toward liberal principles, one that subtends the broader invocation of democratic aspiration and vital diversity. That we see these principles primarily through their negation does not undermine their force or
the power of Ellison's liberalism, which we might dub as not so much bleak
as rather a version of the blues, in that it refuses a starkly tragic attitude,
instead promoting an artistic working through of individual and collective
struggle, one not afraid to dwell in difficulty.

THE GOLDEN NOTEBOOK

Doris Lessing's *The Golden Notebook* has been widely interpreted and discussed as a major text of second-wave feminism that is also a brilliant experimental novel. But *The Golden Notebook* is also a text highly pertinent to
the broader political history of the novel in the twentieth century, given
its powerful engagement with the aspirations and disappointments of the
progressive Left. Along with its trenchant treatment of sexual relations and
gender ideology, it responds to the political crises of the twentieth century
both retrospectively, in its treatment of the failure of the communist dream,
and prospectively, in its heightened anxiety about nuclear war. Lessing's
text is not oblivious to the larger geopolitical scale invoked by Cleary, as the
treatment of the African experience shows. But even as the text registers defining power struggles over nationalism and communism on the periphery,
it more centrally treats the fate of communist aspiration across an international constellation of movements in England, Europe, and America as well
as the international realignments of the cold war era. The formal experi-

mentation of the text is to a significant degree aiming to come to terms with what sort of politics, and what relation between aesthetics and politics, will be adequate to the bleak conditions of the contemporary era. For this reason it serves as a rich concluding object of analysis for the present book, and especially for the question of how resourceful and various the modernist liberal aesthetic is, as it simultaneously acknowledges and transforms strategies evident in the realist engagement with liberalism, both its nineteenth-century exemplars and in later instances of existential realism evident in the twentieth century (as discussed in the previous chapter).

The Golden Notebook is a complex, multivoiced text, comprising a frame novel titled *Free Women*, four notebooks written by Anna Wulf (the main character of the frame novel), and a fifth special notebook, the golden notebook (also by Anna), which seeks to integrate the divided texts. A black notebook chronicles time Anna spent in Africa during World War II, in the company of a political group negotiating the competing demands of nationalism and communism and of race, class, and gender. A red notebook treats Anna's experiences with the Communist Party in England, including fraught and shifting experiences of allegiance and detachment. The yellow notebook is a novel written by Anna, about a female character named Ella who is herself writing a novel about a character planning suicide. And the blue notebook is simply a sort of journal, often trained on sexual and romantic relations, as well as Anna's relationship with her close friend Molly; in this it seems to shadow *Free Women* in many ways.

My analysis of *The Golden Notebook* argues for an interpretation of the work centered on what is arguably the text's crux, the dual ending. At the close of the inset golden notebook section of the novel, which occurs very late in the text, we discover that Anna is in fact the author of *Free Women*: this means that the ostensible frame novel is not the orienting objective reality behind Anna and her notebooks, but simply another fictional text written by Anna, like the yellow notebook, and like *Frontiers of War* (a novel Anna has written about the African experience, which figures in the red notebook).[23] Various discrepancies between the blue notebook and *Free Women* now can be attributed to the fictional license of the latter, including several key facts about Tommy (who attempts suicide and is blinded in the frame novel but not in the blue notebook, and who marries in the blue notebook but not in the frame novel). The key fact that emerges from the ending of the golden notebook, however, is that Anna ends up a writer and not, as she claims at the end of *Free Women*, someone who has abandoned writing and plans to join the Labour Party, work in marriage counseling, and tutor delinquent kids.

This revelation might appear as an ironic treatment of a progressive message and of the consolations of conventional novelistic closure, but it is complicated in that the characters within *Free Women* seem also to treat their own "endings" ironically, as a form of capitulation and failure. In general, I argue, any idea that metafictional irony trumps realism in this text is not a satisfactory solution to the major interpretive questions posed by Lessing's novel. That characters named Anna and Molly (as well as others) appear in both the blue notebook and *Free Women*, while other characters appear under altered names, creates an ongoing dynamic of confusion and irresolution. Similarly, while it may seem that we are witnessing a metafictional performance, there are ways a more intimate tension between modernism and realism orients the ongoing narrative, with the emphasis on subjectivity, perspective, alienation, and isolation brought very much to the fore in the stories of mental breakdown in the blue and golden notebooks and the realist counterforce evident not only in the "frame" novel but to varying degrees in all the notebooks.

Fundamentally, the novel is as much about a crisis of realism and what it stands for as about a crisis of political commitment. Moreover, the two are related, though not in a simple one-to-one correspondence. Early in the novel, in the black notebook, within the context of a critique of the contemporary literary form of the "novel-report," we hear from Anna that she values above all the type of novel used to make "philosophical statements about life," such as those by Thomas Mann, "the last of the writers in the old sense."[24] The novel-report, by contrast, is a style of ethnography, trained on particular forms of life rather than a larger social whole and a guiding moral framework. The problem is not so much that individuals are failing to write traditional humanist novels, but that the conditions of life have changed. Like the forms of unity and totality with which they are associated, and which they aim to comprehend, philosophical novels are not possible in the present situation. But there is a suggestion, even as Anna asserts her own incapacity, that a new sort of novel might be possible, one that still taps into the philosophical and moral resources evident in earlier writers even as it adapts to altered conditions. Anna writes, "I am incapable of writing the only kind of novel that interests me: a book powered with an intellectual or moral passion strong enough to create order, to create a new way of looking at life" (59). Yet it is arguable that under the challenging sociological, historical, and psychological conditions *The Golden Notebook* presents, Lessing herself does succeed in writing the type of novel that interests Anna.

The reasons for loss of belief in realist totality are complex. First, there is the loss of the dream of unity that Marxism promised. Second, there are a range of forces and conditions that thwart the will to unity and control, including human psychology and human violence, the vicissitudes of desire, and the challenges of the gender divide between men and women. While these conditions are presented to a large degree as recalcitrant facts of nature, the apprehension of their force has occurred within history, particularly with respect to disappointed political aspirations: disenchantment is thus a distinctly modern predicament. A concentration of distinctive negative forces, moreover, emerges from the extreme violence of the twentieth century, including the threat of nuclear annihilation and the effects of those forms of anomie, isolation, uniformity, and massification that mark modern capitalist and communist societies. The most striking example of such anomie is represented in the novel by modern population control through housing, as revealed in the yellow notebook in an interesting conversation between Ella and Paul (to which I will return).

An interesting question begins to take shape within the recognition that wholeness and unity are no longer possible: Are there actually positive potentials that issue from fragmentation and disunity, particularly psychological fragmentation? Protection from extreme forms of psychic disintegration is surely desirable, the text makes clear, and in fact much of what is moving about the relationship between Saul and Anna has to do with the support they provide one another in the face of the severe challenges to psychic stability they each face in their different ways. Yet at the same time, experimentation with selfhood is valorized at certain points, as is a certain plasticity or even fracturing of personality. The most significant of such moments occurs in a conversation between Anna and the Jungian psychoanalyst Mrs. Marks, when Anna says:

> "If I'd said, Yesterday I met a man at a party and suddenly he said something, and I thought: *Yes*, there's a hint of something—there's a crack in that man's personality like a gap in a dam, and through that gap the future might pour in a different shape—terrible perhaps, or marvelous, but something new—if I said that, you'd frown." (453; emphasis in the original)

And of course the form of the text could be said implicitly to endorse experimentation and multiplicity. Even in the sphere of politics, where internal divisions and reactive self-definition are repeatedly shown to afflict party dynamics, there is a fleeting suggestion that a new "fluid" and "experimental" form of protest politics—represented in the blue notebook by Tommy and the new socialists—might be enabling or worth welcoming (489).

The text's approach to formal and aesthetic questions shares in the divided appraisal of fragmentation and disunity evident elsewhere in the novel, and any satisfactory account of the novel's dual ending must take into account the text's full range of aesthetic values. As I have already indicated, very early on Anna expresses her admiration for humanist realism. It is no accident that this endorsement occurs in the black notebook, which records an early political commitment to communism within a complex historical and cultural field comprising a range of national, racial, gendered, and class divisions. (All indications are that the setting is Rhodesia.)[25] Notably, additional aesthetic values are given concrete expression in this section of the book, including the importance of personality as a privileged object of artistic capture and the need for updated literary themes in order to render moral realism relevant to contemporary concerns.

The focus on personality is presented as a replacement for the leftist obsession with the "question of morality in art": "All I care about is that I should describe Willi and Maryrose so that a reader can feel their reality" (68). The idea of adapted literary convention materializes in response to the sense of moral demand issuing out of the concrete situation in which George Hounslow, an older member of the group and a "roads man," finds himself (97). He is having an illicit affair with the cook's wife at the Boothby hotel in Mashopi, where the group goes to unwind, and has fathered an unacknowledged biracial child who passes as one of the cook's children. A discussion of this situation among Anna, Willi, and George directly addresses the limits of Marxist ideology and the need for an expanded realism to address the challenges of their time and place. When George reveals that he is troubled by the deprivations his illegitimate child will face while his own legitimate children have the prospect of a university education before them, the following exchange occurs:

> "What is the point?" said Willi. "Your blood? Your sacred sperm, or what?"
>
> Both George and I were shocked. Willi saw it with a tightening of his face, and it remained angry as George said: "No, it's the responsibility. It's the gap between what I believe in and what I do."
>
> Willi shrugged and we were silent. Through the heavy midday hush came the sound of Johnnie's drumming fingers.
>
> George looked at me again, and I rallied myself to fight Willie. Looking back I want to laugh—because I automatically chose to argue in literary terms, just as he automatically answered in political terms. But at the time it didn't seem extraordinary to George either, who sat nodding as I spoke.

"Look," I said. "In the nineteenth century literature was full of this. It was a sort of moral touchstone. Like Resurrection, for instance. But now you just shrug your shoulders and say it doesn't matter?"

"I haven't noticed that I shrugged," said Willi. "But perhaps it is true that the moral dilemma of a society is no longer crystallised by the fact of an illegitimate child?"

"Why not?" I asked.

"Why not?" said George, very fierce. (124)

The retrospective Anna treats the appeal to a literary framework with dismissive laughter, but the terms of the argument are actually at once literary and moral: the moral orientation of nineteenth-century realism is invoked to identify the complexity of the sociological context in which they live now. This is a rich moment, drawing attention to the significance of George's situation, its importance not only to the historical context but also to the novelistic art of the moment. The suggestion is that mixed-race illegitimacy does capture something important about present conditions. It is implied, moreover, that George's relation to his dilemma, his anguished self-consciousness, is morally admirable.[26] This exchange in no way involves a simplistic appeal to moral clarity. It speaks rather to a reimagined moral realism adequate to the time—to the historical moment, to the colonial situation, to the realities of sexuality and desire and divided intentions, to the failure of total moral control or political correctness. It is a moment of moral self-consciousness underwritten by awareness of disunity and pain.

If this scene in the black notebook emphasizes a moral realism adapted for the times, many other aspects of the text stress aesthetic ideas associated with radical forms of perspectivalism, indeterminacy, and the limits of language and narrative. At one point in the red notebook, Anna stresses "the thinning of language against the density of our experience" (288); in a transition between the yellow and blue notebooks, she states that "literature is analysis after the event" (216). Both of these moments seem to suggest that language and conventional forms remain inadequate to experience as it is lived, and the experiment in which Anna seeks to record a single day also seems to run aground in its attempt to capture experience in its immediacy, oriented as it is toward the expectation of a lover's arrival that doesn't occur. But if these elements of the text privilege existence over its representation, there are other ways representation shapes and limits experience; for example, it becomes clear that not only do stories impose the laws of dissolution onto the relationships they describe, they also begin to work into one's consciousness of ongoing experience, as in the case of the many ideas for stories in the yellow notebook that seem to shape the "real" experience of Anna and Saul in the blue notebook. And of course in a larger and more consequential revelation, we find that what we thought was a realist rendering of events is a novel written by Anna.

Arguably, then, the shaping question of the novel concerns how we are to think about the problem of unity and fragmentation in relation to the problem of form. The novel seems, on the one hand, to employ a realism meant to accommodate the complexities of historical, sociological, and psychological fragmentation, as well as experiential relations to representation and language themselves. On the other hand, it includes elements of indeterminacy that constitute forms of outright ontological incommensurability (as in the gap between the "frame" novel and the notebooks, or the multiple versions of Anna and others who appear under the same names across different representational worlds). There have been a number of critical approaches to this problem. My reading of the novel will be allied with those interpretations that see the entire novelistic project, despite its complex experimentalism, in terms of a humanist-existential struggle, one that ultimately seeks to assert meaningfulness under conditions of fragmentation, inevitable failure, and bleakness. By this account, Anna works toward affirmation by traveling through breakdown and fragmentation, and the journey is as much a psychic as an artistic one. Such an approach takes the modernist and metafictional elements seriously, but it sees them as ultimately in the service of an aspirational struggle that is clear about its difficulties, moves through extreme states, and courts breakdown in order to acknowledge modern conditions and thereby build something new. The culminating complexities of this struggle are seen as housed in the golden notebook and in Anna's relationship with Saul, and the achievement that ensues is represented by the fact that both Anna and Saul are able to write in the wake of their tortured but ultimately mutually supportive relationship. Indeed, that Saul gives Anna the first words of *Free Women* is read by some as indicating that not only does Anna write *Free Women*, but she is the creator/editor of *The Golden Notebook* itself.[27]

It is worth noting that those who do address the dual ending tend to belittle *Free Women* and elevate the golden and blue notebooks. Gayle Green, who sides with those who view Anna as the author of the whole, states, "If *Free Women* is all Anna writes as a result of her breakthrough, it hardly seems worth the effort."[28] Beth Boehm argues that the revelation that *Free Women* is Anna's novel, and the dramatic discrepancy between her fate in that novel and the future provided by Saul's gesture at the end of the golden notebook reveals that "the conventional novel reduces experience to cliché, that literature as 'analysis after the event,' is false."[29]

By contrast, I propose a reading that holds the two endings in suspended balance, treating them as part of a live tension.[30] Two elements within the novel are particularly relevant to this reading: the emphasis on personality and attitude (and the moral and aesthetic value they are perceived to hold) and the turn, at the end of *Free Women*, to practical and institutional responses to current needs. Part of the dismissal of *Free Women* results from the view that it diminishes forms of experience represented in the blue and golden notebooks, transforming the psychologically turbulent Saul into the rather thinly drawn character of Milt and rendering the tensions in the sexual relationship, and the psychic distress of the characters, far less potent. This dilution of experiential intensity is seen as continuous with the bland progressivism of Anna's choice to be a marriage counselor and to join the Labour Party rather than to write. A certain relief at being able to dismiss the ending of *Free Women*, that is, seems to carry over into relief at being able to dismiss the resigned political attitude represented by Anna's practical choices and to redirect attention toward the existentially inspiring forms of disenchantment and anticonventionality that mark the attitudes of Saul and Anna in the blue and golden notebooks.

However, Anna's choices at the end of *Free Women* comport with a line of argument we see elsewhere in the novel, most prominently in the advocacy of "boulder pushing" by the character Paul in the yellow notebook, a position then echoed and refined by a composite figure, at once Paul and Michael, in Anna's dream in the golden notebook.[31] "You and I are the boulder-pushers," Paul says to Anna. "All our lives, you and I, we'll put all our energies, all our talents, into pushing a great boulder up a mountain. The boulder is the truth that the great men know by instinct, and the mountain is the stupidity of mankind" (199). The truths known by the "great men" pertain to enlightened progressive reform—that solitary confinement makes people worse, that ruling the poor through fear and oppression degrades the humanity of all, that violence begets violence (199). Boulder pushing involves striving to make things better with the awareness that it will produce only minimal gains at best and is an endless task. The view is recognizably liberal rather than radical, but it is distinctly bleak in tenor, reflecting a commitment to struggle amid diminished expectations.[32] How do we assess this line of argument, in light of the text's strong investment in radicalism? And how does its presence in the novel affect our understanding of the dual ending?

A fictional character in the yellow notebook, Paul is the lover of Ella, the central character in the notebook/novel, a woman who works on an advice column for a magazine and is herself writing a novel. She shares similarities with Anna and is in fact avowed by Anna as a fictional version of herself. The reference to "boulder pushing" emerges out of a series of conversations between Ella and Paul, conversations that foreground Ella's dark views of contemporary life and Paul's tempered acknowledgment of some forms of progress. In a drive through the English suburbs, Ella remarks on the ugliness and monotony of their surroundings, while Paul emphasizes advances that have been made in employment and overall welfare. Ella responds: "I can't understand how anyone can see what's happening to this country and not hate it. On the surface everything's fine — all quiet and tame and suburban. But underneath it's poisonous. It's full of hatred and envy and people being lonely" (179). This claim is subtended by what Ella characterizes as a "personal vision" that appeared when she was in the hospital with tuberculosis, "a vision of some dark, impersonal destructive force that worked at the roots of life and that expressed itself in war and cruelty and violence" (179). Ella's outlook in the conversation thus comprehends recalcitrant facts of nature (and human nature) as well as the dehumanizing aspects of contemporary forms of life. Against such a vision, all talk of social policy and social progress appears fundamentally irrelevant and blinkered. This exchange with Paul resonates with Anna's discussion of her writer's block with Mrs. Marks ("Why can't you understand that . . . I can't pick up a newspaper without what's in it seeming so overwhelmingly terrible that nothing I could write would seem to have any point at all?" [240]), as well as with a number of passages throughout the various sections of *The Golden Notebook* that emphasize destructiveness and violence, epitomized in the darkly vivid "joy in spite" figure who recurs in Anna's dreams (457).

One might assume that Ella, through whom the narrative is focalized, carries more authority in the conversation and that Paul is expressing a naive position relative to the searing insights of the novel. But there are crucial elements in the presentation of Paul that signal his function as an exemplar in political attitude. His character significantly inflects the treatment of political life in the novel given its movement from a disenchanted communism to the socialist tradition of the Labour Party as well as the primacy of institutional reform and individual betterment. It is not possible to fully disentangle the novel's investments in socialist principles and in liberal ones, but it is certain that to the extent that the values and aims of a failed communist effort live on within the political aspirations of the exemplary characters, they are filtered through recognizable liberal orientations — chastened expectations, steady aspirations, therapeutic responses, and a focus on temperament (or attitude) itself. And as I will show, through the character of Paul we are prompted to consider the value of a reflective liberal response to the challenges of the era.

Attitude is actually one of the most important elements of the lifeworld of *The Golden Notebook*: cynicism and bitterness are ubiquitous, and they issue from political disenchantment as well as more general acknowledgment of conditions of power and tendencies toward destructiveness, dissolution, and antagonism in all forms of relation, from the sexual couple to the political group and beyond. The number of statements in the novel that are accompanied by a "laugh" is remarkable, and they are rarely moments of high-spirited affirmation, to put it mildly.[33] But even as disappointment and irony seem to express a prevalent mood in and of the novel, at the same time the reader encounters an ongoing critique of cynicism and bitterness as distinctly negative qualities, as lamentable consequences of disappointed idealism or experiences of personal frustration in the face of existing power dynamics. For these reasons, the representation of Paul, a medical doctor from a working-class background, is noteworthy. At one point he describes the exclusionary effects of class-based communications at his workplace, his inability to understand and respond to his upper-class colleagues' ritualized speech interactions. When Anna asks whether he is the only working-class doctor in the hospital, he clarifies that he is the only one in his particular section and that "they never let you forget it" and are "not even conscious of doing it" (178). We then read: "This was good-humoured, humourous. It was also bitter. But the bitterness was from old habit, and had no sting in it" (178). Similarly, Ella is drawn to the "tones" of Paul's voice, which include "delicacy, irony, and compassion" (177). At another point Paul is distinguished for his dual stance, the complete "change of his whole personality" when he switches from his "critical stories" about the medical establishment (marked by "a delighted malicious irony") to discussing his actual patients (which he does with "an extraordinary delicacy of kindness, and with an angry compassion" [188]). This capacity for complex tonal harmonics marks an achievement at once critical and characterological: it stands out in a text where bitterness and irony typically seem calcified rather than, as we see here, supple and blended with leavening affects. It is also worth noting that this is a conception of achieved personality, or personality actively layered by experience, rather than the aesthetics of personality based on gesture or image, as we see in the black notebook, or the more vanguard conception of the future as a new shape pouring in through a crack in one's personality (453).

Paul thus functions as a characterological exemplar in political terms, even as he increasingly comes across negatively as the relationship progresses (or devolves). This reading rests in part on the constellation of moments within the text that develop and endorse the political attitude he holds, including the later dream sequence when he is absorbed into a composite figure and a related description of the political leader Mr. Mathlong. Note that for many critics the intensity of the gender divide between the men and women characters—and the sense of doom attending romantic attachment—would dwarf into near irrelevance the progressive or aspirational force of the political dimension I am tracing. But one could argue that the emphasis on sexuality and gender in the history of the novel's reception has occluded the significance of the text as a response to the specific political conditions of the postwar period. Paul's character is certainly functioning in the context of that particular thematic.[34]

Just as Paul is a fictional character within a novel Anna is writing, Mr. Mathlong never appears directly in the book: we learn of him as a friend of Anna's from conversations in *Free Women*. This seems to underscore the possibility that these figures are imagined characterological ideals. A black African imprisoned for his role in national liberation struggles, Mr. Mathlong is described by Anna as a political "saint" by virtue of his dedication, his integrity, his courteousness, and his capacity for detachment (493). He is contrasted with another political figure who is seen as deficient: Charlie Themba, the bombastic union leader. A key summation of Mr. Mathlong's value occurs during Anna's meditative state akin to film viewing, which comes during the period with Saul and is recorded in the blue notebook. Anna first observes that Mr. Mathlong has not appeared before her in the long procession of people she has known. Then she aspires to be him, to merge with him. "He was the man who performed actions, played roles, that he believed to be necessary for the good of others, even while he preserved an ironic doubt about the results of his actions. It seemed to me that this particular kind of detachment was something we needed very badly in this time, but that very few people had it, and it was certainly a long way from me" (570). The double stance represented by both Paul and Mr. Mathlong, along with Anna's desire to achieve Mr. Mathlong's combination of practical action and ironic skepticism, signals an aspirational ideal that seems to answer to the conditions of political disenchantment.

The more bitter and cynical responses to political disenchantment within the novel carry a different charge, expressing a failure of imagination and moral strength, but also the depth of the original investment in a transformed world. Paul and Mr. Mathlong, by contrast, model a combination of aspiration and detachment, compassion and critique. They can successfully access critical knowingness without letting it corrode the personality, and in this way they can come to terms with the ways larger forces—systemic, natural, psychological—condition and even dictate the commitment to boulder pushing, or piecemeal reform. It is a liberal temperament adapted to the times, reflective not of tolerance or impartiality, but rather of the capacity to act in the face of long odds and in the name of incremental gains. Unlike the aesthetic of personality as "that unique flame," counterposed in the black notebook to the moral strictures of political art, this form of personality not only refuses the constrained terms of debate over communism and literature, it proposes a temperament refined through its engaged participation in those debates as well as the chastened experience of ongoing crisis (69).

The Golden Notebook emphasizes a progressive politics committed to the tenets of socialism and the welfare state as well as to many of the ideals of progressive liberal reform. But the text belongs unmistakably to the tradition of bleak liberalism I have been tracking throughout this book precisely in its elevation of individual attitude or temperament, both as a political ideal and as an aesthetic topos. In this text, Lessing is certainly interested in the historical reality and role of broader collective movements, as the extensive treatment of the communist experience shows. And there is a crucial discussion of collective revolutionary movements, one we might pair with the boulder-pushing motif, in the conversation between Tommy and Anna, on the night leading up to his suicide attempt in *Free Women*. In answer to a pressing question from Tommy demanding she explain her philosophy, Anna states:

> "Every so often, perhaps once in a century, there's a sort of—act of faith. A well of faith fills up, and there's an enormous heave forward in one country or another, and that's a forward movement for the whole world. Because it's an act of imagination—of what is possible for the whole world. In our century it was 1917 in Russia. And in China. Then the well runs dry, because . . . the cruelty and the ugliness are too strong. Then the well slowly fills again. And then there's another painful lurch forward." (263)

In some ways this description parallels the dynamic described in the boulder-pushing passages, though it applies the dynamic to radical rather than liberal actions, thereby recruiting them to a longer perspective on struggle under bleak conditions. But beyond this interest in historical transformation is a specific and persistent emphasis on political attitude.

The larger significance of the dual stance exemplified by Paul and Mr. Mathlong is underscored by its being formally mirrored by the novel itself, with the "frame" novel and its close representing an achieved set of political commitments, subtended by the hovering awareness—which animates the ending of the notebooks proper—of writerly vocation achieved in and through experiences of disintegration, violence, annihilation, joy-in-spite. It doesn't make sense to belittle or dismiss the ending of the "frame" novel, elevating the more romantic struggles of the blue and golden notebooks, since precisely what those struggles yield is the art of *Free Women*. Saying that in one ending Anna is an artist and in another she dedicates herself to institutional reform fails to come to terms with the fact that through her novel Anna the artist affirms a commitment to progressive reform informed by noncorrosive ironic detachment.

In its focus on emotional needs and practical institutions, moreover, the ending of *Free Women* speaks to the most existentially intense and politically consequential struggles of the notebooks. Anna reveals her intention to become a marriage counselor in Dr. North's clinic and also to teach delinquent kids. The first of these forms of social work is fundamentally therapeutic: it involves recognizing a need to provide care in the face of suffering and implicitly acknowledging the difficulty of making peace with society. We are witnessing not simply political work in the name of reform, but participation in a medico-institutional complex that aims to salve suffering. In this sense the ending of *Free Women* is very bleak indeed, as it recognizes the power of those forces that perpetuate suffering. Teaching delinquent kids is perhaps more aspirational, linked as it is to education's potential to generate options, while joining the Labour Party involves a belief in the meaningfulness of political participation of the most basic sort. But in this constellation of efforts, and with the inclusion of the therapeutic dimension, Lessing implicitly insists that political response ideally involves attending to entrenched forms of psychic suffering as well as other modes of practical political engagement.

What's important about the ending of *Free Women* is thus the way Anna's choices signal a broader conception of need than one finds in socialism. This is in fact a defining feature of Lessing's contribution to postwar political literature, and it dovetails with her treatment of the sexual and romantic relationships in the novel. What helps both Anna and Saul work through fragmentation and psychic extremity to the possibility of creative reengagement with the world is their support of one another, however laced with aggression, withdrawal, and mistrust that support can be at times. Through their relationship, a claim is being made for friendship as a crucial stay against disintegration, one linked to the possibility of forms of detachment or reflexivity that can be alleviated by talk, laughter, and acknowledgment, as they are in many of the exchanges between the two. This mode of relating, crucial in the Anna-Saul friendship, is distilled into more stable form in the *Free Women* rendition of the Anna-Milt relationship. The novel lays particular stress on the unflinching working through of psychic and emotional needs, and it holds up a friendship made possible only in the wake of romantic disenchantment. This movement parallels the resolution of the political disenchantment, in which we see a movement from radicalism to reform.

Ultimately, *The Golden Notebook* can be seen to enact a bleak liberalism characterized by a version of the dual stance that marked *Bleak House* over a century earlier and that has been evident across a number of texts, examined in this book, that have tried to navigate the poles of critique and aspiration. Interestingly, just as suspicion is seen to corrode character in Dickens, cynicism or bitterness corrodes character in Lessing. The novels are responding to different social and historical contexts, but they belong within a longer genealogy of literary responses to some of the most intractable challenges of modern social and political life. In both cases the novels use formal experimentation with realism to insist on a productively unresolved tension between forms of critical detachment and lived commitments to ethico-political ideals. It has been my ongoing argument that such formal expression of this characteristically liberal tension is various and complex, in ways that previous literary history has failed to appreciate. This book has sought to begin the task of analyzing the liberal aesthetic as it took shape in nineteenth-century realism, in the subgenre of the political novel throughout the nineteenth and twentieth centuries, then finally in the literature informed by the rise of modernism and the debates over politics and aesthetics among the progressive thinkers and writers of the twentieth century.

Notes

INTRODUCTION

1. Alan Brinkley, "Liberalism and Belief," in *Liberalism for a New Century*, ed. Neil Jumonville and Kevin Mattson (Berkeley: University of California Press, 2007), 75–89.

2. The phrases listed here are in some cases associated with specific thinkers: "liberal vices" (Shklar); "value pluralism" (Berlin); "the tragedy of history" (Niebuhr).

3. John Stuart Mill, *On Liberty*, in *Mill: "The Spirit of the Age," "On Liberty," "The Subjection of Women,"* ed. Alan Ryan (New York: Norton, 1997).

4. John Wyon Burrow, *Whigs and Liberals: Continuity and Change in English Political Thought* (Oxford: Clarendon Press, 1988). Subsequent page references will be given parenthetically in the text.

5. Giorgio Agamben, *Homo Sacer: Sovereign Power and Bare Life*, trans. Daniel Heller-Roazen (Stanford, CA: Stanford University Press, 1998), 121.

6. Timothy Brennan, *Wars of Position: The Cultural Politics of Left and Right* (New York: Columbia University Press, 2006); John Brenkman, *The Cultural Contradictions of Democracy: Political Thought Since September 11* (Princeton, NJ: Princeton University Press, 2007).

7. Dominick LaCapra, *History in Transit: Experience, Identity, Critical Theory* (Ithaca, NY: Cornell University Press, 2004).

8. Sean McCann and Michael Szalay, "Do You Believe in Magic? Literary Thinking after the New Left," *Yale Journal of Criticism* 18, no. 2 (2005): 435–68.

9. Franz Kafka, *The Trial*, trans. Breon Mitchell (New York: Schocken Books, 1998), 217.

10. Jacques Derrida, "Before the Law," in *Acts of Literature*, ed. Derek Attridge (New York: Routledge, 1992), 208.

11. Jacques Derrida, "Force of Law: The 'Mystical Foundation of Authority,'" in *Deconstruction and the Possibility of Justice*, ed. Drucilla Cornell, Michel Rosenfeld, and David Gray Carlson (New York: Routledge, 1992), 3–67.

12. Agamben, *Homo Sacer*, 57. Subsequent page references will be given parenthetically in the text.

13. Derrida, who discusses the role of the fable within *The Trial*, essentially sees the priest as reprising the role of the doorkeeper. In this reading *The Trial* simply reinforces the effects of the fable rather than significantly situating it within an existential struggle.

14. Lionel Trilling, *The Liberal Imagination: Essays on Literature and Society* (New York: New York Review Books, 2008); Richard Rorty, *Contingency, Irony, Solidarity* (Cambridge: Cambridge

University Press, 1989); and Stefan Collini, "On Variousness; and On Persuasion," *New Left Review* 27 (2004): 65-97.

15. Richard Rorty, "Private Irony and Liberal Hope," in *Contingency, Irony, Solidarity*.

16. Richard Rorty, "Human Rights, Rationality, and Sentimentality," in *On Human Rights: The Oxford Amnesty Lectures 1993*, ed. Susan Hurley and Stephen Shute (New York: Basic Books, 1993), 111-34.

17. Mill, *On Liberty*, 84.

18. Trilling, *Liberal Imagination*, 301. Subsequent page references will be given parenthetically in the text.

19. Harvey M. Teres, *Renewing the Left: Politics, Imagination, and the New York Intellectuals* (New York: Oxford University Press, 1996), 260-61.

20. Trilling, *Liberal Imagination*, xx-xxi.

21. See Martha C. Nussbaum, *Love's Knowledge: Essays on Philosophy and Literature* (New York: Oxford University Press, 1990).

22. John Dewey, "Creative Democracy: The Task before Us," in *John Dewey: The Later Works, 1925-1953*, vol. 14, *1939-1941*, ed. Jo Ann Boydston (Carbondale: Southern Illinois University Press, 1988), 224-30. See also George Kateb, "Aestheticism and Morality: Their Cooperation and Hostility," *Political Theory* 28, no. 1 (2000): 5-37. Kateb has an interesting discussion of "democratic aestheticism," which seems to bridge the aesthetic and the political in a harmonious, productive way, but the ideal is advanced in the context of an acute discussion of the many ways aesthetics can channel negative forms of morality and politics. Kateb's ideal is thus set in relation to an apprehension of the very negative forces I am interested in exploring.

23. Michael Warner, *The Letters of the Republic: Publication and the Public Sphere in Eighteenth-Century America* (Cambridge, MA: Harvard University Press, 1990); Pam Morris, *Imagining Inclusive Society in Nineteenth-Century Novels: The Code of Sincerity in the Public Sphere* (Baltimore: Johns Hopkins University Press, 2004); and John Plotz, *The Crowd: British Literature and Public Politics* (Berkeley: University of California Press, 2000).

24. D. A. Miller, *The Novel and the Police* (Berkeley: University of California Press, 1988); Nancy Armstrong, *Desire and Domestic Fiction: A Political History of the Novel* (New York: Oxford University Press, 1987); Bruce Robbins, *Upward Mobility and the Common Good: Toward a Literary History of the Welfare State* (Princeton, NJ: Princeton University Press, 2007); Lauren M. E. Goodlad, *Victorian Literature and the Victorian State: Character and Governance in a Liberal Society* (Baltimore: Johns Hopkins University Press, 2003); and Michael Szalay, *New Deal Modernism: American Literature and the Invention of the Welfare State* (Durham, NC: Duke University Press, 2000).

25. David Wayne Thomas, *Cultivating Victorians: Liberal Culture and the Aesthetic* (Philadelphia: University of Pennsylvania Press, 2004); Stefan Collini, *Public Moralists: Political Thought and Intellectual Life in Britain, 1850-1930* (Oxford: Clarendon Press, 1991); and Martha C. Nussbaum, *Poetic Justice: The Literary Imagination and Public Life* (Boston: Beacon Press, 1995). Also worthy of mention here is Daniel Malachuk, *Perfection, the State, and Victorian Liberalism* (New York: Palgrave Macmillan, 2005), which interestingly participates in both a renewed defense of individual practices of moral perfectionism and a critique of anti-statism (especially insofar as it fundamentally misunderstands nineteenth-century thinking about the state).

26. Elaine Hadley, *Living Liberalism: Practical Citizenship in Mid-Victorian Britain* (Chicago: University of Chicago Press, 2010).

CHAPTER ONE

1. See Amanda Anderson, *The Way We Argue Now: A Study in the Cultures of Theory* (Princeton, NJ: Princeton University Press, 2006), 136-38.

2. The most probing and comprehensive study of the historical exclusions attending the rise of liberalism, both within bodies of thought and with respect to the historical emergence of modern

democratic states, is Domenico Losurdo's *Liberalism: A Counter-History* (New York: Verso, 2011). Losurdo argues that liberalism and racial slavery must be seen in terms of a "twin birth" and challenges the idea that exclusions can be explained historically.

3. The headnote to Howe's piece is illuminating: "By the 1950s, few of the New York Intellectuals were Marxists any longer; some viewed themselves as democratic socialists or liberal humanists or cosmopolitan intellectuals, while still others in later years grew increasingly conservative on cultural and political issues. The literary criticism of the best of the New York Intellectuals, especially that of Rahv (e.g., the collection *Literature and the Sixth Sense*, 1969) and Trilling (e.g., *The Liberal Imagination*, 1950) remains stimulating. Yet even this work has come to seem dated, for it dramatizes the need that many once felt for a sharp, self-aware integration of literary and political commentary. Now, after the cold war has ended, many younger readers find much of the writing of the New York Intellectuals hard to understand; its fighting tone, edgy rhythms, and political contexts and cultural references are far from their reality." This strangely dismissive commentary is all we hear of a complex debate over form and content, politics and literature, one that significantly affected the fate of liberalism within the literary wing of the academic Left. See Vincent B. Leitch, ed., *The Norton Anthology of Theory and Criticism* (New York: Norton, 2001), 1532. Nothing about this has changed in the second edition of the *Norton Anthology* (2010), which claims to have an entirely updated section on the twentieth century.

4. Michael Kimmage, *The Conservative Turn: Lionel Trilling, Whittaker Chambers, and the Lessons of Anti-Communism* (Cambridge, MA: Harvard University Press, 2009).

5. Alan M. Wald, *The New York Intellectuals: The Rise and Decline of the Anti-Stalinist Left from the 1930s to the 1980s* (Chapel Hill: University of North Carolina Press, 1987), 352. Wald's book laments the abandonment and therefore missed actualization of the most promising force to emerge during this era: a revolutionary anti-Stalinism.

6. For example, in the afterword to the 1988 edition of *The End of Ideology*, Daniel Bell criticizes the movements of the sixties for being moralistic rather than substantively political, and for being cultural rather than economic and political in emphasis. Trilling resisted the energies behind the 1968 uprising at Columbia and was denounced for it. Isaiah Berlin wrote equivocally on Vietnam and was attacked by Perry Anderson in the *New Left Review* for liberal complacency. See Daniel Bell, *The End of Ideology: On the Exhaustion of Political Ideas in the Fifties* (Cambridge, MA: Harvard University Press, 2000), 409-47; Kimmage, *Conservative Turn*, 312; Michael Ignatieff, *Isaiah Berlin: A Life* (London: Vintage, 2000), 234, 244-58.

7. Arthur M. Schlesinger Jr., *The Vital Center: The Politics of Freedom* (New Brunswick, NJ: Transaction, 1998), 169; Bell, *End of Ideology*, 300.

8. See especially Michel Foucault, "The Ethic of Care for the Self as a Practice of Freedom: An Interview with Michel Foucault on January 20, 1984," by Raúl Fornet-Betancourt, Helmut Becker, and Alfredo Gomez-Müller, trans. J. D. Gauthier S.J., in *The Final Foucault*, ed. James Bernauer and David Rasmussen (Cambridge, MA: MIT Press, 1988).

9. See John Brenkman, *The Cultural Contradictions of Democracy: Political Thought Since September 11* (Princeton, NJ: Princeton University Press, 2007); Timothy Brennan, *Wars of Position: The Cultural Politics of Left and Right* (New York: Columbia University Press, 2006); and Dominick LaCapra, *History in Transit: Experience, Identity, Critical Theory* (Ithaca, NY: Cornell University Press, 2004).

10. Schlesinger, *Vital Center*, xx-xxi.

11. Granville Hicks, "On Attitudes and Ideas," *Partisan Review* 14, no. 2 (1947): 124.

12. See Kimmage, "Toward an Anti-Communism of the Left and an Anti-Communism of the Right," in *Conservative Turn*, 140-72.

13. Raymond Aron, *The Opium of the Intellectuals* (New Brunswick, NJ: Transaction, 2001), xx. When Aron uses the term American liberalism he is referring to a spectrum of liberalism that includes social democrats and communists—this was a common usage at the time, one Trilling also employed.

14. Isaiah Berlin, "Two Concepts of Liberty," in *Liberty: Incorporating Four Essays on Liberty*, ed. Henry Hardy (Oxford: Oxford University Press, 2002), 198.

15. Schlesinger, *Vital Center*, 245-46.

16. Richard Rorty, "Private Irony and Liberal Hope," in *Contingency, Irony, and Solidarity* (Cambridge: Cambridge University Press, 1989), 73-95.

17. Quoted in Richard Fox, *Reinhold Niebuhr: A Biography* (New York: Pantheon Books, 1985), 220.

18. Sidney Hook, "The New Failure of Nerve," *Partisan Review* 10, no. 1 (1943): 2-23, and "The Failure of the Left," *Partisan Review* 10, no. 2 (1943): 165-77.

19. Hook failed to acknowledge in his attack that many of the bleak liberals entirely endorsed the power of science and instrumental action in the field of piecemeal reform. Acknowledging the limits of rationalism and the dangers of overvaluing reason did not translate into a wholesale rejection of its uses within practically defined contexts. For a discussion of this failure of acknowledgment in Hook's understanding of Niebuhr, see Fox, *Reinhold Niebuhr*, 216-17.

20. Hook, "Failure of the Left," 169.

21. Lionel Trilling, *The Liberal Imagination: Essays on Literature and Society* (New York: New York Review Books, 2008), 87. Subsequent page references will be given parenthetically in the text.

22. Lionel Trilling, "Elements That Are Wanted," *Partisan Review* 7, no. 5 (1940): 376-77.

23. Ronald Aronson, *Camus and Sartre: The Story of a Friendship and the Quarrel That Ended It* (Chicago: University of Chicago Press, 2004).

24. Albert Camus, *The Rebel: An Essay on Man in Revolt*, trans. Anthony Bower (New York: Vintage, 1991), 11. Subsequent page references will be given parenthetically in the text.

25. Wald, *New York Intellectuals*, 217-18.

26. For an interesting discussion of later formations of liberalism fundamentally conditioned by the aftermath of World War II, see Tony Judt's discussion of the distinctive contributions of Eastern European liberals of the seventies and beyond. Judt discusses figures such as Adam Michnik, Václav Havel, Leszek Kołakowski, and Czesław Miłosz, showing how they could be seen to extend the project of earlier cold war liberals and emphasizing distinctive aesthetic and philosophical features of their political thought. Judt has been a major voice writing on behalf of a more balanced, less accusatory understanding of the cold war liberals. For an overview, see Tony Judt (with Timothy Snyder), *Thinking the Twentieth Century* (New York: Penguin, 2012), 195-283.

27. John Stuart Mill, *On Liberty* in *Mill: "Spirit of the Age," "On Liberty," "The Subjection of Women,"* ed. Alan Ryan (New York: Norton, 1997), 114.

28. John Stuart Mill, *The Subjection of Women* in *"Spirit of the Age," "On Liberty," and "The Subjection of Women,"* 139.

29. Mill, *On Liberty*, 45, 44. Subsequent page references will be given parenthetically in the text.

30. Mill, *Subjection of Women*, 141.

31. See Stefan Collini, "New Liberal Theorist," in *Liberalism and Sociology: L. T. Hobhouse and Political Argument in England, 1880-1914* (Cambridge: Cambridge University Press, 1979), 121-46. Collini discusses the relation between Hobhouse and Green and situates Hobhouse's work within the broader tradition of liberal thought and emerging sociology.

32. L. T. Hobhouse, *Hobhouse: Liberalism and Other Writings*, ed. James Meadowcroft (Cambridge: Cambridge University Press, 1994), 8. Subsequent page references will be given parenthetically in the text.

33. As Collini notes in the epilogue of *Liberalism and Sociology*, Hobhouse elevated the art of nineteenth-century realism, and George Eliot in particular, while lamenting what he saw as the moral deficiency of modernism, with its investment in will, instinct, and impulse. This attitude, it should be noted, emerged as part of his wartime pessimism. Hobhouse's hopes for political progress were seriously undercut by the experience of World War I (see 245-53).

34. Michel Foucault, *The Birth of Biopolitics: Lectures at the Collège de France, 1978-79*, ed.

Michel Senellart, trans. Graham Burchell (London: Palgrave Macmillan, 2008), 13, 15-16. Subsequent page references will be given parenthetically in the text.

35. Michael C. Behrent, "Liberalism without Humanism: Michel Foucault and the Free Market Creed, 1976-1979," *Modern Intellectual History* 6, no. 3 (2009): 539-68; Daniel Zamora, "Can We Criticize Foucault?," *Jacobin*, December 10, 2014, accessed January 25, 2015, https://www.jacobinmag.com/2014/12/foucault-interview.

36. See especially Wendy Brown, "Neoliberalism and the End of Liberal Democracy," in *Edgework: Critical Essays on Knowledge and Politics* (Princeton, NJ: Princeton University Press, 2005), 37-59. Since this first discussion of Foucault's lectures, Brown has published a major study of neoliberalism that moves well beyond Foucault's analysis. See Brown, *Undoing the Demos: Neoliberalism's Stealth Revolution* (Cambridge, MA: MIT Press, 2015).

37. Brown, "Neoliberalism and the End of Liberal Democracy," 49.

38. David Harvey, *A Brief History of Neoliberalism* (Oxford: Oxford University Press, 2007), 116. Subsequent page references will be given parenthetically in the text.

39. William E. Connolly, *The Fragility of Things: Self-Organizing Processes, Neoliberal Fantasies, and Democratic Activism* (Durham, NC: Duke University Press, 2013), 68-69.

40. Brown, "Neoliberalism and the End of Liberal Democracy," 57.

41. Harvey, *Brief History of Neoliberalism*, 11. Note that Harvey cites a number of authors who use this term. Subsequent page references will be given parenthetically in the text.

42. Brown, "Neoliberalism and the End of Liberal Democracy," 43.

43. Harvey, *Brief History of Neoliberalism*, 167-68.

CHAPTER TWO

1. Ian Watt, *The Rise of the Novel: Studies in Defoe, Richardson, and Fielding* (Berkeley: University of California Press, 1957); Georg Lukács, *The Theory of the Novel*, trans. Anna Bostock (Cambridge, MA: MIT Press, 1971); Raymond Williams, *The English Novel: From Dickens to Lawrence* (London: Chatto and Windus, 1970); and Nancy Armstrong, *Desire and Domestic Fiction: A Political History of the Novel* (New York: Oxford University Press, 1987).

2. Robert Pippin, *Modernism as a Philosophical Problem: On the Dissatisfactions of European High Culture*, 2nd ed. (Oxford: Blackwell, 1999).

3. D. A. Miller, *The Novel and the Police* (Berkeley: University of California Press, 1988).

4. Lionel Trilling, *Sincerity and Authenticity* (Cambridge, MA: Harvard University Press, 1971).

5. Instances of this form of criticism include certain Marxist accounts, Marxist-inflected poststructuralist accounts, and Foucauldian accounts. See Terry Eagleton, *Criticism and Ideology: A Study in Marxist Literary Theory* (London: New Left Books, 1976); Rosalind Coward and John Ellis, *Language and Materialism: Developments in Semiology and the Theory of the Subject* (London: Routledge and Kegan Paul, 1977); and Miller, *Novel and the Police*. Harry Shaw provides a fine analysis of these accounts, noting that they in turn provoked a number of important critiques and supplements, including George Levine's *Realistic Imagination*, David Lodge's *After Bakhtin*, and Roland Barthes's *S/Z*, which gives to realism, as did others, a self-undermining dynamic. My interest is in the afterlife of the ideological critique of realism, and in particular the beleaguered position in which it has placed the concept and theory of liberalism. See Harry E. Shaw, *Narrating Reality* (Ithaca, NY: Cornell University Press, 1999), 1-37.

6. Charles Dickens, *Bleak House* (New York: Penguin, 1996), 29. Subsequent page references will be given parenthetically in the text.

7. Eagleton, *Criticism and Ideology*, 129-30; Raymond Williams, *The Country and the City* (New York: Oxford University Press, 1973), 156. Also see Bruce Robbins, "Telescopic Philanthropy: Professionalism and Responsibility in *Bleak House*," in *Nation and Narration*, ed. Homi K. Bhabha (New York: Routledge, 1990), 213-39.

8. Amanda Claybaugh, *The Novel of Purpose: Literature and Social Reform in the Anglo-American World* (Ithaca, NY: Cornell University Press, 2007), 52-84.

9. Walter Bagehot, "Charles Dickens," in *Literary Studies* (London: J. M. Dent, 1932), 2: 189, 191.

10. George Orwell, "Charles Dickens," in *A Collection of Essays* (New York: Harvest, 1981), 86, 51.

11. Lauren M. E. Goodlad, *Victorian Literature and the Victorian State: Character and Governance in a Liberal Society* (Baltimore: Johns Hopkins University Press, 2003), 91.

12. Bruce Robbins makes a related argument in "Telescopic Philanthropy," claiming that throughout the novel Dickens is disclosing the risks and gains of a systemic or impersonal perspective. However, he reads Woodcourt quite differently, as more in line with a limited professionalism, and sees the novel as animated by ambivalence rather than mediation.

13. Woodcourt also has a near-narratorial ability to read character and physiognomy, as is demonstrated in a conversation with Esther about Richard in which Woodcourt presents a complex description of how Richard has changed: " 'It is not,' said Mr. Woodcourt, 'his being so much younger or older, or thinner or fatter, or paler or ruddier, as there being upon his face such a singular expression. I never saw so remarkable a look in a young person. One cannot say that it is all anxiety or all weariness; yet it is both, and like ungrown despair' " (707).

14. I am indebted in this reading of Woodcourt's position in Yorkshire to an unpublished seminar paper by Maggie Vintner, titled "Great Effects—Family Patterns in *Bleak House*" (unpublished seminar paper, Johns Hopkins University, 2007). Vintner rightly points out that other readings of the novel, notably Lauren Goodlad's, have mistakenly read the life and work characterizing Woodcourt and Esther's marriage as a domestic and rural retreat.

15. Anthony Trollope, *An Autobiography* (Oxford: Oxford University Press, 1998), 166. Despite the reference to mode ("humour," "pathos") as well as plot, it is clear from remarks elsewhere in the *Autobiography* that for Trollope plot is the key point of contrast to character. See especially 232-33. Subsequent page references will be given parenthetically in the text.

16. Trilling, *Sincerity and Authenticity*.

17. I recognize that *sincerity* and *honesty* are terms used with different emphases in Trollope. In the most general terms, *honesty* is characterological, while *sincerity* is a feature of communicative interactions (it is thus always social). However, both terms are pertinent to an analysis of Trollope in light of Trilling's schema, precisely because the forms of moral integrity that mark Trilling's ideal of sincerity would be captured by Trollope's concept of honesty.

18. In *Sincerity and Authenticity* Trilling generally portrays the Victorian novelists as stalled within a distinctly unglamorous sincerity topos, one that gives way to a kind of liberating reversal in the modern tradition, whereby art becomes antinormative rather than normative. Associated with duty, earnestness, work, and seriousness, writers such as Matthew Arnold, Charles Dickens, and George Eliot might understand various threats to the forms of belief and social custom that make up the sincerity paradigm, but they defend the ideal nonetheless: "The best of the novelists of the nineteenth century and of the beginning of our own epoch were anything but confident that the old vision of the noble life could be realized. But in the degree to which Balzac, Stendhal, Dickens, Trollope, Flaubert, and Henry James were aware of the probability of its defeat in actuality, they cherished and celebrated the lovely dream" (40).

19. See Trollope, *Autobiography*, 39-40. For key passages in the novels, see Trollope, *The Eustace Diamonds* (New York: Penguin, 1986), 71-72, 582-83, and Trollope, *The Prime Minister* (New York: Penguin, 1994), 588. Subsequent page references to *An Autobiography* will be given parenthetically in the text.

20. Trollope, *The Way We Live Now* (New York: Penguin, 1994), 204. Subsequent page references will be given parenthetically in the text. Similarly, Lady Carbury, the representative of modern literary puffery, says of Melmotte, "One cannot measure such men by the ordinary rule." Lady Carbury makes claims for the greater good achieved by the belief he inspires (in this case, in the railway venture): "If a thing can be made great and beneficent, a boon to humanity, sim-

ply by creating a belief in it, does not a man become a benefactor to his race by creating that belief?" (231).

21. Mrs. Hurtle eulogizes Melmotte at some length. In response to Paul's comment that she may find her idol has feet of clay, she responds, "Ah,—you mean that he is bold in breaking those precepts of yours about coveting worldly wealth. All men and women break that commandment, but they do so in a stealthy fashion, half drawing back the grasping hand, praying to be delivered from temptation while they filch only a little, pretending to despise the only thing that is dear to them in the world. Here is a man who boldly says that he recognises no such law; that wealth is power, and that power is good, and that the more a man has of wealth the greater and the stronger and the nobler he can be. I love a man who can turn the hobgoblins inside out and burn the wooden bogies that he meets" (204).

22. For an example see John Kucich, *The Power of Lies: Transgression in Victorian Fiction* (Ithaca, NY: Cornell University Press, 1994).

23. For the relevant discussion in the *Autobiography*, see 355: "The book has the fault which is to be attributed to almost all satires, whether in prose or verse. The accusations are exaggerated. The vices implied are coloured so as to make effect rather than to represent truth. Who, when the lash of objurgation is in his hands, can so moderate his arm as never to strike harder than justice would require? The spirit which produces the satire is honest enough, but the very desire which moves the satirist to do his work energetically makes him dishonest." In the case of the earlier revisionist readings, I have in mind Ruth apRoberts's influential reading of Trollope as a situation ethicist or A. O. J. Cockshut's claim that Trollope's vision darkened in his later novels. See Ruth apRoberts, *The Moral Trollope* (Athens: Ohio University Press, 1971), and A. O. J. Cockshut, *Anthony Trollope: A Critical Study* (New York: New York University Press, 1968).

24. Anthony Trollope, *Barchester Towers* (New York: Penguin, 2003), 50–51. Subsequent page references will be given parenthetically in the text.

25. And indeed it is important to note that Melmotte is never explicitly identified as a Jew. Rather, characters in the novel so identify him, which is to say, the larger society does. See Paul Delany, "Land, Money, and the Jews in the Later Trollope," *Studies in English Literature, 1500–1900* 32, no. 4 (1992): 775.

26. It is also significant to this reading of Trollope's emphasis on the counterposing effects of a communicative model of sincerity that his critique of society involves a vivid portrayal of the many ways language can be recruited to the forces of dishonesty. From the opening treatment of various forms of what he in the *Autobiography* calls "literary dishonesty," to the naming of Melmotte (*mal mot*), to the treatment of how damaging to bonds of affection or friendship can be the mere use of an accusatory word, Trollope makes it clear that a high-stakes battle is being waged over the linguistic register. Again, we might read this as evidence of Trollope's prescient linguistic turn, but it has far more to do with his profound investment in a broadly conceived sincerity paradigm, one that ambivalently intimates its own (fragile, regulative) ideal against a potent awareness of all the forces that work to undermine truthful communication.

27. Shirley Robin Letwin, *The Gentleman in Trollope: Individuality and Moral Conduct* (Cambridge, MA: Harvard University Press, 1982).

28. It is interesting, however, that Trollope suggests it would be in Georgiana's best moral interests to bind her character, as it were, to Brehgert. Which is to say, as I stressed before, that the emphasis on critique remains compatible with a valuing of character and does not simply displace it.

29. The significance of certain characters who pragmatically understand the economic dimensions of their own courtship scenarios was brought to my attention by Naomi Fry, "Trollope's *The Way We Live Now* and the Location of the Substantial Real" (unpublished seminar paper, Johns Hopkins University, 2003). Focusing especially on Marie Melmotte and Lord Nidderdale, Fry analyzes the importance of friendships forged through the shared experience, and mutual understanding, of financially driven courtship scenarios. This would be another, albeit more pragmatic, version of the value of lucid critique in Trollope.

30. George Eliot, "Prelude," in *Middlemarch* (New York: Penguin, 2003), 3.

31. Suzanne Graver, *George Eliot and Community: A Study in Social Theory and Fictional Form* (Berkeley: University of California Press, 1984).

32. Amanda Anderson, "Living Theory: Personality and Doctrine in Eliot," in *A Companion to George Eliot*, ed. Amanda Anderson and Harry E. Shaw (Malden, MA: Wiley-Blackwell, 2013), 442–56.

33. For an interesting discussion of this aspect of Eliot's work, see Stefanie Markovits, *The Crisis of Action in Nineteenth-Century English Literature* (Columbus: Ohio State University Press, 2006).

34. George Levine provides a skeptical reading of Will Ladislaw's entry into politics based on this fact. See Levine, *The Realistic Imagination: English Fiction from Frankenstein to Lady Chatterley* (Chicago: University of Chicago Press, 1981), 299.

35. Eliot, *Middlemarch* (New York: Penguin, 2003), 145. Subsequent page references will be given parenthetically in the text.

36. Elaine Hadley points to this scene to argue that *Middlemarch* provides an "unsettled" treatment of the relation between principle and personality and places it next to the more radical undermining of the informing principles of a liberalizing democratic politics in the scene of Mr. Brooke on the hustings, where rational debate and self-reflexivity are mocked and rendered dysfunctional. See Elaine Hadley, *Living Liberalism: Practical Citizenship in Mid-Victorian Britain* (Chicago: University of Chicago Press, 2010), 300–305. I argue instead that the story of Will's dedication to liberal politics presents a different conception of action and commitment than we find in the ethically focused narratives.

37. Henry Staten, "Is *Middlemarch* Ahistorical?," *PMLA* 115, no. 5 (2000): 991–1005.

38. D. A. Miller, *Narrative and Its Discontents: Problems of Closure in the Traditional Novel* (Princeton, NJ: Princeton University Press, 1981), 130, 153. Subsequent page references will be given parenthetically in the text.

39. I would argue that Eliot's idealism is aware of limits. It is aspirational and chastened at the same time. It reflects a kind of acceptance and wisdom and undimmed energy.

40. Eliot, *Middlemarch*, 836. Subsequent page references will be given parenthetically in the text.

41. Deronda's sense of his own mission does include liberal-democratic elements, such as reflective endorsement and deliberative debate, but Will's is more trained on the ongoing liberal democratic process of eliminating exclusion, wrong, and injury. For a discussion of Daniel Deronda's politics, see Amanda Anderson, *The Powers of Distance: Cosmopolitanism and the Cultivation of Detachment* (Princeton, NJ: Princeton University Press, 2001), 119–46.

42. Staten, "Is *Middlemarch* Ahistorical?"

43. Henry James, "Unsigned review, *Galaxy*, March 1873," in *George Eliot: The Critical Heritage*, ed. David Carroll (London: Routledge, 1971), 355. In an 1873 review, Sidney Colvin writes, "[Dorothea] marries the man of her choice, and bears him children; but we have been made to feel all along that he is hardly worthy of her." Sidney Colvin, "Review, *Fortnightly Review*, January 1873," in *George Eliot: The Critical Heritage*, ed. Carroll, 337. And A. V. Dicey calls Will "the least satisfactory character in the book." A. V. Dicey, "Unsigned review, *Nation*, January 1873," in *George Eliot: The Critical Heritage*, ed. Carroll, 349. For an interesting assessment of the varying responses to Will from a feminist perspective, see Kathleen Blake, "'Middlemarch': Vocation, Love and the Woman Question," in *Middlemarch*, ed. John Peck, New Casebooks (New York: St. Martin's Press, 1992), 146–47.

44. Others have noted and attempted to account for Will's anomalousness, the way he doesn't quite fit into the value system of the narrative itself. George Levine suggests that insofar as Will is "enmeshed in compromise and the ideal at the same time," he is like his creator and serves as a "novelist *manqué*." Raymond Williams suggests that he indicates Eliot's thinking beyond the terms of the interconnected web she otherwise endorses, introducing a "thread to the future" and a form of freedom and mobility that is at odds with the novel and that explains the many dissatis-

factions with Will's character. See Levine, *Realistic Imagination*, 301, 304, and Williams, *English Novel*, 92-94.

CHAPTER THREE

1. Some sections of the following text, as well as a few paragraphs in my readings of the various novels, are adapted from my essay "Dickens, Charlotte Brontë, Gaskell: Politics and Its Limits," in *The Cambridge History of the English Novel*, ed. Robert L. Caserio and Clement Hawes (Cambridge: Cambridge University Press, 2012).

2. There is a rich and complex body of work one might reference here, but among some of the key texts, influential in their own right and also in the work they have generated, I would include Fredric Jameson, *The Political Unconscious: Narrative as Socially Symbolic Act* (Ithaca, NY: Cornell University Press, 1981); Benedict Anderson, *Imagined Communities: Reflections on the Origin and Spread of Nationalism* (London: Verso, 1983); Nancy Armstrong, *Desire and Domestic Fiction: A Political History of the Novel* (New York: Oxford University Press, 1987); Franco Moretti, *The Way of the World: The "Bildungsroman" in European Culture* (London: Verso, 1987); and D. A. Miller, *The Novel and the Police* (Berkeley: University of California Press, 1988).

3. Jacques Rancière, *The Politics of Literature*, trans. Julie Rose (Cambridge: Polity Press, 2011), 11. Subsequent page references will be given parenthetically in the text.

4. Rancière, it should be added, links this modernist movement to the depth hermeneutics introduced by Marx and Freud.

5. Theodor Adorno, "Commitment," trans. Francis McDonagh, in Adorno et al., *Aesthetics and Politics: The Key Texts of the Classical Debate within German Marxism*, trans. Anya Bostock et al., ed. Ronald Taylor (London: New Left Books, 1977), 188. Subsequent page references will be given parenthetically in the text.

6. While Rancière has some interesting things to say about the dynamic set in play between the narrator (whom he does not distinguish from Flaubert) and the character Emma, his remarks mainly have to do with a scapegoating mechanism that seeks to establish a difference between good and bad approaches to the relation between art and life.

7. Raymond Williams, *Culture and Society: 1780-1850* (New York: Columbia University Press, 1958), 87-109.

8. One sees examples of this particularly in the history of feminist critics and queer theory, though also in the Marxist tradition. For a discussion of the formation within feminism, see Amanda Anderson, "The Temptations of Aggrandized Agency," in *The Way We Argue Now: A Study in the Cultures of Theory* (Princeton, NJ: Princeton University Press, 2006), 46-66.

9. Irving Howe, *Politics and the Novel* (Chicago: Ivan R. Dee, 2002).

10. For key examples of the two approaches specified, see Ruth Bernard Yeazell, "Why Political Novels Have Heroines: *Sybil, Mary Barton*, and *Felix Holt*," *Novel* 18, no. 2 (1985): 126-44, and Catherine Gallagher, "Causality versus Conscience: The Problem of Form in *Mary Barton*," in *The Industrial Reformation of English Fiction: Social Discourse and Narrative Form, 1832-1867* (Chicago: University of Chicago Press, 1985), 62-87.

11. F. R. Leavis, *The Great Tradition: George Eliot, Henry James, Joseph Conrad* (New York: New York University Press, 1964), and David Lodge, *Working with Structuralism: Essays and Reviews on Nineteenth and Twentieth Century Literature* (Boston: Routledge and Kegan Paul, 1981).

12. Charles Dickens, *Hard Times* (New York: Norton, 2001), 21. Subsequent page references will be given parenthetically in the text.

13. Utilitarianism can be designated a "radical" ideology because of its aim to remake identity at the root, manufacturing a new form of human subject who is governed by facts alone and extending its principles to all social and political institutions.

14. Dickens uses the terms distort and maim as well, for example, in an early rhetorical second-person address to M'Choakumchild: "Say, good M'Choakumchild. When from thy boiling store,

thou shalt fill each jar brim full by-and-by, dost thou think that thou wilt always kill outright the robber Fancy lurking within—or sometimes only maim him and distort him!" (10).

15. See Leavis, *Great Tradition*, and Humphrey House, *The Dickens World* (London: Oxford University Press, 1960).

16. Lodge, *Working with Structuralism*.

17. I use the term *character-character dialogue* here rather than *character-character argument* to register the distinction between conversations that function critically as a form of mediated telling without being overt or serious political arguments by one or more of the parties and those that do engage in such overt argument.

18. Interestingly, Leavis parenthetically acknowledges this very exchange as a kind of counterweight to his critique of Dickens's representation of the trade unions. See Leavis, *Great Tradition*, 245-46.

19. Seymour Chatman, *Story and Discourse: Narrative Structure in Fiction and Film* (Ithaca, NY: Cornell University Press, 1980).

20. James Phelan, "Rhetoric, Ethics, and Narrative Communication, or From Story and Discourse to Authors, Resources, and Audiences," *Soundings* 94, no. 1 (2011): 64.

21. This description draws on my discussion of the scene in *Tainted Souls and Painted Faces: The Rhetoric of Fallenness in Victorian Culture* (Ithaca, NY: Cornell University Press, 1993), 117.

22. Elizabeth Gaskell, *North and South* (New York: Norton, 2005), 112-13. Subsequent page references will be given parenthetically in the text.

23. Simon During, *Against Democracy: Literary Experience in the Era of Emancipations* (New York: Fordham University Press, 2012).

24. E. M. Forster, *Howards End* (New York: Norton, 1998), 218-19. Subsequent page references will be given parenthetically in the text.

CHAPTER FOUR

1. See Martin Jay, *The Dialectical Imagination: A History of the Frankfurt School and the Institute of Social Research, 1923-1950* (Boston: Little, Brown, 1973), 121-24, for a summary of this critique and for an analysis of key arguments made by Max Horkheimer and Herbert Marcuse along these lines.

2. See Giorgio Agamben, *Homo Sacer: Sovereign Power and Bare Life*, trans. Daniel Heller-Roazen (Stanford, CA: Stanford University Press, 1998).

3. For a recent exception to this tendency, see Elaine Hadley, *Living Liberalism: Practical Citizenship in Mid-Victorian Britain* (Chicago: University of Chicago Press, 2010).

4. For a local study of this phenomenon, see Jock Macleod, "Between Culture and Politics: Liberal Journalism and Literary Cultural Discourse at the Fin de Siècle," *English Literature in Transition, 1800-1920* 51, no. 1 (2008): 5-22. For a broader discussion of the concepts of literary-philosophical overlaps and literary-academic hybrids, see Randall Collins, *The Sociology of Philosophies: A Global Theory of Intellectual Change* (Cambridge, MA: Harvard University Press, 1998), 754-84. Collins's central example is French existentialism, but there are resonances with the New York intellectuals and Frankfurt school thinkers under discussion here.

5. On the former, see Adam Kirsch, *Why Trilling Matters* (New Haven, CT: Yale University Press, 2011), and Morris Dickstein, *Double Agent: The Critic and Society* (Oxford: Oxford University Press 1992). For a further discussion of the latter, see chapter 1.

6. On the former, see Mark Krupnick, *Lionel Trilling and the Fate of Cultural Criticism* (Evanston, IL: Northwestern University Press, 1986); on the latter, see Alan M. Wald, *The New York Intellectuals: The Rise and Decline of the Anti-Stalinist Left from the 1930s to the 1980s* (Chapel Hill: University of North Carolina Press, 1987), and Russell J. Reising, "Lionel Trilling, The Liberal Imagination, and the Emergence of the Cultural Discourse of Anti-Stalinism," *boundary* 2 20, no. 1 (1993): 94-124.

7. See Tom Samet, "The Modulated Vision: Lionel Trilling's 'Larger Naturalism,'" *Critical Inquiry* 4, no. 3 (1978): 539-57; Dickstein, *Double Agent*, 78-79; and Donald E. Pease, "Negative Interpellations: From Oklahoma City to the Trilling-Matthiessen Transmission," *boundary* 2 23, no. 1 (1996): 1-33. The phrase "dissent from the orthodoxies of dissent" comes from Lionel Trilling, "Reality in America," in *The Liberal Imagination: Essays on Literature and Society* (New York: New York Review Books, 2008), 9.

8. For the former, see Krupnick, *Lionel Trilling and the Fate of Cultural Criticism*, 16; for the latter, see Kirsch, *Why Trilling Matters*, 22.

9. On the minimal interaction between the New York intellectuals and the Frankfurt school, as well as the striking resonances between "the American liberal critique of liberalism and the German anti-liberal critique of liberalism," see Ross Possnock, *The Trial of Curiosity: Henry James, William James, and the Challenge of Modernity* (Oxford: Oxford University Press, 1991), 78-79. Also see Thomas Wheatland, *The Frankfurt School in Exile* (Minneapolis: University of Minnesota Press, 2009). Interestingly, one direct interaction that did occur, and that Wheatland treats, was a debate between Horkheimer and Hook on science and instrumental reason. As I have noted, Hook was of course at a remove from the bleak liberal distrust of instrumental reason. His pragmatic Marxism was fundamentally at odds with the dialectical methods favored by the Frankfurt school, and Horkheimer saw Hook's pragmatism as a form of positivism, expressing "a limitless trust in the existing world" (quoted in Wheatland, *Frankfurt School*, 113). Part of the reason there was limited interaction was Horkheimer's policy of noninvolvement in politics: he wanted to safeguard the security and reputation of the group (141). Wheatland argues that the real points of conjuncture were the critique of mass culture and the valorization of modernism, and he notes that there was a missed dialogue on these matters (171).

10. Theodor W. Adorno, "Cultural Criticism and Society," in *Prisms*, trans. Samuel Weber and Shierry Weber Nicholsen (Cambridge, MA: MIT Press, 1967), 32. My account here is indebted to Jay, *Dialectical Imagination*, which contains a comprehensive history and analysis of these features of the Frankfurt school.

11. See Jay, *Dialectical Imagination*, 227, for a notable exception: the shift toward "democratic" rather than radical emphases in some of the empirical work of the 1940s.

12. See Krupnick, *Lionel Trilling and the Fate of Cultural Criticism*, 117-34, for an account of this shift in Trilling's thinking. It is also worth noting that Adorno singles out for dismissal the sort of attitude evinced in Trilling's earlier moral reading of Freud. See Adorno, *Aesthetic Theory*, trans. and ed. Robert Hullot-Kentor (Minneapolis: University of Minnesota Press, 1997), 8.

13. Adorno, "Commitment," trans. Francis McDonagh, in Adorno et al., *Aesthetics and Politics: The Key Texts of the Classical Debate within German Marxism*, trans. Anya Bostock et al., ed. Ronald Taylor (London: New Left Books, 1977), 180. Subsequent page references will be given parenthetically in the text.

14. As I will discuss later, Trilling himself espoused what he termed moral realism (in *The Liberal Imagination*), but the literary position of his that I am exploring here, one more keyed to the question of ideology and its limits, is in some sense more broadly defined than moral realism.

15. See Irving Howe, *Politics and the Novel* (Chicago: Ivan R. Dee, 2002).

16. See Philip Rahv, "Paleface and Redskin" and "The Cult of Experience in American Writing," in *Essays on Literature and Politics, 1932-1972*, ed. Arabel J. Porter and Andrew J. Dvosin (Boston: Houghton Mifflin, 1978), 3-22.

17. Rahv, "Cult of Experience in American Writing," 17-18.

18. See Trilling, "Elements That Are Wanted," *Partisan Review* 7, no. 5 (1940): 376n.

19. André Malraux, *Man's Fate*, trans. Haakon M. Chevalier (New York: Vintage, 1968), 142.

20. It is of course a central premise of this chapter and book that the bleakness derives, historically speaking, from the experience of catastrophe; my point here is to analyze what seems to motivate it within the conceptual economy of their respective thinking.

21. For a recent and far-reaching discussion of the significance of the anthropological inquiry

in the interwar and postwar era, see Mark Greif, *The Age of the Crisis of Man: Thought and Fiction in America, 1933-1973* (Princeton, NJ: Princeton University Press, 2015). Greif links the sense of concern around this issue to the cascading sense of crisis in the twentieth century.

22. For a useful analysis of this aspect of Adorno's work see Stefan Breuer, "The Long Friendship: On Theoretical Differences between Adorno and Horkheimer," in *On Max Horkheimer: New Perspectives*, ed. Seyla Benhabib, Wolfgang Bonss, and John McCole (Cambridge, MA: MIT Press, 1993), 257-79.

23. Adorno, *Aesthetic Theory*, 301. See also Adorno, "Notes on Kafka," 262, and Simon Jarvis, *Adorno: A Critical Introduction* (New York: Routledge, 1998), 122.

24. Trilling, "The Poet as Hero: Keats in His Letters," in *The Opposing Self: Nine Essays in Criticism* (New York: Viking Press, 1955), 39. Subsequent page references will be given parenthetically in the text.

25. Trilling, "The Fate of Pleasure," in *Beyond Culture: Essays on Literature and Learning* (New York: Viking Press, 1965), 79. Subsequent page references will be given parenthetically in the text.

26. Trilling, "Art and Fortune," in *The Liberal Imagination*, 275.

27. I am indebted here to Chris Westcott's insight into the dynamics of ideological propping in this novel, which he analyzes by means of Slavoj Žižek's account of liberalism. See Christopher Westcott, "Lionel Trilling and the Liberal Imaginary" (unpublished seminar paper, Johns Hopkins University, 2010).

28. Trilling, *The Middle of the Journey* (New York: New York Review Books, 2002), 134. Subsequent page references will be given parenthetically in the text.

29. There is little indication within the novel of what Trilling's ideal of political life would be, though it is surely significant that Laskell works on housing—a core element of progressive urban social policy linked to basic welfare and melioration rather than wholesale transformation and linked also to the conditions of daily existence rather than larger ambitions. But of course even such liberal progressivism is shown to be irrelevant to the primal experience of life-threatening illness and the changes it brings. It is interesting that in Trilling's introduction to the 1975 edition he retrospectively gives a negative indication of what sort of politics he favors: "It might be wondered whether the Communist-oriented intellectuals of the late forties did have what is properly to be called a political life. It must sometimes seem that their only political purpose was to express their disgust with politics and make an end of it once and for all, that their whole concern was to do away with those defining elements of politics which are repugnant to reason and virtue, such as mere opinion, contingency, conflicts of interest and clashes of will and the compromises they lead to" (Trilling, "Introduction to the 1975 Edition," *The Middle of the Journey*, xxx-xxxi).

30. Trilling, "The Sense of the Past," in *The Liberal Imagination*, 183.

31. Trilling, "Manners, Morals, and the Novel," in *The Liberal Imagination*, 221.

32. Michel Foucault, "The Ethic of Care for the Self as a Practice of Freedom: An Interview with Michel Foucault on January 20, 1984," by Raúl Fornet-Betancourt, Helmut Becker, and Alfredo Gomez-Müller, trans. J. D. Gauthier S.J., in *The Final Foucault*, ed. James Bernauer and David Rasmussen (Cambridge, MA: MIT Press, 1988), 18.

33. Trilling, preface to *The Liberal Imagination*, xxi.

CHAPTER FIVE

1. See Georg Lukács, *Realism in Our Time: Literature and the Class Struggle*, trans. John and Necke Mander (New York: Harper and Row, 1964).

2. See Theodor Adorno, "Reconciliation under Duress," trans. Rodney Livingstone, in Adorno et al., *Aesthetics and Politics: The Key Texts of the Classic Debate within German Marxism*, trans. Anya Bostock et al., ed. Ronald Taylor (London: New Left Books, 1977), 151-76.

3. Joe Cleary, "Realism after Modernism and the Literary World-System," *Modern Language*

Quarterly 73, no. 3 (2012): 255–68. Subsequent page references will be given parenthetically in the text.

4. While I will focus on Ellison's distinctive views on the sociology and history of race relations in the United States as what sets him apart from liberal contemporaries, it has also been argued that Ellison's political history is more complicated than assumptions about the novel's anticommunism assume. See Barbara Foley, *Wrestling with the Left: The Making of Ralph Ellison's "Invisible Man"* (Durham, NC: Duke University Press, 2010).

5. Ralph Ellison, "Society, Morality, and the Novel," in *Going to the Territory* (New York: Random House, 1986), 257.

6. Irving Howe, "Black Boys and Native Sons," in *Selected Writings, 1950–1990* (New York: Harcourt, 1990), 120.

7. Ralph Ellison, "The World and the Jug," in *Shadow and Act* (New York: Vintage, 1995), 111.

8. Ellison, "That Same Pain, That Same Pleasure," in *Shadow and Act*, 15.

9. Lionel Trilling, "Reality in America," in *The Liberal Imagination: Essays on Literature and Society* (New York: New York Review Books, 2008), 19.

10. Ellison, "World and the Jug," 115, 112.

11. For a rich and useful discussion of the psychological complexity of Ellison's treatment of race relations and its reliance on both Hegel and W. E. B. Du Bois, see Jesse Wolfe, "'Ambivalent Man': Ellison's Rejection of Communism," *African American Review* 34, no. 4 (2000): 621–37.

12. Ellison, "Twentieth-Century Fiction and the Black Mask of Humanity," in *Shadow and Act*, 33, 32. Subsequent page references will be given parenthetically in the text.

13. Ellison, *Invisible Man* (New York: Vintage, 1995), 342. Subsequent page references will be given parenthetically in the text.

14. Kenneth W. Warren argues this point persuasively, directing attention to Ellison's attempt to establish cultural authority within and through the novel itself. See Warren, "Ralph Ellison and the Problem of Cultural Authority," *boundary 2* 30, no. 2 (2003): 169–70.

15. For the full argument along these lines, see Ellison, "Twentieth-Century Fiction and the Black Mask of Humanity," in *Shadow and Act*, 24–44.

16. Ellison, "World and the Jug," 137.

17. Ellison, *Invisible Man*, 581.

18. Ellison, introduction to *Shadow and Act*, xvii.

19. Ellison, "The Charlie Christian Story," in *Shadow and Act*, 234. See William J. Maxwell, "Ralph Ellison and the Constitution of Jazzocracy," *Journal of Popular Music Studies* 16, no. 1 (2004): 51.

20. Ellison, "Remembering Jimmy," in *Shadow and Act*, 246. Subsequent page references will be given parenthetically in the text.

21. Ellison, *Invisible Man*, 143. Subsequent page references will be given parenthetically in the text.

22. There is a parallel here with Trollope, surprising as it may seem, though Trollope resides within the buffered world of the novel of manners whereas Ellison is pursuing a more complex and less protected world of aggression and violence. Nonetheless, both imagine writing as a space somewhat protected from the workings of power that plague embodied interactions. See chapter 2.

23. Of course, given the way "Anna" is a character who takes on different identities in *Free Women* and the various notebooks, it is not uncontroversial to refer to Anna as I do in this sentence—the locution is adopted simply to clarify a basic distinction between the "frame" novel and the notebooks.

24. Doris Lessing, *The Golden Notebook* (New York: Harper, 2008), 59, 58. Subsequent page references will be given parenthetically in the text.

25. *Frontiers of War* is set in the "the Rhodesian veld." The Allied air force training facility in

the black notebook, and the fact that *Frontiers of War* grows out of the experience recorded there, suggest that the black notebook is set there as well (58).

26. George is one of the people characterized as "good" in the moral catalog of characters Anna provides in the black notebook, a catalog generated within the context of an assertion about the basic moral judgments that attend encounters with other people, even as the simple designations of "good" or "nice" are not considered sufficient for novelistic depiction of character (104).

27. For examples of the emphasis on a humanist existential struggle, see John L. Carey, "Art and Reality in *The Golden Notebook*," *Contemporary Literature* 14, no. 4 (1973): 437–56; Joseph Hynes, "The Construction of *The Golden Notebook*," *Iowa Review* 4, no. 3 (1973): 100–113; Anne M. Mulkeen, "Twentieth-Century Realism: The 'Grid' Structure of *The Golden Notebook*," *Studies in the Novel* 4, no. 2 (1972): 262–74; and Dennis Porter, "Realism and Failure in *The Golden Notebook*," *Modern Language Quarterly* 35, no. 1 (1974): 56–65. For readings that also fall within this general category but shift to a stronger emphasis on multiplicity and deconstructive models, see Gayle Greene, *Doris Lessing: The Poetics of Change* (Ann Arbor: University of Michigan Press, 1994), 93–121, and Molly Hite, *The Other Side of the Story: Structures and Strategies of Contemporary Feminist Narrative* (Ithaca, NY: Cornell University Press, 1989), 55–102. Both Greene and Hite see Lessing as mounting a strong critique of realism and the various ideologies it underwrites, but they also maintain a focus on the existential significance of the critique. For a counterexample that stresses the novel's ultimate insistence on the unknowability of the relation between fiction and the real, see Beth A. Boehm, "Reeducating Readers: Creating New Expectations for *The Golden Notebook*," *Narrative* 5, no. 1 (1997): 88–98.

28. Greene, *Doris Lessing*, 118.

29. Boehm, "Reeducating Readers," 94.

30. Hite could be seen as taking the same view when she argues that the two narratives are "irreconcilable" and that "neither can be construed as taking precedence over the other" (99). But she goes on to say that both narratives, the realist narrative of reform and the modernist narrative of artistic becoming, "emerge as profoundly unsatisfactory" (99). For Hite, the text points instead to multiplicity as the promising condition for new experiences. By contrast, I will argue for the significance of the two endings held in suspension.

31. Lessing, *Golden Notebook*, 589. Subsequent page references will be given parenthetically in the text. The composite figure differs from Paul in not characterizing Anna and himself as "failures," and the implication is that he is stronger, and less defeated, than Paul. However, as I will argue, Paul's own stance is cast as a kind of achievement, and he, like the dream figure, projects composite qualities as an alternative to negative attitudes.

32. As Paul says in another discussion with Ella, "If you had your way, building the new Jerusalem, it would be like killing a plant by suddenly moving it into the wrong soil. There's a continuity, some kind of invisible logic to what happens. You'd kill the spirit of people if you had your way" (180). Again, this establishes him as a liberal and reformist in relation to her revolutionary radicalism.

33. I was alerted to this aspect of the text by Jerrine Tan's seminar paper "The Humorous Ironist; The Cruel Clown" (unpublished seminar paper, Brown University, 2013).

34. Along these lines, Betsy Draine suggests that Paul represents the political aspect of Anna's identity, while Ella represents the romantic. See Draine, *Substance under Pressure: Artistic Coherence and Evolving Form in the Novels of Doris Lessing* (Madison: University of Wisconsin Press, 1983), 79. For a useful survey of feminist responses to the novel, including those that emphasize the sexual divide, see Greene, *Doris Lessing*, 96–97.

Bibliography

Adorno, Theodor W. *Aesthetic Theory*. Translated and edited by Robert Hullot-Kentor. Minneapolis: University of Minnesota Press, 1997.

——. "Commitment." Translated by Francis McDonagh. In Adorno et al., *Aesthetics and Politics: The Key Texts of the Classic Debate within German Marxism*, translated by Anya Bostock et al., edited by Ronald Taylor, 177–95. London: New Left Books, 1977.

——. "Cultural Criticism and Society." In *Prisms*, translated by Samuel Weber and Shierry Weber Nicholsen, 17–34. Cambridge, MA: MIT Press, 1967.

——. "Notes on Kafka." In *Prisms*, translated by Samuel Weber and Shierry Weber Nicholsen, 243–71. Cambridge, MA: MIT Press, 1967.

——. "Reconciliation under Duress." Translated by Rodney Livingstone. In Adorno et al., *Aesthetics and Politics: The Key Texts of the Classic Debate within German Marxism*, translated by Anya Bostock et al., edited by Ronald Taylor, 151–76. London: New Left Books, 1977.

Agamben, Giorgio. *Homo Sacer: Sovereign Power and Bare Life*. Translated by Daniel Heller-Roazen. Stanford, CA: Stanford University Press, 1998.

Anderson, Amanda. "Dickens, Charlotte Brontë, Gaskell: Politics and Its Limits." In *The Cambridge History of the English Novel*, edited by Robert L. Caserio and Clement Hawes, 341–56. Cambridge: Cambridge University Press, 2012.

——. "Living Theory: Personality and Doctrine in Eliot." In *A Companion to George Eliot*, edited by Amanda Anderson and Harry E. Shaw, 442–56. Malden, MA: Wiley-Blackwell, 2013.

——. *The Powers of Distance: Cosmopolitanism and the Cultivation of Detachment*. Princeton, NJ: Princeton University Press, 2001.

——. *Tainted Souls and Painted Faces: The Rhetoric of Fallenness in Victorian Culture*. Ithaca, NY: Cornell University Press, 1993.

——. *The Way We Argue Now: A Study in the Cultures of Theory*. Princeton, NJ: Princeton University Press, 2006.

Anderson, Amanda and Harry E. Shaw, ed. *A Companion to George Eliot*. Malden, MA: Wiley-Blackwell, 2013.

Anderson, Benedict. *Imagined Communities: Reflections on the Origin and Spread of Nationalism*. London: Verso, 1983.

ApRoberts, Ruth. *The Moral Trollope*. Athens: Ohio University Press, 1971.

Armstrong, Nancy. *Desire and Domestic Fiction: A Political History of the Novel.* New York: Oxford University Press, 1987.

Aron, Raymond. *The Opium of the Intellectuals.* New Brunswick, NJ: Transaction, 2001.

Aronson, Ronald. *Camus and Sartre: The Story of a Friendship and the Quarrel That Ended It.* Chicago: University of Chicago Press, 2004.

Bagehot, Walter. "Charles Dickens." In *Literary Studies,* 2:164–97. London: J. M. Dent, 1932.

Behrent, Michael C. "Liberalism without Humanism: Michel Foucault and the Free Market Creed, 1976–1979." *Modern Intellectual History* 6, no. 3 (2009): 538–68.

Bell, Daniel. *The End of Ideology: On the Exhaustion of Political Ideas in the Fifties.* Cambridge, MA: Harvard University Press, 2000.

Berlin, Isaiah. *Liberty: Incorporating Four Essays on Liberty.* Edited by Henry Hardy. Oxford: Oxford University Press, 2002.

Blake, Kathleen. "'Middlemarch': Vocation, Love and the Woman Question." In *Middlemarch,* edited by John Peck, 144–54. New Casebooks. New York: St. Martin's Press, 1992.

Boehm, Beth A. "Reeducating Readers: Creating New Expectations for *The Golden Notebook.*" *Narrative* 5, no. 1 (1997): 88–98.

Brenkman, John. *The Cultural Contradictions of Democracy: Political Thought since September 11.* Princeton, NJ: Princeton University Press, 2007.

Brennan, Timothy. *Wars of Position: The Cultural Politics of Left and Right.* New York: Columbia University Press, 2006.

Breuer, Stefan. "The Long Friendship: On Theoretical Differences between Adorno and Horkheimer." In *On Max Horkheimer: New Perspectives,* edited by Seyla Benhabib, Wolfgang Bonss, and John McCole, 257–79. Cambridge, MA: MIT Press, 1993.

Brinkley, Alan. "Liberalism and Belief." In *Liberalism for a New Century,* edited by Alan Jumonville and Kevin Mattson, 75–89. Berkeley: University of California Press, 2007.

Brown, Wendy. *Edgework: Critical Essays on Knowledge and Politics.* Princeton, NJ: Princeton University Press, 2005.

———. *Undoing the Demos: Neoliberalism's Stealth Revolution.* Cambridge, MA: MIT Press, 2015.

Burrow, John Wyon. *Whigs and Liberals: Continuity and Change in English Political Thought.* Oxford: Clarendon Press, 1988.

Camus, Albert. *The Rebel: An Essay on Man in Revolt.* Translated by Anthony Bower. New York: Vintage, 1991.

Carey, John L. "Art and Reality in *The Golden Notebook.*" *Contemporary Literature* 14, no. 4 (1973): 437–56.

Carroll, David, ed. *George Eliot: The Critical Heritage.* London: Routledge, 1971.

Chatman, Seymour. *Story and Discourse: Narrative Structure in Fiction and Film.* Ithaca, NY: Cornell University Press, 1980.

Claybaugh, Amanda. *The Novel of Purpose: Literature and Social Reform in the Anglo-American World.* Ithaca, NY: Cornell University Press, 2007.

Cleary, Joe. "Realism after Modernism and the Literary World-System." *Modern Language Quarterly* 73, no. 3 (2012): 255–68.

Cockshut, A. O. J. *Anthony Trollope: A Critical Study.* New York: New York University Press, 1968.

Collini, Stefan. *Liberalism and Sociology: L. T. Hobhouse and Political Argument in England, 1800–1914.* Cambridge: Cambridge University Press, 1979.

———. "On Variousness; and on Persuasion." *New Left Review* 27 (2004): 65–97.

———. *Public Moralists: Political Thought and Intellectual Life in Britain, 1850–1930.* Oxford: Clarendon Press, 1991.

Collins, Randall. *The Sociology of Philosophies: A Global Theory of Intellectual Change.* Cambridge, MA: Harvard University Press, 1998.

Colvin, Sidney. "Review, *Fortnightly Review,* January 1873." In *George Eliot: The Critical Heritage,* edited by David Carroll, 331–38. London: Routledge, 1971.

Connolly, William E. *The Fragility of Things: Self-Organizing Processes, Neoliberal Fantasies, and Democratic Activism*. Durham, NC: Duke University Press, 2013.

Coward, Rosalind, and John Ellis. *Language and Materialism: Developments in Semiology and the Theory of the Subject*. London: Routledge and Kegan Paul, 1977.

Delany, Paul. "Land, Money, and the Jews in the Later Trollope." *Studies in English Literature, 1500–1900* 32, no. 4 (1992): 765–87.

Derrida, Jacques. "Before the Law." In *Acts of Literature*, edited by Derek Attridge, 181–220. New York: Routledge, 1992.

———. "Force of Law: The 'Mystical Foundation of Authority.'" In *Deconstruction and the Possibility of Justice*, edited by Drucilla Cornell, Michel Rosenfeld, and David Gray Carlson, 3–67. New York: Routledge, 1992.

Dewey, John. "Creative Democracy: The Task before Us." In *John Dewey: The Later Works, 1925–1953*, vol. 14, *1939–1941*, edited by Jo Ann Boydston, 224–30. Carbondale: Southern Illinois University Press, 1988.

Dicey, A. V. "Unsigned review, *Nation*, January 1873." In *George Eliot: The Critical Heritage*, edited by David Carroll, 339–52. London: Routledge, 1971.

Dickens, Charles. *Bleak House*. New York, Penguin, 1996.

———. *Hard Times*. New York: Norton, 2001.

Dickstein, Morris. *Double Agent: The Critic and Society*. Oxford: Oxford University Press, 1992.

Draine, Betsy. *Substance under Pressure: Artistic Coherence and Evolving Form in the Novels of Doris Lessing*. Madison: University of Wisconsin Press, 1983.

During, Simon. *Against Democracy: Literary Experience in the Era of Emancipations*. New York: Fordham University Press, 2012.

Eagleton, Terry. *Criticism and Ideology: A Study in Marxist Literary Theory*. London: New Left Books, 1976.

Eliot, George. *Middlemarch*. New York: Penguin, 2003.

Ellison, Ralph. *Invisible Man*. New York: Vintage, 1995.

———. *Shadow and Act*. New York: Vintage, 1995.

———. "Society, Morality, and the Novel." In *Going to the Territory*, 239–74. New York: Random House, 1986.

Foley, Barbara. *Wrestling with the Left: The Making of Ralph Ellison's "Invisible Man."* Durham, NC: Duke University Press, 2010.

Forster, E. M. *Howards End*. New York: Norton, 1998.

Foucault, Michel. *The Birth of Biopolitics: Lectures at the Collège de France, 1978–79*. Edited by Michel Senellart. Translated by Graham Burchell. London: Palgrave Macmillan, 2008.

———. "The Ethic of Care for the Self as a Practice of Freedom: An Interview with Michel Foucault on January 20, 1984." By Raúl Fornet-Betancourt, Helmut Becker, and Alfredo Gomez-Müller. Translated by J. D. Gauthier S.J. In *The Final Foucault*, edited by James Bernauer and David Rasmussen, 1–20. Cambridge, MA: MIT Press, 1988.

Fox, Richard. *Reinhold Niebuhr: A Biography*. New York: Pantheon Books, 1985.

Fry, Naomi. "Trollope's *The Way We Live Now* and the Location of the Substantial Real." Unpublished seminar paper, Johns Hopkins University, 2003.

Gallagher, Catherine. *The Industrial Reformation of English Fiction: Social Discourse and Narrative Form, 1832–1867*. Chicago: University of Chicago Press, 1985.

Gaskell, Elizabeth. *North and South*. New York: Norton, 2005.

Goodlad, Lauren M. E. *Victorian Literature and the Victorian State: Character and Governance in a Liberal Society*. Baltimore: Johns Hopkins University Press, 2003.

Graver, Suzanne. *George Eliot and Community: A Study in Social Theory and Fictional Form*. Berkeley: University of California Press, 1984.

Greene, Gayle. *Doris Lessing: The Poetics of Change*. Ann Arbor: University of Michigan Press, 1994.

Greif, Mark. *The Age of the Crisis of Man: Thought and Fiction in America, 1933–1973*. Princeton, NJ: Princeton University Press, 2015.

Hadley, Elaine. *Living Liberalism: Practical Citizenship in Mid-Victorian Britain*. Chicago: University of Chicago Press, 2010.

Harvey, David. *A Brief History of Neoliberalism*. Oxford: Oxford University Press, 2007.

Hicks, Granville. "On Attitudes and Ideas." *Partisan Review* 14, no. 2 (1947): 117–29.

Hite, Molly. *The Other Side of the Story: Structures and Strategies of Contemporary Feminist Narrative*. Ithaca, NY: Cornell University Press, 1989.

Hobhouse, L. T. *Hobhouse: Liberalism and Other Writings*. Edited by James Meadowcroft. Cambridge: Cambridge University Press, 1994.

Hook, Sidney. "The Failure of the Left." *Partisan Review* 10, no. 2 (1943): 165–77.

———. "The New Failure of Nerve." *Partisan Review* 10, no. 1 (1943): 2–23.

House, Humphrey. *The Dickens World*. London: Oxford University Press, 1960.

Howe, Irving. "Black Boys and Native Sons." In *Selected Writings 1950–1990*. New York: Harcourt, 1990.

———. *Politics and the Novel*. Chicago: Ivan R. Dee, 2002.

Hynes, Joseph. "The Construction of *The Golden Notebook*." *Iowa Review* 4, no. 3 (1973): 100–113.

Ignatieff, Michael. *Isaiah Berlin: A Life*. London: Vintage, 2000.

James, Henry. "Unsigned review, *Galaxy*, March 1873." In *George Eliot: The Critical Heritage*, edited by David Carroll, 353–59. London: Routledge, 1971.

Jameson, Fredric. *The Political Unconscious: Narrative as Socially Symbolic Act*. Ithaca, NY: Cornell University Press, 1981.

Jarvis, Simon. *Adorno: A Critical Introduction*. New York: Routledge, 1998.

Jay, Martin. *The Dialectical Imagination: A History of the Frankfurt School and the Institute of Social Research, 1923–1950*. Boston: Little, Brown, 1973.

Judt, Tony (with Timothy Snyder). *Thinking the Twentieth Century*. New York: Penguin, 2012.

Kafka, Franz. *The Trial*. Translated by Breon Mitchell. New York: Schocken Books, 1998.

Kateb, George. "Aestheticism and Morality: Their Cooperation and Hostility." *Political Theory* 28, no. 1 (2000): 5–37.

Kimmage, Michael. *The Conservative Turn: Lionel Trilling, Whittaker Chambers, and the Lessons of Anti-Communism*. Cambridge, MA: Harvard University Press, 2009.

Kirsch, Adam. *Why Trilling Matters*. New Haven, CT: Yale University Press, 2011.

Krupnick, Mark. *Lionel Trilling and the Fate of Cultural Criticism*. Evanston, IL: Northwestern University Press, 1986.

Kucich, John. *The Power of Lies: Transgression in Victorian Fiction*. Ithaca, NY: Cornell University Press, 1994.

LaCapra, Dominick. *History in Transit: Experience, Identity, Critical Theory*. Ithaca, NY: Cornell University Press, 2004.

Leavis, F. R. *The Great Tradition: George Eliot, Henry James, Joseph Conrad*. New York: New York University Press, 1964.

Leitch, Vincent B., ed. *The Norton Anthology of Theory and Criticism*. New York: Norton, 2001.

Lessing, Doris. *The Golden Notebook*. New York: Harper, 2008.

Letwin, Shirley Robin. *The Gentleman in Trollope: Individuality and Moral Conduct*. Cambridge, MA: Harvard University Press, 1982.

Levine, George. *The Realistic Imagination: English Fiction from Frankenstein to Lady Chatterley*. Chicago: University of Chicago Press, 1981.

Lodge, David. *Working with Structuralism: Essays and Reviews on Nineteenth and Twentieth Century Literature*. Boston: Routledge and Kegan Paul, 1981.

Losurdo, Domenico. *Liberalism: A Counter-History* (New York: Verso, 2011).

Lukács, Georg. *Realism in Our Time: Literature and the Class Struggle*. Translated by John and Necke Mander. New York: Harper and Row, 1964.

———. *The Theory of the Novel*. Translated by Anna Bostock. Cambridge, MA: MIT Press, 1971.

Macleod, Jock. "Between Culture and Politics: Liberal Journalism and Literary Cultural Discourse at the Fin de Siècle." *English Literature in Transition, 1800–1920* 51, no. 1 (2008): 5–22.

Malachuk, Daniel. *Perfection, the State, and Victorian Liberalism*. New York: Palgrave Macmillan, 2005.

Malraux, André. *Man's Fate*. Translated by Haakon M. Chevalier. New York: Vintage, 1968.

Markovits, Stefanie. *The Crisis of Action in Nineteenth-Century English Literature*. Columbus: Ohio State University Press, 2006.

Maxwell, William J. "Ralph Ellison and the Constitution of Jazzocracy." *Journal of Popular Music Studies* 16, no. 1 (2004): 40–57.

McCann, Sean, and Michael Szalay. "Do You Believe in Magic?: Literary Thinking after the New Left." *Yale Journal of Criticism* 18, no. 2 (2005): 435–68.

Mill, John Stuart. *Mill: "The Spirit of the Age," "On Liberty," and "The Subjection of Women."* Edited by Alan Ryan. New York: Norton, 1997.

Miller, D. A. *Narrative and Its Discontents: Problems of Closure in the Traditional Novel*. Princeton, NJ: Princeton University Press, 1981.

———. *The Novel and the Police*. Berkeley: University of California Press, 1988.

Moretti, Franco. *The Way of the World: The "Bildungsroman" in European Culture*. London: Verso, 1987.

Morris, Pam. *Imagining Inclusive Society in Nineteenth-Century Novels: The Code of Sincerity in the Public Sphere*. Baltimore: Johns Hopkins University Press, 2004.

Mulkeen, Anne M. "Twentieth-Century Realism: The 'Grid' Structure of *The Golden Notebook*." *Studies in the Novel* 4, no. 2 (1972): 262–74.

Nussbaum, Martha C. *Love's Knowledge: Essays on Philosophy and Literature*. New York: Oxford University Press, 1990.

———. *Poetic Justice: The Literary Imagination and Public Life*. Boston: Beacon Press, 1995.

Orwell, George. "Charles Dickens." In *A Collection of Essays*, 48–103. New York: Harvest, 1981.

Pease, Donald E. "Negative Interpellations: From Oklahoma City to the Trilling-Matthiessen Transmission." *boundary 2* 23, no. 1 (1996): 1–33.

Phelan, James. "Rhetoric, Ethics, and Narrative Communication, or From Story and Discourse to Authors, Resources, and Audiences." *Soundings* 94, no. 1 (2011): 55–75.

Pippin, Robert. *Modernism as a Philosophical Problem: On the Dissatisfactions of European High Culture*. 2nd ed. Oxford: Blackwell, 1999.

Plotz, John. *The Crowd: British Literature and Public Politics*. Berkeley: University of California Press, 2000.

Porter, Dennis. "Realism and Failure in *The Golden Notebook*." *Modern Language Quarterly* 35, no. 1 (1974): 56–65.

Possnock, Ross. *The Trial of Curiosity: Henry James, William James, and the Challenge of Modernity*. Oxford: Oxford University Press, 1991.

Rahv, Philip. "The Cult of Experience in American Writing." In *Essays on Literature and Politics, 1932–1972*, edited by Arabel J. Porter and Andrew J. Dvosin, 8–22. Boston: Houghton Mifflin, 1978.

———. "Paleface and Redskin." In *Essays on Literature and Politics*, edited by Arabel J. Porter and Andrew J. Dvosin, 3–7. Boston: Houghton Mifflin, 1978.

Rancière, Jacques. *The Politics of Literature*. Translated by Julie Rose. Cambridge: Polity Press, 2011.

Reising, Russell J. "Lionel Trilling, *The Liberal Imagination*, and the Emergence of the Cultural Discourse of Anti-Stalinism." *boundary 2* 20, no. 1 (1993): 94–124.

Robbins, Bruce. "Telescopic Philanthropy: Professionalism and Responsibility in *Bleak House*." In *Nation and Narration*, edited by Homi K. Bhabha, 213–39. New York: Routledge, 1990.

———. *Upward Mobility and the Common Good: Toward a Literary History of the Welfare State.* Princeton, NJ: Princeton University Press, 2007.

Rorty, Richard. *Contingency, Irony, Solidarity.* Cambridge: Cambridge University Press, 1989.

———. "Human Rights, Rationality, and Sentimentality." In *On Human Rights: The Oxford Amnesty Lectures 1993,* edited by Susan Hurley and Stephen Shute, 111–34. New York: Basic Books, 1993.

Samet, Tom. "The Modulated Vision: Lionel Trilling's 'Larger Naturalism.'" *Critical Inquiry* 4, no. 3 (1978): 539–57.

Schlesinger, Arthur M., Jr. *The Vital Center: The Politics of Freedom.* New Brunswick, NJ: Transaction, 1998.

Shaw, Harry E. *Narrating Reality.* Ithaca, NY: Cornell University Press, 1999.

Staten, Henry. "Is *Middlemarch* Ahistorical?" *PMLA* 115, no. 5 (2000): 991–1005.

Szalay, Michael. *New Deal Modernism: American Literature and the Invention of the Welfare State.* Durham, NC: Duke University Press, 2000.

Tan, Jerrine. "The Humorous Ironist; The Cruel Clown." Unpublished seminar paper, Brown University, 2013.

Teres, Harvey M. *Renewing the Left: Politics, Imagination, and the New York Intellectuals.* New York: Oxford University Press, 1996.

Thomas, David Wayne. *Cultivating Victorians: Liberal Culture and the Aesthetic.* Philadelphia: University of Pennsylvania Press, 2004.

Trilling, Lionel. "Elements That Are Wanted." *Partisan Review* 7, no. 5 (1940): 367–79.

———. "The Fate of Pleasure." In *Beyond Culture: Essays on Literature and Learning,* 57–87. New York: Viking Press, 1965.

———. *The Liberal Imagination: Essays on Literature and Society.* New York: New York Review Books, 2008.

———. *The Middle of the Journey.* New York: New York Review Books, 2002.

———. "The Poet as Hero: Keats in His Letters." In *The Opposing Self: Nine Essays in Criticism,* 3–49. New York: Viking Press, 1955.

———. *Sincerity and Authenticity.* Cambridge, MA: Harvard University Press, 1971.

Trollope, Anthony. *An Autobiography.* Oxford: Oxford University Press, 1998.

———. *Barchester Towers.* New York: Penguin, 2003.

———. *The Eustace Diamonds.* New York: Penguin, 1986.

———. *The Prime Minister.* New York: Penguin, 1994.

———. *The Way We Live Now.* New York: Penguin, 1994.

Vintner, Maggie. "Great Effects–Family Patterns in *Bleak House.*" Unpublished seminar paper, Johns Hopkins University 2007.

Wald, Alan M. *The New York Intellectuals: The Rise and Decline of the Anti-Stalinist Left from the 1930s to the 1980s.* Chapel Hill: University of North Carolina Press, 1987.

Watt, Ian. *The Rise of the Novel: Studies in Defoe, Richardson, and Fielding.* Berkeley: University of California Press, 1957.

Warner, Michael. *The Letters of the Republic: Publication and the Public Sphere in Eighteenth-Century America.* Cambridge, MA: Harvard University Press, 1990.

Warren, Kenneth W. "Ralph Ellison and the Problem of Cultural Authority." *boundary 2* 30, no. 2 (2003): 169–70.

Westcott, Christopher. "Lionel Trilling and the Liberal Imaginary." Unpublished seminar paper, Johns Hopkins University, 2010.

Wheatland, Thomas. *The Frankfurt School in Exile.* Minneapolis: University of Minnesota Press, 2009.

Williams, Raymond. *The Country and the City.* New York: Oxford University Press, 1973.

———. *Culture and Society: 1780–1850.* New York: Columbia University Press, 1958.

———. *The English Novel: From Dickens to Lawrence*. London: Chatto and Windus, 1970.

Wolfe, Jesse. "'Ambivalent Man': Ellison's Rejection of Communism." *African American Review* 34, no. 4 (2000): 621–37.

Yeazell, Ruth Bernard. "Why Political Novels Have Heroines: *Sybil*, *Mary Barton*, and *Felix Holt*." *Novel* 18, no. 2 (1985): 126–44.

Zamora, Daniel. "Can We Criticize Foucault?" *Jacobin*, December 10, 2014. Accessed January 25, 2015. https://www.jacobinmag.com/2014/12/foucault-interview.

Index

ideological novel of manners (*continued*)
of, 108-10, 114, 119-20; Trilling's approach to, 32, 99, 108-10, 114-15, 118.
See also *The Middle of the Journey*
ideology critique: privileging of interests over
character in, 19; of realism, 47, 147n5
individualism, 11, 14-15, 38, 46-47, 50-54
industrial novels, 16-17, 35, 79. *See also* political novel
Invisible Man (Ellison), 17, 114, 118-28;
black cultural expression in, 121-24, 128,
155n14; democratic ideals in, 120-23,
128; experimental prose style of, 123-24,
128; liberal principles of debate and lived
political commitment in, 124-28, 155n22

James, Henry, 30, 76
Jay, Martin, 153nn10-11
Judt, Tony, 146n26

Kafka, Franz, 83; Adorno's view of, 104, 106,
113; "Before the Law," 7-11, 143n13; *The
Trial*, 7, 10, 143n13; Trilling's view of,
106-7
Kateb, George, 144n22
Keats, John, 106-7
Keynesian economics, 39
Kinsey report, 30
Koestler, Arthur, 29
Kołakowski, Leszek, 146n26
Kristol, Irving, 24

LaCapra, Dominick, 6
Leavis, F. R., 5, 84, 152n18
Lessing, Doris, 17, 22, 98, 114-15, 128. See
also *The Golden Notebook*
Letwin, Shirley, 67
Levine, George, 147n5, 150n44
liberal aesthetics. *See* aesthetic liberalism
Liberal Imagination, The (Trilling), 12-13, 108,
112-13, 119
liberalism, 1-17; aesthetics and, 11-17;
conventional political interpretations of,
1-2, 4, 18-19; critical examination of,
4-12, 19-20; description of, 1; ethos and
character in, 20-22; existential challenges
of, 3-4, 24, 29, 32-33, 97-98, 104-5;
formal and conceptual complexity of,
1-4, 13-17, 22-24, 38-39, 45, 99-101,
111-14, 117-18, 141; Frankfurt school
critiques of, 5, 17, 23, 99-103; incremen-

tal approach to reform in, 114; individualism and, 50-54; law of consequences of,
68-69; pragmatic forms of, 28-29, 101,
153n9; temperament and, 14-15
Liberalism (Hobhouse), 38
liberal politics. *See* political liberalism
literary liberalism, 6-11; in cold war-era
bleak liberalism, 15, 17, 18-45, 141; formal and conceptual complexity of, 13-17;
in the ideological novel of manners, 13,
17, 88, 98-115, 118-20; ideology critique
practices and, 19, 47, 147n5; in modernist literature, 17, 115-41; in the political
novel, 16-17, 78-98; in realist novels of
the nineteenth-century, 15-16, 35, 46-77;
relation to modernity of, 46-48; on state
power, 13-14; textual dynamics of, 10
Locke, John, 39
Lodge, David, 84, 86, 147n5
Losurdo, Domenico, 144-45n2
Lukács, Georg, 29-30, 46; Adorno's critique
of, 83; on modernism, 117; on subjective
interiority, 116

Malachuk, Daniel, 144n25
Malraux, André, 29, 104-5; *Man's Fate*, 105
Mann, Thomas, 130
Man's Fate (Malraux), 105
market liberalism, 19, 22, 39, 41. *See also*
neoliberalism
Marxism, 25; literary analysis in, 13, 50, 83,
100; Sartre's turn to, 32. *See also* Adorno,
Theodor
Mary Barton (Gaskell), 90, 94
Maxwell, William, 124
McCann, Sean, 6
Michnik, Adam, 146n26
Middlemarch (Eliot), 16, 48, 68-77; Dorothea's moral idealism in, 71-75; Will Ladislaw's political reform project in, 69-73,
75-77, 150n36, 150n41, 150nn43-44
Middle of the Journey, The (Trilling), 17,
32, 78-79, 98, 108-14; character-to-
character argument in, 110-12, 115,
154n29; dynamic tension in, 98, 111-12;
elusiveness of causality in, 112; John
Laskell in, 108-15, 154n29; psychological
dynamics and individual temperament in,
108-10, 114-16, 119-20
Mill, John Stuart, 2-3, 30-31; *Autobiography*,
35; *Considerations on Representative Govern-*

queer theory, 5, 151n8

Rahv, Philip, 104–5
Rancière, Jacques, 97, 151n4; *The Politics of Literature*, 80–81
Rawls, John, 2, 13, 100–101
realism, 47, 83, 104, 106, 112; Camus on, 33; social forms of, 116; Soviet form of, 29; Trilling and "moral realism," 112
realism/modernism debates, 29–30, 83, 104, 106, 115–18
realist novels of the nineteenth century, 15–16, 35, 46–77; Cleary's account of, 116–17; Dickens's *Bleak House*, 48–56, 70, 111; dynamics of character and virtue in, 48, 56–59, 69–71, 76–78, 148n15; Eliot's *Middlemarch*, 68–77; ideology critique on, 47, 147n5; industrial novels of, 35; Lessing's examination of, 130, 132–33; modernity and, 46–48; power and violence in, 16, 79, 88, 117; third-person narration in, 48–49, 54–56, 70, 111, 115–17; Trollope's *The Way We Live Now*, 56–68
Rebel, The (Camus), 32–33
Robbins, Bruce, 148n12
Romola (Eliot), 70
Roosevelt, Franklin D., 21, 29, 44
Rorty, Richard, 11–14, 28; "Private Irony and Liberal Hope," 11–12
Rushing, Jimmy, 124

Sartre, Jean-Paul, 32, 80–81, 104
Schlesinger, Arthur M., Jr., 101, 118; *The Vital Center*, 24, 26, 28–29. *See also* New York intellectuals
Schmitt, Carl, 5
Shadow and Act (Ellison), 124
Shaw, Harry, 147n5
Shklar, Judith N., 2
Silone, Ignazio, 29, 104–5; *Bread and Wine*, 105
sincerity: in Ellison's *Invisible Man*, 124–28; Trilling's analysis of, 57–59, 148n17; Trollope's ideal of, 57, 59–68, 148nn17–18
Smith, Adam, 3, 39
social-problem novel. *See* political novel
"Society, Morality, and the Novel" (Ellison), 118
Southern Agrarian movement, 5
Spencer, Herbert, 38

Subjection of Women, The (Mill), 36–37
Szalay, Michael, 6

temperament, 14–15, 22–23; in *The Golden Notebook*, 136–39; liberal aesthetics and, 11; in Trilling, 112, 114
Temps Modernes, Les, 32
theory, 4, 23, 25, 101, 106
Thomas, David Wayne, 14
Tocqueville, Alexis de, 2, 34
Toynbee, Arnold, 26
Trial, The (Kafka), 7, 10, 143n13
Trilling, Lionel, 2, 11–13, 17, 78–79, 101–6, 153n7; comparison with Adorno of, 99, 103–7, 113–14; comparison with Ellison of, 118–20; comparison with Foucault of, 112–13; on complexity of identity, 30, 119–20; on the conservative turn, 24, 145n6; on Dreiser's determinism, 119; "Elements That Are Wanted," 31–32; existential realism of, 99, 103–6, 109–14, 123–24, 153n14, 154n29; "The Fate of Pleasure," 107; on Freud, 103, 153n12; *The Liberal Imagination*, 12–13, 108, 112–13, 119; on modern literary art and readerly experience, 30–32, 47, 104–8, 113–14; on moral realism, 112, 153n14; on practices of the self, 112–14; "The Princess of Cassamassima," 30; on race, 22; rejection of progressive optimism by, 26–27, 30, 103; on sincerity and authenticity, 57–59, 148n17. *See also The Middle of the Journey*
Trollope, Anthony, 16; *An Autobiography*, 57–60, 148n15, 149n23, 149n26; *Barchester Towers*, 57, 61–63; centrality of character for, 56–59, 66, 148n15; ideals of honesty and sincerity of, 57, 59–68, 148nn17–18; on satire and dishonesty, 60, 149n23, 149n26; value of tradition for, 68. *See also The Way We Live Now*
Trotsky, Leon, 23
Twain, Mark, 120–21
"Two Concepts of Liberty" (Berlin), 27

utilitarianism, 35, 84–86, 151nn13–14

Vintner, Maggie, 148n14
Vital Center, The (Schlesinger), 24, 26, 28–29

Printed and bound by CPI Group (UK) Ltd, Croydon, CR0 4YY

09/06/2025

14685684-0001